Praise for Marianne Richmond

"Marianne Richmond's early life was shaped by trauma and obfuscation, but in *If You Were My Daughter* she explores the covenant of motherhood and—with clarity, compassion, and wit—reclaims her own story."

—Jeannette Walls, *New York Times* bestselling author of *The Glass Castle*

"In her beautiful memoir, Richmond bravely finds her way through a legacy of emotional trauma, pulling us into her courageous, tender heart while bringing us closer to our own...a stunning story."

—Kelly McDaniel, LPC, author of *Mother Hunger*

"Marianne's portrayal of epilepsy and the impact of seizures is spot on. Her story resonates with what others in the epilepsy community are saying—Epilepsy is more than seizures. It's seizures AND all the other 'stuff' that comes with it—fear, stigma, anxiety. Very hard to fathom a child navigating epilepsy without the loving support of parents. You really captured it—and I could feel it through your words. I know others will identify and benefit from your story—both those with epilepsy and those that love someone with epilepsy."

—Vicki Kopplin, executive director, Hemophilia Foundation of Minnesota/Dakota, former executive director, Epilepsy Foundation of Minnesota

"*If You Were My Daughter* is a powerful and inspirational book, and it will resonate with readers who yearn to connect to a warm maternal voice. The wisdom, insights, and life lessons shared by Marianne Richmond provide guidance on self-love, resilience, and personal growth. I personally really appreciated the authenticity, vulnerability, and emotional depth portrayed in her writing of her childhood adversity and how it impacted her physical and emotional health. This book is a compelling and empowering read for anyone seeking motivation, encouragement, and a deeper understanding of life's challenges and triumphs."

—Dr. Gillian O'Shea Brown, LCSW, author, complex trauma psychotherapist and adjunct professor, New York University

"Having long admired Marianne Richmond's beloved picture books, I was curious about her backstory. Now I understand. This evocative memoir reveals a graceful soul who desires to put into the world for others what her own heart needed."

—Ami McConnell, bestselling author of *Faithful Daughter*

Also by Marianne Richmond

Marianne is best known for her beloved
children's books that have touched the lives of millions.
Some of her bestselling favorites include:

The Gift of an Angel
The Gift of a Memory
Hooray for You
I Love You So...
I Wished for You: An Adoption Story
If I Could Keep You Little
Be Brave Little One
I Love You All Ways
The World Is Awaiting You

A memoir of Healing
an Unmothered Heart

IF YOU WERE MY DAUGHTER

Marianne Richmond

Published by Sourcebooks
P.O. Box 4410, Naperville, Illinois 60567-4410
(630) 961-3900
sourcebooks.com

Library of Congress Cataloging-in-Publication Data

Names: Richmond, Marianne, author.
Title: If you were my daughter : a memoir of healing an unmothered heart /
   Marianne Richmond.
Description: Naperville, Illinois : Sourcebooks, [2025] | Summary: "From
   beloved bestselling children's author Marianne Richmond (9.5 million
   books sold), a compelling and poignant memoir about how growing up with
   misdiagnosed epilepsy and an emotionally unavailable mother caused her
   to question her sanity and self-worth before finding forgiveness as her
   greatest path to healing"-- Provided by publisher.
Identifiers: LCCN 2024043304 (print) | LCCN 2024043305 (ebook) | (hardcover) | (epub) | (pdf)
Subjects: LCSH: Richmond, Marianne. | Richmond, Marianne--Health. |
   Richmond, Marianne--Family. | Mothers and daughters--United
   States--Biography. | Epilepsy--Diagnosis. | Forgiveness. | Authors,
   American--20th century--Biography. | Authors, American--21st
   century--Biography.
Classification: LCC PS3568.I35158 Z46 2025 (print) | LCC PS3568.I35158
   (ebook) | DDC 818/.5403 [B]--dc23/eng/20241028
LC record available at https://lccn.loc.gov/2024043304
LC ebook record available at https://lccn.loc.gov/2024043305

Printed and bound in the United States of America.
MA 10 9 8 7 6 5 4 3 2 1

Hello dear reader,

I am grateful to have this book in your hands. It's been a yearslong project through many drafts and iterations. "Choose the story you want to tell," advised numerous mentors, teachers and friends. Simple and far from easy! But a decade later, I believe I have.

When Kelly McDaniel, licensed therapist and author of *Mother Hunger*, agreed to endorse my work, I felt elated *and* affirmed. "We heal by being witnessed," she said during one of our several conversations. This moment solidified my greatest hope for *If You Were My Daughter*: that my story illuminates healing as an ongoing, unpredictable and surprising journey. And that my words are a witness to you and your heart.

A special note to the epilepsy community, I realize the vocabulary around this neurological disorder has changed over time. My language in this story is reflective of the terms used when I was experiencing my challenges.

With love and appreciation,

Marianne Richmond

Contents

PART II

PART III

Forgiveness costs you your story.

REV. JOHN MCCLEAN

Holy Cross Cemetery

Philadelphia, October 2018

M
Y CELL PHONE ALARM RINGS. The sun peeks through the dirty apartment window, highlighting the dancing dust.

It takes me a second to remember where I am—lying next to my husband, Jim, in "Michael's Airbnb," a drab apartment in Old City Philadelphia—before the *why* comes rushing back. I get up, dress in yesterday's clothes, and rouse Jim, who makes coffee and calls an Uber while I search the crumb-filled kitchen drawers for two tablespoons we can use later for shovels. Then we carry our travel mugs and duffel bag to the elevator, meet our driver out front, and head to the airport to rent a car.

It's just five miles from Philadelphia International to Holy Cross Cemetery in Yeadon, an adjacent borough. Jim's presence is a comfort, and he calmly navigates the bumpy streets, a patchwork of new tar over old, while I look out my window at the tired storefronts lining either side. Main Street Market. Super Stars Barber Shop. Zesty Pizza. Power lines crisscross above, electric tightropes dissecting a clear autumn sky. Two tall and lanky boys amble down the sidewalk, throwing fake punches while laughing. Four policemen lounge against a cement wall, drinking coffee from white to-go cups. I glance at the digital clock on the dash—11:11, a divine reminder to pay attention to my thoughts, though I don't need reminding.

I've been thinking about this for forty years.

In the back seat sits our small Nike gym bag holding the Bounty Hunter Junior metal detector Jim ordered online. Small enough to fit in our checked luggage and, according to the website, powerful enough to "detect coin-sized objects buried up to five inches deep." I root around in my purse for my cell phone and call the cemetery to tell Lois, the office manager, I'm on my way. She and I've talked several times over the past months when I couldn't find my grandma's whereabouts using their online search.

"She's here, honey," Lois reassured. "Plot HCJ45."

Twenty minutes later, we pass through the official entrance flanked by two massive concrete pillars and wind our way through 225 acres of grave sites to a small building, white and nondescript, in a back corner. Inside, sitting behind a heavy old desk, is a dark-skinned woman with barely there hair and funky plastic eyeglasses. Dozens of manila file folders and breast cancer pamphlets clutter her desktop; family photos and kid art hang on the wall behind her, plus a large sign to cemetery customers still owing money for their burial plots: *When you die, please let us be your pallbearers. We carried you so long, we'd like to finish the job.*

"Lois?" I say.

"Marianne!" She jumps up, a wide smile lighting her face. Short and compact, her fuchsia pink *Find the Cure* T-shirt shouts *Bold and Fearless* in capital letters, and I have no doubt. A silver-link choker with a weighty heart charm dangles from her neck. In a flutter of movement, Lois grabs a paper from the pile on her desk—she knows right where it is—and slides it over the tall counter between us: a photocopy of the burial order for Rozalia Sokas, Mom's mom, my grandmother. My eyes scan the details. The deed owner is my uncle Pete, Mom's brother, who paid $109.00 in 1971 to have his mother buried. Cause of death: general arteriosclerosis. Heart disease.

"Joe will take you to the grave site," Lois offers.

A man with thick black hair and wearing a gray suit has slipped into the room behind us, his plaid shirt and striped tie a mismatch. He nods our way to confirm his presence. Pinned to his jacket lapel is a gold rectangular badge, *Catholic Cemeteries* etched across the top and *Joe, Family Services Counselor* etched below it. I don't want an escort, but Joe is eager to oblige, so we get back into our car and follow his long white Buick past countless grave markers to a cross-shaped headstone smack-dab in the middle of a main roundabout. Jim and I connect eyeballs, telegraphing panic. Grandma couldn't be more conspicuous, center stage in one of the busiest intersections in the entire cemetery. We may as well erect a marquee for our upcoming performance.

The three of us gather around the headstone. Its inscription shows the family name, Sokas, in bold caps with three names underneath: *Alexander, 1879–1945; Rozalia, 1890–1971; and Juliana, 1920–*. I know for sure from a cousin that my aunt Julie, Mom's middle sister, is dead and buried here too, her end date oddly never inscribed.

"Established in 1890..." Joe drones on about the history of the cemetery while numerous cars drive by, spilling out mourners to new and nearby graves.

Move along, Joe, I silently will, but he keeps talking.

"Youse guys still have two plots availerbul," he says in his thick Philly accent, his right hand resting atop the marble cross, the other in his pants pocket.

"Thanks, I'll let you know if we want them," I promise, turning slightly to dismiss him.

Finally alone, Jim and I fetch the gym bag, curving our bodies to shield our extracting of the two-foot-long wand with a large metal circle

on one end. Fresh batteries are in, and we brought extras in case. Jim
flicks on the power button and waves his wedding ring underneath.

Beeeeep. A piercing squeal punctuates the quiet.

"Turn that thing down!" I shush, laughing nervously while looking
over my shoulder.

Google didn't tell me metal detecting at a grave site is illegal, but it
isn't "morally recommended" either. A burial is starting behind us, the
reverend welcoming mourners with a deep and somber intonation.
A bugle's wail travels on the breeze. They are oblivious to us for now,
thankfully, and I have preplanned my excuse if anyone asks. "I lost my
ring last time I was here," I'll say. It's a loose version of the truth.

"I buried it at my mother's grave site."

Mom's long-ago words float across my brain. This single sentence
is all I know about the whereabouts of her wedding ring. I was eleven
when she returned from a visit to Philadelphia without it and told Dad
what she did. I remember Dad's face too, crushed and confused. Now
standing in the cemetery, I envision Mom solo and discreet, pressing
her silver band into the earth next to the headstone, using extra effort
from her thumb to sink it deeper. Was it day or night? Was she calm,
nervous, desperate? Crying? Or feeling bold and victorious?

Can she see me here today?

Jim begins circling the wand around the grave. We work together for
thirty minutes, me scraping away grass with my spoon tips, expecting
the quick shrill of success. A few random beeps from small rocks, then
nothing. Jim moves the wand slower. Wider.

Still nothing.

"Maybe she buried it over her mom's body," I suggest, and we
move further from the headstone, imagining Grandma six feet below
us, way deeper than our five-inch reach. We look and dig and look
some more.

Forty-five minutes later, I sit back on my heels, slow acceptance settling in.

"Are you gonna take it if you find it?" my friend Jane asked when I first told her my plan.

"Of course!" I said smugly, believing I'd have the choice. But as the trip grew closer, I wasn't as sure. Mom had her reasons, though what they were, I'd never fully know. Perhaps her ring isn't even here, "my mother's gravestone" code for *I threw it in the trash*. I'm guessing her intention wasn't for me to go looking for it forty years later.

So why, exactly, am I doing this? The best answer I can give myself is curiosity and, perhaps more accurately, the satisfaction of a final truth dig. To see her story anew, the one to which I'd long turned a deaf and incompassionate ear. And for her to see me too, moving toward her.

My daughter journey has been one long effort to know this woman who didn't know me back. To try countless times to get her to see and meet me in the ways I needed. And to make peace with the certainty of this never happening because she forgot her part in my pain, and I forgave it so I could free myself of this tired storyline. And to know—for sure—it was never about me and my lovability. Sensitive me, born to fractured her, was a setup for my lifetime of inner loneliness.

BEEP. BEEP. BEEP. BEEP.

The detector is screaming. Jim and I meet eyes, and I toss my spoons aside. Using my bare fingers, I dig up the grass where the detector is hot, piling it to the side. The beep stops. Jim moves the wand over to the grassy clump, and it screeches again.

I feel metal....

Marianne and her mother, 1967.

PART I

Kitchen Floor

I AM NINE YEARS OLD, WANDERING the house looking for something to do.

Weekends are like this. Mom and Dad rarely make plans for us except eleven o'clock mass on Sunday morning and donuts after from Grebe's Bakery, but only if Tony, George, and I behave: no elbow wars during the readings, no whispering during the sermon, and no resting our butts on the pew while kneeling.

I pause by the back door, its window overlooking the small concrete patio. Our summer picnic table sits lonely in the center. Mom's two metal clothesline poles jut skyward, useless without wet laundry hanging between them. Wisconsin usually has snow by now, six-foot mountains of it lining our driveway, but this year, nothing. Our grass pokes upright, unseasonably green. Low clouds mute the January sky, typical of the endless stretch between Christmas and Easter when dark comes early and neighbors on Laura Lane go from their cars to garages to houses, smoke curling from chimneys no matter the time of day. Not from ours, though. "Too messy," Dad says about making a real fire in our fireplace. Plus, it's located in a dumb spot in the family room, built into the brown paneled wall in a pass-by part of the room; we pass by it to get to the TV part.

Mom is cleaning the kitchen table after lunch, corralling sandwich crumbs with her dishcloth, while my two older brothers watch the last of the Saturday cartoon lineup from their spot on the beige garage-sale couch that is hardly a couch. With no armrests and unattached back cushions that fall to the ground constantly, it's more a stiff bench. George is picking at his lower lip, a habit Mom is trying to help him break. George split his mouth open while sledding, and when the doctor stitched him up, he left George with a lip bump that's become an oral fixation. "Stop picking," Mom reminds him from the kitchen.

Down the hallway, I find Dad in his bedroom, rummaging through the top drawer of his fake birchwood dresser, the one he calls his "chesta-drawers" and where he keeps his white undershirts, leather billfold, and camera. Dad is the family picture-taker and keeper, the output of his infrequent efforts slid into one narrow-but-thick green photo album he stores on the highest shelf in his closet—the one I need his permission to look at, which seems silly—hiding away our only family memories. Sometimes it takes Dad a full year to use and develop one roll of film with his frugal cadence: One photo on Mother's Day. Another on the first day of school. Two snaps on a birthday or Christmas. I can grow two inches between rolls.

It feels strange to be in Mom and Dad's room, so tidy, sparse, and seemingly off-limits. Their room holds a certain smell too, like unwashed hair. They make their bed in the morning, Dad's side stiffened with raw plywood under the aged mattress, then don't return until nighttime. Every so often, I slip into their room to look through Mom's dresser drawers, unfolding her stash of delicate embroidered hankies and holding up her huge white bras to my nothing chest, marveling at the two-inch-wide shoulder straps, the D cups, and the four hooks needed to secure the back. Or I take out Tony's and George's baptism outfits, two matching sets of doll-sized white seersucker overalls with short-sleeved, button-down white cotton shirts. When I ask Mom about my baptism clothes, she says she borrowed a "beautiful white gown" from a church friend and had to give it back.

"Hi, Dad," I say loudly.

Dad looks more like a grandpa than a dad, his hair gray and thinning. He wears hearing aids in both ears too, each a chunk of molded plastic, yellowed from earwax and connected to his eyeglasses by short cloudy tubes. I never knew Dad without his hearing problem. It started in his midtwenties in the army in Virginia when, after a long day of shooting practice, he couldn't hear normal talking. Then he failed a hearing test on the base. "Nerve loss," the doctors said, and then they discharged him.

As aggravating as his ears are for him, they come in handy for us when we talk at supper about what we got him for Christmas or when there's something he doesn't need to know—like Tony accidentally shooting our neighbor's dog, Brandy, with his BB gun, and Mom and Tony quietly paying for the dog's pellet-removal surgery out of Tony's newspaper route money, Dad none the wiser. Honestly, we got so used to Mom talking and Dad not that it was sometimes easy to forget he was part of the family, except for one time when his frustration over feeling invisible boiled over. He stood up, slammed his dinner plate on the table so hard his peas jumped off the dish, and stormed out of the kitchen. None of us said a thing, staring at the table with remorse.

Dad turns his gaze.

"Hi," I repeat, looking him in the eyes so he can read my lips.

"Marianne-o," he says, surprised to see me. "What can I do for you?"

Dad is the only one who calls me Marianne-o, and the simple o tacked onto my name makes me feel special—and victorious. Mom named me after the Blessed Virgin Mary and the Virgin's mother, Saint Anne. Hearing this was the first I knew the Virgin had a mother.

"The spelling was written across my forehead in a dream," Mom says, squiggling her right index finger across her real forehead whenever she recounts the story. "One word, with an *i* in the middle so no one can give you a nickname." As if she can control this.

"Can I use your camera?" I ask. Dad is protective of his stuff, especially his money. "I want to go outside. Take pictures of the day. I don't have anything else to..."

My *do* is interrupted by a pinch in my left pinky. I look at my hand, expecting to see an obvious cause. But nothing. Instead, a prickly numbness is pulsing in my little finger, quickly spreading into the adjacent fingers, and slowly curling my hand into a claw. What is happening?

Panicked, I grab my left hand with my right, trying to unbend my rigid fingers with no luck.

"Whatsa matter, honey?" Dad asks, confused.

"I don't know!" I whimper with alarm. "My hand—it's, it's *numb*!" The pulsing is marching up my left arm now, raising it upward.

I bolt from their bedroom.

"*Mom!*" I scream, running back toward the kitchen with my left arm overhead like a ballerina, forcing me off-balance.

Mom's back is facing me—she's doing the dishes now—as I round into the room and collapse awkwardly with a thud, my head just missing the corner of the table. I land hard on my right shoulder before rolling onto my back. Mom rushes to kneel at my side, her hands dripping with soapy water. My arms and legs, stiff and extended, begin convulsing, my head hitting the floor with a rhythmic cadence. I struggle to stay conscious but am drowning in a torrent of sensation, feeling as if my body will surely split in two. I am awake but can't speak.

"Hail Mary...full of grace, the Lord is with thee..." Mom implores, her head bowed, stopping only to command Tony and George to call the ambulance.

"Call nine-one-one!" she shouts, knowing Dad won't hear her plea.

"Blessed are you among women, and blessed is the fruit of thy womb, Jesus..."

I fade in and out of black, my brain filled with my screams, reverberating in the tunnels of unconsciousness. "Help me!" I shout inside my head. "Mom, help me, me, me...!"

"Holy Mary, Mother of God."

And then two minutes, five minutes, an hour later, I can't tell, my body quiets; the storm abates. Sprawled and spent on our gold linoleum floor, I watch the kitchen cabinets come slowly into focus, Mom still kneeling to my right.

"What was *that*?" I ask, desperately hoping whatever it was is over for sure.

"I don't know, dear. I don't know," she says, her face pale and drawn.

Tony bounds into the kitchen, leading two Greendale paramedics with a stretcher.

"Ambulance is here," he says.

They scoop me up, cover me with a scratchy blue blanket, and ferry me back through the family room and out the front door to a waiting ambulance. Its flashing light quietly spins, sending an intermittent and eerie red glow into the neighborhood.

I'm an emergency, I think. *Make some noise.*

Lying on my back, damp cold stings my cheeks. My across-the-street neighbors, whose names I don't know, stand on their front step, the Mrs. holding her kitchen towel in one hand, her other arm around the Mr.'s waist. They watch as I'm loaded into the back of the ambulance. No "Hope you're okay!" Nothing, just watching. My only other ambulance ride was when I was six and I stuffed a fake plastic lipstick tube, part of my pretend beauty set, up my nose, and I couldn't get it back out by blowing. "Breathe through your mouth, breathe through your mouth," the paramedic repeated the whole way to the hospital until the ER doctor sucked out the lipstick with a teeny, tiny tube that looked like a miniature vacuum cleaner.

We drive in silence. Mom sits on a built-in bench to my right, her hand on my thigh. Exhaustion pins me down. My eyeballs strain to take in my surroundings, metal walls jam-packed with tubes, bandages, and scary-looking medical equipment. Tears trickle down my cheeks, catching in my ears.

What happened? Is it going to happen again? When? Does Dad know we're gone or where we're going? I don't know where I'm going.

Finally we stop.

"Trinity Memorial Hospital," Mom announces.

The ambulance doors open, and the two guys pull me out headfirst. I read *Emergency Room* on a sign as I wheel by, through the double doors and waiting area, until they deposit me onto a narrow bed in an exam room.

"Take care, young lady," the taller guy offers, yanking a curtain around my tiny space.

A few minutes later, a nurse appears to take my temperature and blood pressure and to ask me to pee in a cup. She pricks my index finger and squeezes out a few drops of blood. Is the answer inside me? A doctor appears next and asks Mom for the backstory. Lying there, I wonder how his looking in my ears and up my nose is going to explain why a tornado ripped through my body, leaving me a scared rag doll.

The nurse returns.

"Labs are normal," she says in a friendly voice.

The doctor scratches some notes on a piece of paper and hands it to Mom.

"Acute strain brachial plexus," she reads his diagnosis aloud.

"Basically, a pinched nerve," he explains and instructs us to see our family physician.

I push myself to upright and slowly get down from the bed on unsteady feet. A pinched nerve can do all this? And I don't know how I pinched it in the first place. Mom gathers her coat and purse, and we walk back to the waiting room, where Dad is now sitting. She must have called Tony or George to tell him where we were.

The three of us drive home. Sitting in the back seat of our station wagon, I hug my knees to my chest and gaze out my window, replaying the afternoon over and over in my mind. Nothing has changed, and everything has changed. Outside is still cold and gray, Laura Lane still quiet. The nosy neighbors are back inside. But I am completely disassembled and rearranged.

Where there once was me, there is now a shell. And fear—big, desperate, and all-consuming—has scooped out my insides, leaving me hollow. We pull into the garage, and the three of us file into the house, the automatic door closing with a heavy thud behind us.

Dr. A

TWO DAYS LATER, INSTEAD OF me sitting at my desk in fourth
grade, Mom and I sit in the front seat of our station wagon in
the parking lot outside Dr. A's office, the car engine running to keep the
heat going. Tony, George, and I go to St. Alphonsus, the old Catholic
school attached to our church, while the other neighborhood kids go
to Highland View, the public school five minutes from our house. Most
mornings, I watch the Highland View group talk and laugh their way
up the street, wanting to be part of them. They don't have to wear a
uniform, walk two miles through Scout Lake Park to get to school, or
go to Friday morning mass. Because no matter how much God I get
during the week, I still have to go on Sunday morning too.

Both of us stare out the windshield, not saying much. Slouched in
my puffy winter coat, I hold my left hand gently with my right like a
wounded bird, staring at my fingers—as if by watching them, I can control their behavior. Every moment my body is still is now a moment I
wonder when it won't be. Every random twitch and twinge in my hands
convinces me another "episode" is imminent.

"They should be open now," Mom says, glancing at her wristwatch.

Dr. Fernando Alvarez—Dr. A—is our longtime family doctor, a short
man with thin lips, shiny black hair with a deep side part, and skin the
color of Dad's coffee. Mom counts on his opinion and remedies for most

of our mild ills and occasional strep throat, and his name and phone number are prominently displayed on one of the many lists, notes, and school schedules taped on the inside of our kitchen cupboards. Mom treats Dr. A's office with emboldened familiarity and, in my view, an expectation they will fit her in when she needs to be fit. "Mary Helf," she announces over the phone to the receptionist, and next thing I know, we can come right over.

"Good morning, Mah de ann," Dr. A. pats the crunchy white paper, his fragmented pronunciation of my name unique to my ears. Mom explains Dr. A's family is from the Philippines which means nothing to me, only that it sounds exotic and far away. I don't understand she's conveying the backstory of his dialect. His three daughter's go to my school, but I am not interested in being friends with anyone whose dad sees me in my underwear. "Come up," he directs my focus.

I sit on the edge, my legs dangling, half listening to Mom, half looking at the pictures on the wall.

"After lunch. Left hand. Fell. Spasm. Hospital. Brachial plexus," Mom relays.

Spasm. Her choice of words bugs me, but I don't know what to call it either. Spasm is what happens in Dad's back after he mows the lawn. Or in my calf in the middle of the night. A muscle cramp. Not the head-banging hurricane that flattened me on Saturday.

Dr. A taps my knees with his rubber mallet, nodding at my automatic kick. I notice his small hands and fingers, nearly black in the creases of his knuckles. He looks in my ears and down my throat. Shines a penlight in my eyes.

"Deep breaths," he says and listens through his stethoscope, his hand on my back underneath my shirt.

"Do you have a headache?" he asks.

"No."

"Do you see okay?"

"Fine."

"Anything else to tell me?"

"No."

But this is a lie, because what I want to say is this: "Look deeper. Longer. Harder. Tell me what's wrong with me and do something to guarantee I will never *ever* again have to go through what happened on Saturday."

"You can get down," Dr. A says, then tells me to wait out front while he talks to Mom in private.

Alone? I panic. Being in public is newly unnerving. What if it happens while I'm out there? In front of everybody? But I go and sit and wait, willing Mom to hurry.

Back in our car, we buckle in.

"So what did he say?" I ask, hopeful.

"He called it a 'conversion reaction,'" Mom says, explaining how it's something more in my mind than in my body. And how, if my mind is stressed, it can make my body do strange things. This makes no sense either. I wasn't stressed when all this started.

"Dr. A believes you're psychologically holding on to me," Mom continues, relaying his theory that when a child—in this case, me—thinks she'll be separated from her parent, she'll often go to "great lengths" to keep the parent's attention.

"So he thinks I'm making this up," I conclude, confused and deflated. I don't yet understand that conversion reaction is a real diagnosis in the medical community, defined as a person having sudden neurological symptoms with no underlying medical illness or injury.

All I hear is it's my doing.

The only separating Mom and I do is me going to school, same as I've been doing successfully since kindergarten, and I can think of a lot less terrifying ways to get her attention besides falling on the floor, shaking uncontrollably, and going unconscious.

The next morning, after saying my problem is more in my head, Dr. A sends Mom and me to Family Hospital in Milwaukee for two tests to see what's actually in my head. The first is a brain X-ray called a CT scan. I lie as still as possible, face up on a narrow table, as the radiologist slides me backward into a circular machine, like going into the hole of a big white donut. It doesn't hurt except for getting a shot full of dye in the crook of my elbow that makes my arm feel ice cold, and my mouth taste like metal.

"To light up your brain," he says.

Next is an EEG.

"Short for *electroencephalogram*," the technician enunciates.

Separating my hair with his blue-latex-gloved fingers, he pastes twenty wires to my scalp with white glue that looks like toothpaste. Then I lie on another padded table in a dimly lit room while he sits in an attached room to record my brain waves for an hour.

"Blink, take deep breaths, stare at the strobe light while hyperventilating," his deep voice instructs from behind a dark window.

Looking into the flashing light while forcing myself to pant as fast as I can, I'm certain I'll have a spasm right here, but I don't.

Later, Dr. A calls Mom to tell us my brain scan came back normal, but my EEG didn't. I have some irregular waves in the back part of my brain called the *occipital lobe*, he says, with more on the right side than the left. But no one—not Mom, Dr. A, or the hospital—is worried enough to do anything else about it, and Dr. A dismisses the results as "typical" for a kid my age. Typical maybe, but I don't like my brain waves being irregular.

My world feels before and after. Before Saturday, I was a Brownie ready to "fly up" to being a Girl Scout. I don't want to be a Girl Scout anymore. Before Saturday, I was taking baton-twirling classes at the community center and piano lessons from Mrs. Patterson down the street. I don't want to twirl or play piano anymore either. And before Saturday, I played Barbies with Kris, a neighbor girl who says she'd rather be a boy, and Mary, my other neighbor friend, who is okay with being a girl. Now I don't want to leave my bedroom or my house. And school? Never again.

The *L* Section

WE MOVED TO GREENDALE, WISCONSIN, when I was two, from Madison where I was born.

"You were the only one I was awake for," Mom says, telling me how she was "drugged up" with my two brothers, Tony taking his sweet time coming into the world, but Georgie coming so fast, she had to keep her legs crossed until the doctor got to the hospital from the golf course. Mom concludes George lost oxygen to his brain, and that's why he's so dark in his baby photo. Standing in the hallway, I inspect our three framed black-and-white pictures hanging next to the thermostat, and sure enough, George's face looks a shade or two darker than Tony's and mine.

Other than that, "It's alllll a blur," Mom says, waving her hand in the air as if dismissing a bothersome insect.

"How can you not remember *anything* else?" I ask, annoyed, looking for more. More stories of first words and steps, favorite books, and toys. Proof to me I existed and that she cared I did. I can't explain why this matters to me, only that it does, and I equate her forgetting with me being forgettable.

Mom blames her bad memory on having three kids in five years, the last, me, at age forty-two. "When other moms were sending kids to college, not preschool," she says, longhand for "I was tired." Instead,

I ask Dad for the green photo album to see what I did before I could remember for myself. Dad's careful and clever recollections, written around the white border of each photo in his perfect tiny penmanship, connect me to my beginnings in a way Mom cannot. *How green was the grass, fragrant the clover, adventuresome the children,* he wrote on a photo of toddler George and baby me trying to crawl off a blanket, George's small hand on my shoulder. I savor these souvenirs of time otherwise lost.

Laura Lane is in the *L* section, near other streets with *L* names—Lilac, Leroy, Lory, and Lakeview, which doesn't have a lake to view. Eleven-ish miles south of Milwaukee, Greendale is organized by letter, one of three Greenbelt Towns planted by the federal government after the Great Depression—the other two, Greenhills, Ohio, and Greenbelt, Maryland. In 1936, as part of the New Deal, President Roosevelt wanted to show America what a modern suburb could look like, a nice place to grow grass and kids near a small village center. At the top of our street, in the middle of the cul-de-sac, sits a large circular brick fountain like a cement wedding cake, built when Laura Lane was part of the Parade of Homes in the '60s. Our house was the last available, the model where builders met with potential buyers to pick out the style of house they wanted. Mom thinks that's why our house has only one bathroom, because it was just for show and not for five people who need two bathrooms.

Across from the fountain lives Mr. Bergy, who has ultimate neighborhood power—the on–off switch in his basement. On goes the water for Memorial Day and the Fourth of July, but otherwise, only when Mr. Bergy is in a fountain mood. Tony and his friends poured laundry soap in the base once, sending big sudsy puffs over the edge and into the street and bringing Mr. Bergy out his front door, red-faced and sputtering, "You kids," while threatening that they wouldn't get away "with this mischief," even though they always did, outrunning Mr. Bergy to hide in the bushes.

When two people from Greendale meet up at the Sentry Foods or Coast to Coast Hardware, after the *hi, how are you*s, one always asks the other, "What section do you live in?" if they don't already know, the answer giving a clue to size of house and, to me, bank account. The *F*, *G* and *H*s live in Overlook Farms, the fancy part of town with big houses, expansive yards, and their own brown welcome sign on a post, while the *A*, *B* and *C*s live in Greendale Originals, the first houses built, which are small and close together near the downtown village. The rest of the alphabet has houses like ours, a basic three-bedroom ranch style with the occasional split-level mixed in.

Driving around town, I imagine being an *F*, *G*, or *H*, but Dad acts like we're not even on the alphabet. "Whoa, whoa, whoa!" he yelps whenever I squeeze a long squirt of dish soap into the sink versus three quick drops or notch our heat up one degree in the winter. "Who touched the thermostat?" Dad's voice bellows through the house, his face inches from the dial, even though he knows it's me, because it's always me.

Mom, on the other hand, is content being an *L*. "This house is a *castle*," she says, comparing it to where she grew up in Philadelphia— "Skid row," she calls it—while I mentally redecorate from the JCPenney flyer in the Sunday newspaper. After church, I stretch out on my stomach on our blue shag living room carpeting and pick out matching couches and chairs with bonus end tables and lamps to replace our secondhand mishmash.

"We can get all this for five ninety-nine, no interest," I relay to Dad in his brown and orange flowered recliner, the fabric faded and threadbare, and hold up the ad while he peers over his sports section. He leans forward for a closer look.

"What's wrong with what we have?" he replies, honestly confused.

Every so often, after seeing an idea in his *Popular Mechanics* magazine, Dad goes on a do-it-yourself spree. Like the wall of ten-inch mirror squares he put up in our dining room, each with a peel-away back that he pressed into place to create a scene of two wrought-iron arches. "It'll make this room look so much bigger," he declared with sweeping gestures. I know the room still ends where it always did, but it's a great spot to blow-dry my hair. He put up fake press-and-stick bricks behind the kitchen sink too and sawed out a homemade skylight in our kitchen ceiling, only problem being the attic is above the kitchen, so it doesn't make any difference light-wise. Most elaborate, though, is the solar collector he built in our backyard out of empty beer and soda cans, a ten-foot square swath of aluminum that captures the sunlight and pumps heat into our basement. "Hot air rises," Dad says, explaining how he's helping heat the whole house by heating the basement first, which is ultimately the same reason we camp in our pop-up trailer every summer instead of staying in hotels: to save money.

A few months before a trip, Dad sits at the kitchen table with his large Wisconsin map and chooses a campground within a two- to four-hour radius. We have all the equipment—a Coleman stove and lanterns, plastic dishes and utensils, a vinyl red-checked tablecloth, and a separate screened-in kitchen tent so we can eat without the bugs. Dad built a fifty-pound kitchen cabinet to lug on our trips, a large wooden rectangle on legs with two hinged doors that drop down for easy food access. He painted it green to match the trees. Problem is, it's Mom's job to buy groceries for the cabinet and do all the laundry when we get home. "Jerry," she says, "this is *not* a vacation for me." One year, Mom and I skipped family camping and took the Greyhound bus twelve hours south to Camp Marydale, a Catholic camp in Erlanger, Kentucky. While I rode a horse, made a God's eye out of yarn and twigs, and slept in a dorm with other preteen girls, Mom checked into the "quiet area" and didn't emerge for seven days.

From what I gather, Mom doesn't like being a homemaker. In third grade, I drew a picture of her for our parent open house. The moms and dads were coming to school that night and "Wouldn't it be wonderful," my teacher said enthusiastically, "to decorate the walls with pictures of our moms!" No names, though, she added with a mischievous smile. "It'll be more fun this way, a find-the-mom treasure hunt!" I pulled out my beloved crayons, the sixty-four-count box with built-in sharpener. Two rows of multicolored possibility stood at attention like vibrant helpers awaiting artistic duty. I once tried eating my crayons to see if different colors tasted different, but no, periwinkle blue, maize yellow, and grass green were all the same, hard waxy bits with zero flavor.

Imagining Mom in my favorite dress of hers—a light-green one with tiny colored flowers—I made a peach circle for her face and smaller brown circles for her short wavy hair. Blue dots for eyes, round pink cheeks, and a red line smile. Mom came to life on my paper, standing in her flowered dress, arms straight at her sides under a scribbled blue sky. Last I drew a big talking bubble and filled it with what she says all the time: *I hate cooking. I hate cleaning. I hate laundry.* Leaning back, I admired my drawing, then gave it to my teacher to hang on the wall.

That night, I waited up late, excited for the praise I was certain I'd get. Instead, Dad's angry face appeared in my bedroom doorway, his brow furrowed, jaw clenched. "We found your picture, young lady," he scolded, adding how *embarrassed* and *hurt* Mom was when she saw it. "Of all the nice things she does for the family..." he rambled on, then ordered me to apologize. I stared at the door left ajar. *She* was hurt? What about *me*? I worked hard on my picture, and now I was supposed to be sorry for telling the truth. Maybe Dad was the sad one, because Mom was never sorry for saying it.

I slipped out of my bedroom and tiptoed across the hallway to her bedside, her room dark, except for the faint streetlight glow coming from the road behind our house. Mom was face up under the gold bedspread, staring at the ceiling, her eyes watery. Was she crying because of me? I rarely saw her cry. "I'm sorry," I whispered to the side of her face. She didn't look my way, only nodded slightly, before I scurried back to my room, guilt heavy in my stomach.

"I never wanted to be married," she confides when it's just the two of us, mostly when we're driving on errands. "But your dad's sisters talked me into it."

I can't recall when she first told me this, only that I cannot remember a time of not knowing it. She follows up with reassurances that Tony, George, and I are her "three greatest gifts," but my brain gets stuck on the part about her not wanting to be a wife in the first place. I want to believe Mom and Dad fell in love like a fairy tale and are still that way, but it wasn't like that. They met as pen pals in 1955 while Mom was in the Air Force after college. One day after choir practice in the chapel, she found a copy of *Extension*, a Catholic magazine, in a pew. In the back was information about The Chaperon Club, a letter-writing club where single Catholics placed an ad in hopes of making a "Catholic connection." Mom joined. "Most guys on the base got drunk on the weekends," she said, so as one of few women and a nondrinker, she spent many weekend nights alone. A few months later, and 449 miles away, Dad was looking at the same magazine while visiting his mom's house in Sheboygan, an hour north of Milwaukee.

"I scanned the pages of that little catalog for people with interesting sketches." Dad tells me his side of the story. Mom's ad caught his eye: *Air Force officer from Ohio, interested in bowling, softball, and other sports.* He sent a letter, and Captain Mary M. Sokas answered. Back and forth they wrote for a year, meeting in person when Mom traveled to

Wisconsin for a long weekend. Dad showed her around Milwaukee—a walk along Lake Michigan and dinner at Mader's German restaurant. For a guy who didn't like to venture too far from home, it was a brave undertaking. Dad says he was nervous for Mom to see his hearing aid, which back then was a cumbersome metal box on his chest with wires up to his ears. Dad fell in love. Mom says she didn't. But she was thinking about leaving the military, and a priest counseled her to move to Milwaukee to see if she and Dad could make a go of things.

"Our wedding night was the first time I learned he couldn't hear a thing when he took his hearing aid off," Mom adds to her confiding in me. I don't want to know this. Imagining Mom and Dad quietly lying naked next to each other is not what my daughter brain needs. And it makes me feel sorry for Dad. He never says a bad word about Mom, calling her his "Marie-tay," a playful take on her name, Mary, and "the love of his life." But when I think about it, they rarely show affection. And if they do, Dad initiates. A quick kiss when he leaves for work. Another for good night. They don't hug, hold hands, or go out to dinner just the two of them.

"Your dad's ears make it too hard to socialize," Mom says.

It's easy to know what Mom doesn't like, and I pay attention to what she does: God and church for sure. She goes to mass every weekday morning. Sits in the same forward-left pew too, according to Tony and George when their altar boy duties coincide with her attendance. Her daily two-mile walk around the L section. Trying new diets. Saturday mass and hot chocolate at McDonald's with her friends Bea and Marjorie, and trying to win the daily money prize from WOKY AM radio, her written tally of the growing jackpot lying next to the white oblong radio on the kitchen counter. And what she talks about most happily: her life in Philadelphia before us.

Out of Alignment

THE PINCH IN MY PINKY jolts me awake. My bedside clock radio glows 2:00 a.m. It's been two weeks since my appointment with Dr. A. Days crawl, punctuated by random terror. A switch has seemingly flipped in my body, and I'm at its mercy, having three, sometimes five, big spasms a week. I'm still not back at school, and Mom isn't pressing. She collects my homework from Sister Joyce, my teacher, while I wait in the car. Close to Mom is where I can endure being me with no answers. Anywhere else feels defenseless and alone.

I bolt upright, grab my left hand with my right, and frantically start rubbing. "No, no, no!" my brain screams, my eyes wide, my whole being tight with panic. Day or night, my spasms all start the same—a sudden pulsing in my left pinky, never a different finger or my right hand. "Please, God, don't let it go big," I beg every time as my hand curls into the claw, because sometimes, just sometimes, my pleading works and the numbness subsides at my wrist, my hand slowly unclenching. My wrist is the threshold that, if crossed, means things go all the way to full body. But there is no way to predict it; I just have to wait and see and hope during the first twenty seconds. "Mommmm!" I yell, scrambling out of bed, the numbness deciding to march up my arm. I stumble toward my doorway to get to Mom and Dad's room across the hall, but I don't make it, collapsing on my carpet instead.

My head thuds against my bedroom floor, my limbs splayed like a starfish. I disappear into unconsciousness. But instead of seeing my usual black nothingness, I see a vision of a huge angel hovering over the neighbor's backyard basketball hoop, the setting familiar and unmistakable. The basketball hoop sits atop a sturdy metal pole, and she is behind it, at least ten feet tall. I can't make out her obscured and gauzy face, but she extends her enormous layered pearly-white wings wide.

"You will be healed," she says in a clear, loving voice, filling my mind with peace.

When I come to, Mom is crouched next to me in her nightgown, her hand resting on my shoulder, her lips moving with a silent Hail Mary.

"Did you see the angel?" I whisper. Surely her presence and promise filled my entire bedroom.

"No angel, dear," Mom consoles me.

I blink to clear my confusion. She was as real as anything I've known, but perhaps just wishful dreaming in my delirium. Slowly I get up and crawl back into my bed, pulling the covers to my chest. Mom follows, sitting next to me. My peace dissolves.

"What happens when you die?" I ask. I've started thinking it would be easier than living in constant fear.

"You go to heaven and spend eternity with Jesus," Mom says, not missing a beat.

"What if it's not true, and when you die, you die?" I counter, the dark room mirroring my doubt. The thought of life being over without anything after makes me short of breath.

"The Bible says it's true."

"But what if it's *not*?" I insist.

Truthfully, it all sounds like make-believe. Mom is one hundred percent sure about Jesus and heaven, telling me to talk to God and the Virgin Mary like they're my second dad and mom. "Your heavenly parents," she says, "available anytime." Or not. To me, God feels like an empty cave. I yell my questions and worries into the God Cave and wait for an answer back. But nothing, just quiet. If God answers prayers, why won't he stop what's happening to me? Or like Jesus making the blind guy see or multiplying the bread loaves, this should be an easy fix for one of them.

If my spasms aren't a God problem, they aren't a family problem either; they are a Mom-and-me problem. Dad leaves the house every morning at 7 a.m. to drive to his job in downtown Milwaukee as a tax auditor for the Wisconsin Department of Revenue. It's a good job for him, Mom says, because he rarely needs to talk on the phone, and when he does, his coworker Linda helps listen for him. One time, I overheard Dad telling Mom somebody at his office threw paper clips at him to get his attention, and I wonder how people can be so mean to someone who can't hear. When Dad gets home every night at 5:59 p.m., he wants supper, his recliner, and the newspaper. He doesn't ask about my spasms, I don't talk about them, and I'm unsure what Mom is telling him, if anything.

Tony and George aren't part of my problem either. Three and two years older, it could be twenty for how often we interact. "The boys," Mom calls them. One unit. Separate. I am the odd girl out. The boys can walk to and from school through Scout Lake Park without Mom. They disappear outside for hours, riding bikes and playing backyard baseball. And lately—getting into trouble. A neighbor lady caught George lighting matches and starting tiny fires behind Mr. Bergy's house, while Tony was letting air out of people's car tires with his friend Billy, whose dad blames Tony for turning his Billy into a "hoodlum." I insert myself into Tony and George's roughhousing any chance I can, pinching and poking them to get a rise. Which I do, until they chase me to my bedroom, where I press my door closed from inside with all my might before they barrel in, pin me on my bed, and twist my wrists with snakebites until I cry. Then I tattle to Mom, who punishes them even though I started the whole thing.

Exactly three weeks after my first spasm, Mom tells me she made me an appointment with Dr. Schultz, the chiropractor she goes to for her back pain.

"Why?" I ask.

"To check your spine," Mom says. "Make sure there's nothing out of alignment causing your spasms."

"My back is fine," I say, though I know Mom's isn't.

"My fourth and fifth lumbar are deteriorating," she says, blaming it on her electroshock therapy in the Air Force. "The worst injustice of my life," she declares, a line she says so often, I can mouth it along with her.

Every six weeks, it's time for her adjustment. To what I don't know, but she can't get enough of Dr. Schultz. Dad wants nothing to do with him, preferring a nap and heating pad for his back pain.

On a Wednesday morning, we drive thirty minutes to a part of Milwaukee I've never been. Old houses line the cracked and weathered streets, overhead power lines suspended like tightropes every which way. Where the heck are we? Not in alphabetized Greendale, that's for sure. "*This* is his office?" I say as we pull up to a small beige brick cube of a building. I want to be in my bedroom with its lime-green carpeting and dancing butterflies wallpaper, reading my Little House on the Prairie books or styling my Barbie doll's hair, not going to some back doctor in a worn-out part of town.

A flimsy screen door opens into a plain waiting room with mint-green linoleum flooring like my school cafeteria. It smells minty too, like muscle cream. Straight-backed chairs line the perimeter; soft music comes from overhead. An older couple sits reading books. They smile at me, a nine-year-old girl, not the usual customer. What's wrong with their spines? I sit and pick up a *Highlights* magazine from a small table. "Find the Hidden Picture" is my favorite feature, plus the "Goofus and Gallant" comic strip, where Goofus always screws up and Gallant one-ups him with his perfect behavior. I feel sorry for Goofus, certain he's feeling depressed like me.

"Hi, Mary," a man's voice booms into the waiting room.

Dr. Schultz peeks out from a doorway, a short kind-looking man with plump red cheeks and a big middle jutting over his belt. His dark hair, slicked back and glossy, is perfectly coiffed, and his pleated cuffed pants float above his ankles to showcase polished black shoes.

"And you must be Marianne," he says, meeting my gaze while motioning to the older people to follow him.

Twenty minutes later, it's our turn. Mom forges ahead with the assurance of a regular, while I nervously trail behind down a hallway to a small room on the left. In the middle is a tall machine, an upright padded table with a foot pedal plugged into a square metal base. Other than that, just a bench, filing cabinets, and posters of the human body without skin, a network of bones, muscles, and nerves. A life-size spine is propped in the corner, its movable white vertebrae like giant marsh-mallows. I sit on the bench.

"Has she had any injuries?" Dr. Schultz asks.

"Well, we *were* in a car accident a couple years ago," Mom says, describing the time a guy ran through stop sign and into the passenger-side door on the way home from ice skating lessons. I had to sit in the witness box in a real courtroom and testify Mom had her lights on, even though I honestly couldn't remember.

"That can certainly do it," Dr. Schultz nods, pondering the revelation.

Do what? The accident was scary, but I wasn't physically hurt.

Dr. Schultz pats the machine and replaces the crumpled white paper covering the top pad, soiled with makeup from the previous customer. "Let's take a look at you," he says. The table moves forward, carrying me to a horizontal position. Face down, I stare at the floor through an opening that lets my nose breathe. Dr. Schultz quickly moves down my spine with his fingers, talking to himself the whole way. "Hmmmm. Uh-huh. Yep," he mumbles as he pokes and prods, getting close to my butt. "She's definitely out of alignment. Second cervical. Fifth. Sixth. Third thoracic too. Moved way over."

I don't know any of these words, but it sure sounds like he's hit the spine jackpot in me.

"Can this be causing her spasms?" Mom asks hopefully.

"Indeed," Dr. Schultz assures her, if my vertebrae are pressing on the nerves leading to my left arm and hand. Before I can object, he gives my upper back a downward thrust, its cracking audible. I grunt. Next, he does the same to my middle back, the table giving way, so my spine doesn't crack in two. *This is crazy!* A couple more pushes and shoves, and he presses his foot pedal to raise me back up. I steady myself on the floor.

"You okay?" Dr. Shultz chuckles. I don't laugh back. He invites me to the bench next, extending his arm to show the way. Mom stands in the corner, watching intently, her purse hooked over her elbow. Contorting me like a pretzel, Dr. Schultz coaxes a crack from my hip and leg. Then, with one hand on each side of my jaw, he cranks my head up and sideways—both right and left—nearly throwing me off the bench. One slip and I'm paralyzed. What is Mom *thinking* bringing me here? My back felt fine, or used to, and now Dr. Schultz is listing everything wrong with me.

"When would you like to see us next?" Mom asks.

"Three or four times a week for the first couple weeks," says Dr. Schultz.

No, no, no, I silently object. Life is getter weirder by the day. A month ago, I was normal. Now I'm having spasms that doctors blame on my mind and crooked spine.

But Mom obliges. "We can do that," she says.

We follow Dr. Schultz into his office, a dimly lit room in the back with old brown carpeting and a big wooden desk overflowing with papers. Mom hands him a check. Twenty-five dollars for one visit. Seventy-five dollars a week. *Wait until Dad finds out,* I think, knowing how carefully he divides his paycheck into long white envelopes for Mom, which she keeps in the kitchen drawer. The grocery envelope. Electric bill and haircut envelopes, though she's constantly moving money from one envelope to another. There is no Dr. Schultz envelope to begin with. No Publishers Clearing House sweepstakes envelope either, but that doesn't stop her from playing every time the letter comes in the mail.

"Looks like we might have some answers!" Mom says cheerfully as we get back into the car.

I want to believe them both, to feel their hope and enthusiasm, but deep down, I doubt the answer is as easy as moving my spine around.

"I have to come back three times a week," I say.

"If that's what it takes," Mom replies.

I am not apologizing for the inconvenience; I am repeating the absurdity, hoping she'll change her mind. But Mom loves Dr. Schultz, and if she thinks he's helping, we'll be back as often as he asks.

"Let's go to Leon's Custard," Mom changes the subject. Leon's is an old-fashioned drive-in ice cream place with a big neon cone blinking on its roof.

"Sure," I say. Anything to think about something else for a few minutes. We walk up to the open window, where workers in white paper hats take our order. I get a vanilla and chocolate twist cone, and Mom asks for the same thing she always does—a caramel cashew sundae with two scoops of ice cream, pronouncing it *care-a-mel*, with three syllables, and justifying the calories because cashews are protein.

Wooden Jesus

THE KIDS GATHER AROUND MY desk.

"Why is your mom here?" they ask.

Mom says I can't stay home forever, so she calls Sister Joyce to ask if she can sit outside my classroom in case I have a spasm. I don't know what Mom tells Sister Joyce about my situation, only that her answer is yes. I like Sister Joyce, with her short stylish haircut and bright-pink lipstick outlining a pretty smile. She looks like an everyday person to me in her black flare-leg stretch pants, red ribbed turtleneck, and white crocheted sweater-vest, unlike the other nuns, whose black habits make them look holy and stern.

"She's grading papers," I lie.

Having Mom at school is a huge comfort to me, but I can't say the real reason out loud. I'm not even sure how to describe the reason. I already feel awkward in my body, self-conscious of my crooked bangs Mom cuts with her pinking shears and my even more crooked front teeth that stick out like fangs. "Too expensive," Dad says about braces, so I sit in my bedroom and push my thumbs against my teeth, trying to move them backward, but they don't budge. I make my own retainer too, bending a paper clip into an arc and sticking it in my mouth, but the sharp edges poke into my cheeks and make them bleed.

Being trapped at my desk is torture, my brain obsessing over when, if, and where the next spasm will happen. It's been nearly two months since everything started and two weeks since my last big one. To help me stay put, I hold my left pinky down with my left thumb. Or I flick my pinky over and over, thinking if I keep it busy, it won't have time to go numb. Doing all this under my desk makes me lean forward.

"What's *wrong* with you?" the boy next to me asks, his face twisted in confusion.

"Nothing," I say, releasing my pinky and sitting on my hand instead. If he thinks I'm weird, I try not to care. I am surviving.

A couple times a week, I jump up during class and run out the door, where Mom sits at a child-size desk reading a book. The kids wordlessly watch me flee.

"I think one's coming," I gasp, my eyes wild with fear. She grabs my left hand, rubbing it between hers. "Hail Mary, full of grace," she whispers, massaging each finger. I can't tell what's real anymore. Did I feel something or just think I did?

Maybe Dr. A is right, and I am the problem.

Most days Mom goes home after lunch recess, after she and I wander around the blacktop parking lot eating our peanut butter and jelly sandwiches from brown bags. As much as I depend on her, I am embarrassed by her presence. No one else's mom is hanging out at school. I envy the other kids playing four square and double Dutch jump rope. I want to be playing too, instead of feeling a desperate, lonely ache in my stomach.

Mom promises the afternoons will pass quickly, but they rarely do with my security person gone. It helps to have music class first thing after lunch with Sister Marianne, my second-favorite nun after Sister Joyce, and not just because our names are spelled the same. Her round ruddy face and wide bosom speak motherly comfort to me, her soft and friendly-looking chambray habit hugging her ample figure like a favorite pair of jeans. A weathered wooden cross, two inches in each direction, hangs from a brown leather cord around her neck, her hair kept secret by her veil, leaving me curious about its color, length, and style.

One Tuesday afternoon in April, we file behind Sister Joyce into the music room. Located downstairs in the way-back corner of the school, it's a big rectangular space with white cement walls and high windows looking out, even with the grass. An upright piano and music stand faces three curved rows of chairs on a raised platform. Sister Marianne nods at Sister Joyce as we walk in, confirming she's in charge now. I take my place on a gray metal chair, my hands smoothing the pleats of my green plaid skirt over my bare thighs.

"Hmmmmm," Sister Marianne hums us to attention.

"Hmmmmm," we reply.

And that's when I feel it—the pinch in my left pinky. *No, no, no, no!* I jolt upright, my heart thumping, panic seizing my chest. I look right and left at my row of classmates. Do they see what is happening? No, they are *oohing* and *aahing* with the piano. I grip my left hand with my right, digging my thumb into the spreading numbness in my palm, trying to push it out through my fingers.

Dear God, please, please, please not here. Not now. Help me. Save me.

I haven't had a big spasm at school. So far only at home with Mom. I can't have one in front of everyone. I CAN'T.

But I am. I rub harder, my heart pounding, my mouth sticky, my breathing quick and shallow. Jumping up, I inch sideways down my aisle toward the door. Kids pull in their knees to let me pass, confusion in their eyes while their mouths are busy singing.

"Where. Are. You. Going?" demands Sister Marianne, pausing her fingers on the piano keys. Ignoring her, I push through the chairs in front of me, leaving a clatter in my wake. My left fingers are curling now, the numbness climbing over my wrist. Past the point of no return, I need to get out.

"Marianne, sit down!" scolds Sister Marianne as I open the door with my right hand and flee, her voice trailing after me. "Marianne!!!"

Running down the hallway, my left arm lifts over my head, threatening my balance. Frantically I search for somewhere to hide. An empty classroom. The bathroom. Yes, the bathroom, a stall for privacy. But I don't make it, rounding a corner and falling on the ground, my spasm claiming me against my will and prayers. Convulsions course through my body, my plaid dress askew, my stiffened limbs jerking. My head bounces on the floor. I lose consciousness and hear my familiar screams reverberate inside me.

"Mommmmm! Help meeeeee," I implore. My spasms take me to a faraway place I can't visit when awake, black and disconnected from my body yet filled with my own voice. I see flashes of light and wonder if I'm halfway to heaven before God decides, "Not yet."

Eventually I come to and open my eyes. How much time has passed? The walls come into focus. I am on my side, curved into myself like a comma, unable to move. Mom is not here. Sister Marianne and Sister Joyce aren't here either. An unfamiliar lady's face appears in front of me. She is on her hands and knees like a puppy, tilting her head to match the angle of mine.

"Are you okay?" she asks gently. I look beyond her, tears sliding from

my eyes, over my nose, and puddling by my shoulder on the ground. I
don't answer. "I'll get the nurse," she offers. "She's right down the hall." I
nod. "I'll hurry," she assures me and backs away, keeping her eyes on me.

I wait until the nice lady comes back with Mrs. Rudella, the school
nurse.

"Oh, honey," Mrs. Rudella says, kneeling beside me. "Can you sit up?"

I raise my torso, the two women on either side helping me upright.
Fiftyish steps later, they gingerly place me on a green padded table in a
room that smells like rubbing alcohol.

"Rest," the nurse says and sits on the edge to talk. "Can you tell me
what happened?"

"I have this...this...thing," I try to explain, "where my hand goes
numb and spreads to my body until I fall down." Her furrowing brow
and widening eyes tell me she hasn't been let in on my issues.

She nods. Pats my knee.

"I'll call your mom," she says.

I lay on the green foam, staring at the ceiling. It happened again. It
keeps happening. Why can't anyone make it stop? Mumbled conversation travels around the room.

"Hallway... Found her... Pale... Resting."

The nurse spins on her chair to face me, handing me a small blue
rectangle of paper. *Permit to Leave Building. Reason: Muscle spasm.* "Your
mother is coming to get you in a few minutes. You can wait for her
outside."

Muscle spasm. There it is again, the phrase diminishing my experience. A muscle spasm is small and inconvenient. This is enormous and
mind altering.

Down the empty hallway I walk, and up the four wide stairs, past
the church sanctuary on my left. I stop and peer into the hushed room
that bustles on Sundays with families, organ music, and the Good News

choir. Our family sits in the same front pew every week, underneath an overhead speaker so Dad can better hear the sermon, though it doesn't do much for his singing, which is terribly—and embarrassingly—off tune. He and I often share a missalette, and I help guide his vocal pace with my index finger, moving it onto each word as we sing. Dad wears the same thing every week too: white slacks pulled up too high, with a white belt, white pleather dress shoes, and a blue plaid suit coat. His outfit is like our living room furniture: in need of replacement.

A huge wooden Jesus hangs on a massive cross behind the altar. Muted light filters through stained-glass windows depicting biblical motifs, the confessionals empty. It smells musty. Like holy water and incense combined. I made my First Confession at St. Alphonsus in third grade, sitting in one of the small dark closet confessionals, thinking up something to tell Father Carter, his silhouetted profile visible through the slatted window, me staring at his large right ear. My classmates and I lined up in the center aisle, our teacher tapping our shoulder when it was our turn for the closet.

"Yes, my child. Go ahead," his deep voice invited.

"I'm sorry I lied to my parents," I said quickly, the same thing I said every time, even if I hadn't lied.

"Your sins are forgiven," Father Carter assured me after some gentle counseling, then told me to kneel in a pew and say ten Hail Marys for my penance. I wondered what everyone else was saying in their closets, what big sins us eight-year-olds were hiding.

After my First Communion in first grade, Mom invited Father Carter to our house for lunch. He sat at our dining room table in his black short-sleeved shirt and white clerical collar, eating ham sandwiches and potato chips. A holy hero in our midst. When our family crowded around him for Dad's photo, I flung my arm casually around Father Carter's shoulder before wondering if it was appropriate. Dad invited Mrs. D too, short for Mrs. Dalrymple, the sweet old lady whose upstairs flat he'd rented before getting married and whose hobby is braiding plastic bread bags into beanie-style hats. *What an odd gathering,* I remember thinking. Most people had relatives for special occasions. But ours are dead, far away, or close and missing nonetheless.

"Any time you want to step in is great," I tell Wooden Jesus before walking outside. "It's getting worse."

Standing on the curb in the quiet of early afternoon, my body is wobbly, my brain tired, my eyes still wet. Across the parking lot, I see our newly green station wagon turn in from Loomis Road, Mom inching toward me. Dad recently had it repainted to cover some rust and chose the same flat olive color for every surface, giving our car an army tank look. I slide into the front passenger seat and hand her the blue paper. I don't remember talking on the way home, only that she calls Dr. A first thing.

"He wants us to see a Dr. Strassburg," she says after hanging up. "Milwaukee's leading neurosurgeon." I know enough from science class to know that *neuro* means *nerves.*

Mom calls Dr. Schultz too, who urges us to come see him right away to make sure I'm not out of alignment. We're driving to his office three times a week as is, my appointments quicker and more routine as he does the same thing every time: Face down to crack my back. On the bench for my hip and neck. "How do things feel?" I ask after each adjustment, eager to hear I'm aligned once and for all.

"You're making progress," he says, but always finds a vertebra "slipped" from where it should be. I can't bend into the bathtub now or reach into my closet without wondering what I am undoing in my back. And his treatment isn't working anyway.

A few days after the music class spasm, I have another big one outside Grebe's Bakery after church, while picking out my favorite pink frosted donut with the white cream filling. Just as the lady hands me a brown paper bag, I feel the pinch, drop my donut bag on the bakery floor, shove the glass door open, and collapse on the sidewalk while other people walk in and out of Grebe's for their donuts. Mom races to a nearby pay phone and calls Dr. Schultz at home. "Lucky for us he answered," Mom says, but I don't feel lucky at all. It's Sunday and Dr. Schultz isn't at work, so he tells us to go to St. Michael's Hospital in Cudahy, a twenty-minute drive, where Dr. Berglund, his neurologist friend, is on call. I'm lying in another ER exam room, as Dr. Berglund does the usual looking in my eyes and ears and concludes I am physically normal with "psychological trauma."

There is nothing normal about me anymore. And less so every day.

Hope Dashed

I SIT ALONE IN A GROWN-UP chair across from Dr. Strassburg, my feet hanging midair. Mom isn't in the room, and I don't ask why. He looks at me across his wide wooden desk, his hands folded in front of a yellow pad of lined paper. He doesn't look friendly or unfriendly, his mouth a straight-across line. He wears a white doctor coat with his name embroidered in red thread on the right chest pocket, *Dr. Raymond Strassburg* taking up the entire width. I have survived the past month knowing this appointment was on our May calendar, desperately hoping he is the person who will finally figure out and fix what is wrong with me.

"Tell me what's going on," he says evenly.

So I do, demonstrating how my hand curls into a claw and raises over my head. Explaining how the numbness sometimes stops at my wrist and other times goes through my whole body. How I shake all over and go unconscious. And then wake up a couple minutes later, tired and confused. I'm nervous describing it, afraid my body will think, *Oh, hey, let's show him what she's talking about,* so I press my left pinky down with my left thumb to make sure it doesn't, though sometimes I wish it would. Maybe then the doctors will believe I have nothing to do with it.

"How often does this happen?" he asks.

"Depends," I say. "Three times a week, sometimes more."

He scribbles words on his paper. "At night? During the day?"

"Both. But more at night."

More writing. "Do you have headaches?"

"No," I say.

"Blurry vision? Like you can't see very well?"

"No."

He gets up and walks to my side of the desk. "Stand up and walk across the room," he says, watching me from behind.

I walk away, slowly turning like a runway model.

"Hop on one foot."

I hop.

"The other."

I hop again.

"Put both arms out, and push up while I push down," he says, demonstrating. I match his strength, impressed with myself. Next, he takes out a tiny flashlight from his embroidered pocket.

"Follow the light with your eyes," he says, moving it right, left, up, and down. My eyeballs stretch every which way.

"Now close your eyes and touch your nose with each finger."

I do this too.

"Okay, you can sit down again."

This guy is my last hope. When I'm not having a spasm, I look normal. Talk, walk, and hop normal. But since January, I am not normal. Can't anyone see how desperate this is? How desperate I am? I am terrified to be at home, at school, in the car, in my body, in my life. This guy needs to tell Mom what to do.

"He gave you a prescription for something called Mebaral," Mom says back in our car. "One pill three times a day for thirty days; then we go back to see if it helped."

I don't care if I need to take twenty pills a day if they stop my spasms. Can I finally rest? Live unafraid? Be back to who I was before? I exhale big and loud, slumping into my seat, deep relief and hope enveloping me like a warm blanket. We stop at Walgreens on the way home, pick up my pills, and hope is mine for the first time since January.

But not for long.

I have barely started the medication when Mom marches into my bedroom.

"Mebaral is a *drug*," she announces, exasperated and angry. "Dr. Strassburg said it *wasn't* a drug." I wasn't in the room when he talked to her after talking to me, so I don't know what he said, though it seems odd he'd mix up this detail.

Mom is standing in front of me like a TV preacher, holding open her *Merck Index*—a book listing every drug and side effect—and reads about Mebaral: "*Medical use: sedative, long-acting hypnotic; anticonvulsant. Side effects: drowsiness, vertigo, cutaneous eruptions.*" Pausing, she says loudly, "*Drug. Dependence. May. Occur,*" punching each word for emphasis.

"Who cares?" I say, flopping on my bed, unfazed. I'm delighted to depend on something that will help me. I'll trade side effects for peace of mind and self-confidence. Drowsiness? No big deal. I'll be tired but safe in my body. And eruptions? I'll handle them too, whatever they are, given what I'm handling already.

But Mom ignores my objection. "Because you know how drug sensitive *I* am," she defends her decision.

Oh, I know.

I can't remember a time of not knowing.

I was born into this story.

⌐

The way she tells it, Mom was twenty-nine, working as a secretary for Smith, Kline, and French Labs, a pharmaceutical company in

Philadelphia, when a letter came to her mailbox "out of the blue" from the U.S. Air Force offering college graduates the opportunity to become squadron commanders. Mom went for the interview. "As a joke," she says, but quickly received a direct commission as a first lieutenant and moved from Pennsylvania to Wright-Patterson Air Force Base located southeast of Dayton, Ohio.

Five years later, by then a captain and pen pals with Dad, Mom was thinking about leaving the military when her own ma got sick and went into the hospital. The Air Force was giving Rozalia, a widow and Mom's dependent, a monthly allowance and free medical care, so Mom stayed put and started taking the train back and forth to Philly to visit her. It was a sixteen-hour trip, leaving Friday after work and riding all night Sunday to be back at her desk by Monday morning.

"I was physically and emotionally spent," Mom says.

She went to the clinic on the base, where a doctor diagnosed her with clinical depression and prescribed Thorazine, an antipsychotic. But the side effects were bad.

"My mind was so spaced-out," Mom explains. "I couldn't add two and two, and I turned yellow with jaundice."

Instead of stopping the medication, the doctor checked Mom into the local hospital, then had her flown to Walter Reed National Medical Center in Washington, DC, the top military hospital in the world.

"I don't remember being told why I had to go to Walter Reed," Mom says. "Only that a girlfriend of mine was crying when they put me on the gurney to fly me, tears running down her face."

Once there, Mom was put in a dorm-like building with a lot of other people, and three times a week for five weeks, a nurse woke her up early to take her to a different room.

"They put me on an examining table, stuck a tongue depressor in my mouth, and rubbed grease on my temples," Mom says. The nurse stood behind her and held electrodes to her head while a man in a white jacket—the doctor, she assumed—stood across the room next to a machine. "And pretty soon electricity went into my head, which led to me having a seizure, and I would just pass out."

They didn't give her any muscle relaxers, and Mom says she would have "lost her mind" if not for a nurse who woke her up at sunrise to distribute Holy Communion.

"It saved my life," Mom says. "I pray every day for that nurse."

⁓

Eighteen years later, the two of us in my small bedroom on Laura Lane, Mom's electroshock therapy is still the centerpiece of her life, the story she tells any chance she gets to anyone who'll listen, be it a supermarket cashier, waitress, or bank teller. It's her explanation and justification any time her brain and body falls short—from a forgotten grocery item to a sore finger to her deteriorating vertebrae—and now her reason for not letting me have medication for my spasms.

It doesn't matter I'm a different person than her and maybe my side effects won't be her side effects, if I have any at all. And that I desperately want medication if it stops my spasms and lets me be safe in my body again. But it's not up to me. I am nine, and she is the grown-up in charge of my life.

"I'll let Dr. Strassburg know we're stopping the medication and won't be back," she says.

Mom leaves my room to make her phone call, and I stare at my ceiling in disbelief and exasperation. Over the next couple days, I wean off the pills and go back to pressing down my pinky with my thumb, back to around-the-clock anxiety and moment-by-moment wondering when the next spasm might take me to the ground.

New Kid

SCHOOL ENDS, SUMMER PASSES, AND fifth grade starts. But two months in, I want out. My ten-year-old self doesn't have the words to name what I am feeling—shame, anxiety, despair—only that I can't sit at my desk at St. Alphonsus surrounded by the same kids who now know my secret. I can't walk the same basement hallways that witnessed my collapse.

I beg Mom and Dad to let me switch to Highland View.

"It'll be *so* much cheaper," I tell Dad, who pays hundreds of dollars a year for the three of us to go to Catholic school. And to Mom, "I can walk with Colleen," my new friend on Laura Lane who moved in next to Mr. Bergy.

"Fine," they say begrudgingly, "as long as you go to CCD."

CCD stands for Confraternity of Christian Doctrine, a Wednesday night religion class for public school kids. It's an easy trade-off in my mind, one night a week versus five endless days.

"This is our new student, Marianne," says Mrs. Lenz, my teacher, to her class, extending her arm and smiling in my direction. "Let's make her feel welcome." My face warms from the verbal spotlight. Our desks form a U shape around Mrs. Lenz, a short woman whose lively brown eyes match her cheery demeanor. I sit to her left in my shag hairstyle and new long-sleeved shirt Mom made for me in a fabric I excitedly chose—a white cotton twill with repeating Pepsi logos. My white elastic-waist pants complete the ensemble. No more uniform meant I needed new clothes, and Mom is feeling newly capable in her sewing abilities after taking a beginner class at the Greendale community center. But what seemed like a confident, fashionable clothing choice this morning feels now like the dumbest decision ever, my outfit a walking unpaid advertisement for brown sugar water.

The other girls are wearing snug jeans and cute peasant tops or matching shirt and skirt sets. I don't own anything like that. Most of my clothes are hand-me-downs from a teenage girl neighbor or "practical separates" from JCPenney. But on my first day, a girl named Caryn invites me to her lunch table and to play at recess. *She must be cool,* I think, *if she spells her name with a c and y instead of the usual k and e.*

⟋∘

I find myself on the lookout for other kids I imagine feel as different inside as I do, projecting my self-consciousness onto them. Unlike at St. Alphonsus, I have two Black girls in my class—Amy Wade and Kay Whitman—who are bused in every morning from downtown Milwaukee thanks to Chapter 220, a program created by Wisconsin's government to promote racial integration in mostly white suburban schools.

Amy, tall and heavy-set with large breasts, looks to me like a grown woman, while Kay is a thin and muscular contrast. Soon I'm waiting in the parking lot most mornings for the big yellow bus, empty except for Amy, Kay, and one third-grade boy. What does it feel like to be the only dark faces in a school of white ones? I know feeling conspicuous, but not like this. My difference is invisible until it's not; theirs is outward and all the time.

"Hi," I say, as they bounce down the steps with their backpacks, and we fall in step. Amy and Kay don't ask why I wait for them, readily accepting the companionship.

During one afternoon snack break, Amy extends her hand toward me. "Can I feel your hair?" she asks. I offer my head, and she smooths my fine flyaway hair. "You wash the grease out, and we put it in!" She laughs a big belly laugh, her big smile brightening her entire face.

A few months into the school year, the *Village Life*, Greendale's community newspaper, writes an article about integration, and Mrs. Lenz tells the reporter to interview Amy and me. "Marianne is my best friend," Amy declares, and our photo appears with the story; the two of us smiling side by side, sitting on the playground swings.

Before long, I have a steady group of school friends, a first for me. Some live far away like Amy and Kay while the rest of us live close to one another. "Walking around" is our preferred evening activity. Donna, Patricia, and Julie from the S section pick me up in L before we collect Paula in O, no purpose or destination in mind.

When my friends show up at my house, however, I let them in only as far as our tiny foyer. I don't want them to see our mismatched furniture, Dad's hearing aids, or the "cowboy lamp" in the family room, a table lamp with two crisscrossed black felt pistols on its burlap shade, all while hoping Mom doesn't bless anybody's forehead with her personal stash of holy water she replenishes from the baptismal font at church. "Hi, Mr. Helf," say my new friends, Dad smiling and nodding, and me knowing he can't hear a word they're saying.

At school, we orbit Mrs. Lenz like planets around the sun, sharing with her our fifth-grade dramas and confessions about the cute boys we like. Mrs. Lenz is a mom herself to two kids, and I want her to be my mom too, for how she makes us feel welcome and valued in her presence. Her curious questions and lean-in listening. Her giggling with shared delight. My favorite homework is the creative writing she assigns, where I escape to my imagination to tell stories about the seasons and being lost in the woods or making up how the elephant got its trunk. *This is outstanding and delightful! Your fine effort is easily seen in your finished product.* Mrs. Lenz returns my writings with hand-drawn smiley faces across the top. It's the first time a grown-up affirms something good my brain is doing, and it fills me with something I don't recognize—pride.

⁓

It's been a year since my last big spasm at St. Al's. Why the reprieve, I'm not sure. Perhaps Wooden Jesus finally took my plea to heart. Mom cuts back my chiropractor visits to once a month after forty-two in three months alone. I can't let my guard down though, as I'm still having hand spasms where my left fingers go numb and curl into the claw. When it happens in class, I fake a bathroom emergency and disappear into a stall. If at recess, I hide behind a wide tree trunk or inside the heavy and colorful cement tunnels that host games of hide-and-seek. I launch my familiar plea to the sky: "Please don't let it go big." It's tricky to let my friends know me while hiding me at the same time. The hidden part feels bigger than the rest of me.

If God is giving me a reprieve, Mom isn't. On Saturday mornings after mass and McDonald's, she drives to a health food store near Dr. Schultz to replace our usual cereal, potato chips, and Hostess snacks with foods we don't recognize: carob, raw Brazil nuts, turbinado sugar, and wheat germ. She's now selling Shaklee products door to door too, a line of vitamins and cleaning solutions. "*How* much did you pay for this?" Dad yells after pulling a loaf of seven-grain bread from the freezer and seeing the two-dollar price tag. White bread from Pick 'n Save is fifty cents. Not to mention Mom replaced his beloved raspberry pastry with expensive toast.

When Tony, George, and I come to breakfast, a bowl of beige puffed millet and two plain rice cakes wait where our Life cereal used to be. And a small mountain of vitamins next to our glasses of milk. Picking up a large, half-inch capsule filled with dark-green powder, I inspect it in my palm.

"Blue-green algae," Mom interjects. "A superfood made from the bacteria in lakes and ponds."

Bacteria for breakfast.

"And this?" I point to an enormous gold-colored capsule.

"Cod-liver oil."

"Gross," I say, choking it down with milk.

"It's full of vitamins A and D and omega-three fatty acids," she says.

"Still gross."

I eat a rice cake to cover up the fishy taste.

Mom adds an extra capsule to my vitamin mountain that Tony and George don't have—something called niacin.

"To get your blood flowing" she says.

Which it certainly does. Fifteen minutes after swallowing, I run to the bathroom mirror, my face blazing hot. Pink floods my cheeks, perspiration dampening my bangs. Mom figures more blood circulating in my body will stop my spasms, but I can't go to school looking like a sweaty tomato.

"Save this one for nighttime," I say.

Many days after school, I find Mom doing shoulder stands in the living room, her legs jutting skyward, her hands propping up her hips. Her sewing lessons complete, she signed up for hatha yoga.

"This pose stimulates the thyroid gland," she offers before I ask.

When any of us have a sore throat, she demonstrates the Lion. On hands and knees, fingers spread, she strains her neck forward and extends her tongue toward her chin. "Haaaaaa," she roars, with an audible constricted breath, before leaning back on her haunches. "It washes the throat with blood."

Why can't I suck on Luden's cherry cough drops like normal kids?

Apple cider vinegar becomes Mom's cure-all. She drinks it with honey from a glass measuring cup, combines it with water to clean our kitchen floor, and rubs it full strength in and around Dad's ears, hoping it will improve his hearing.

She still allows us one soda a day, but only if we mix it with Shaklee protein powder. Tony and George stir the pale bland powder into a thimbleful of Sprite to turn it into a paste, then swallow the chalky lump before drinking the rest of their precious soda unspoiled. Tony confides to me he's trading Mom's carob brownies at lunch for Twinkies, but I don't have the heart to tell her, knowing those brownies are likely five dollars each. To her credit, Mom tucks an occasional heart- or clover-shaped sugar cookie in our lunches for Valentine's or St. Patrick's Day, the quarter-inch-thick frosted ones from Grebe's Bakery. I savor those days and calories.

"Money doesn't grow on trees," Dad lectures Mom about her new family diet.

"The Lord will provide," she counters, which sums up their two life philosophies. No matter how much or little Mom has, she gives ten percent to Catholic Charities and Paralyzed Veterans and donates our old clothes to Goodwill. "We were destitutely poor," she says about her own childhood, telling and retelling how she once caught her ma readying to cook their pet rabbit for dinner and how wearing her old-lady neighbor's shoes to school started her bunions.

Mom's parents, Alexander and Rozalia Sokas, came to the U.S. from Lithuania through New York's Ellis Island in the late 1800s. "Didn't speak a lick of English," Mom says. Her dad washed dishes at Horn and Hardart's restaurant for twenty-five cents a week, and her ma washed clothes at a nearby laundry.

Mom was the youngest of four kids, one boy and three girls, born on April Fool's Day in 1923, weighing one pound. It's hard to imagine Mom ever that little, her 160 pounds always twenty more than she wants. "My parents didn't think I'd make it," she says, "so they baptized me in the kitchen sink." They named her after a Mary too: Mary Magdalene. "A slut in the Bible," Mom says, laughing at her own humor whenever she recounts the memory.

I met my grandmother just once, when I was five. Mom's dad died before I was born. Our family drove from Wisconsin to Philadelphia for Christmas. All I remember is throwing up in the back seat after the thirteen-hour trip, and my grandma, a short and stocky woman in a shapeless dress, her hair in a low bun, following me around.

"Do you want coffee? Do you want coffee?" she asked, her small feet shuffling on the wooden floor in oversized slippers.

"She's five, Ma," Mom said gently, steering her away from me. "She doesn't drink coffee."

Mom's two sisters are in Philly too—Emily, a nun and schoolteacher renamed Sister Nicola, and Julianne, who wanted to be a nun but got rejected from the nun program at age thirteen, stayed single, and works at Prange's department store. "She clothed you kids birth to six," Mom says.

Sister Nicola mails me her old school supplies, which I use to keep track of my pretend classroom. "Erika is absent *again*," I admonish aloud from my "desk," which is me sitting on a basement step talking to my imaginary students below, all assigned a favorite boy or girl name I like better than my own.

On my first day of kindergarten, each of us students had to skip around the large blue circle repeating our first name aloud. "To help us get to know each other," said my smiling teacher Mrs. Barczak in a high-pitched friendly voice. I awaited my turn sitting cross-legged, pressing my pleated skirt down between my legs to cover up my underwear. A large name tag shaped like a school bus hung from my neck, my name written in large careful letters. "Marianne, Marianne, Marianne," I skipped and sang, my patent leather shoes tapping the linoleum outside the rug, my name tag flying, my hands pressing my skirt over my bottom. "Hi, Marianne!" the other kids shouted in unison. *Who are they talking to?* I wondered, feeling mismatched to myself. I didn't hear the name of a regular six-year-old girl, rather that of a grown-up church lady.

⌒

Once a month, Mom and Julie talk on the phone, starting out in English, then switching to Lithuanian when she doesn't want us to listen in. Mom says her nightly prayers in Lithuanian too. I stand in her bedroom doorway and watch her kneeling, hands folded, forehead to bedspread, a rush of gibberish coming from her lips. Mom's oldest and only brother, Pete, is my godfather and lives in Maryland. I've never met him, but he mails me fifty dollars for both my birthday and Christmas, which is more than a year's allowance. "He was like a second father to me," Mom says about Pete. He was also the one who convinced her to go to college. Mom wanted to be a gym teacher, but Pete told her to major in chemistry. So she did, proudly quoting Newton's third law whenever it comes in handy, usually when Tony, George, and I get into trouble. "For every action, there is an equal and opposite reaction," she says.

I never met Dad's parents, both gone before I was born. His mother,

Margaret, was a seamstress, and his father, George, a harness maker until a doctor told him, "Either you get out of that smelly harness shop and into the open air, or you die." Dad's parents switched to farming and bought their first farm in the early 1900s in Marathon City, Wisconsin, close to Wausau. Dad was born there in July of 1923, three months after Mom and a world away, the second-youngest of seven kids. But soon after, his parents lost that farm. "World War One had ended," Dad says, "and the price for milk, our main income, fell." His broke parents picked up the pieces and became sharecroppers, leasing a farm from an owner and paying him one-half their receipts for rent. Two more farms followed, the final one in Kiel, Wisconsin, where Dad graduated high school.

"Farm life wasn't for the faint of heart," he says. Milking cows before and after school. Tilling the soil. Corn harvesting time. "And worrying about how much people would pay at the market for our crops, milk, eggs, and Ma's home-baked kuchen and kalachies."

But Dad talked of having fun too: playing football and the oboe, speech club, and hitching a ride to school on the back of a horse-drawn wagon going into town. It's hard for me to reconcile my quiet, antisocial Dad with the outgoing kid he described. His hearing loss seemingly kidnapped his exuberant soul.

Though Mom's family is far away, Dad's six siblings and most of our nineteen first cousins live near Sheboygan, a quick, ninety-minute drive from Greendale.

"Why don't we ever see anyone?" I ask. Early pictures in the green photo album show visits from Sister Nicola and Aunt Julie and Sunday lunches with Dad's family. When I was in first grade, Dad hosted his brothers and sisters in our backyard to play Jarts and eat bratwurst.

But after that, nobody.

"They don't like me," Mom says.

"That's not true, Mary," Dad counters, but she is resolute. Why he doesn't go alone or bring us kids with him, I don't know. He's especially fond of his youngest sister, Jean. It was only the two of them living at home after his older siblings moved out and got married. But whatever his reasons, he refuses to go solo.

"I wish it was different for you," Mom tells me, which makes little sense, given she has the power to change it.

To fill our grandparent void, she "adopts" some from a nearby nursing home, a man and a woman, with the idea we'll visit once a week to hang out with our pretend relatives.

One Sunday afternoon, the four of us go to the nursing home. Dad refuses, content to stay home and read the newspaper. Mom checks us in at the front desk, and the white-haired receptionist leads us back to a community gathering space. Round tables dot the carpeted floor, board games and in-progress puzzles on several. A few residents sit parked about in wheelchairs, some sleeping, others existing. It is uncomfortably quiet; the smell of disinfectant stings my nose. Mom explains our mission to a nurse who gestures to a lone man.

"That's Harold," she says. "He doesn't get many visitors."

Mom walks over, Tony, George, and me trailing behind.

"Hellooo, Harold," she chirps, trying to make eye contact with the elderly guy slumped in his wheelchair, barely cognizant. He gazes at her through cloudy, unresponsive eyes, nodding off for intermittent naps. This is going nowhere. The nurse, sensing futility, takes us next to a private room where Anne resides. Propped up in bed, Anne appears on the younger end of old, awake, and eager to converse. A perky stranger, but a stranger nonetheless. While Mom engages in forced chitchat with Anne, Tony, George, and I hang back in her doorway, wondering when the heck we can get out of here.

Our grandparent experiment lasts exactly one Sunday, and it's back to the five of us. Until Mom announces she's leaving.

City Girl

WHAT? FOR HOW LONG?" I ask, my voice high and shaky. I am playing jacks on the kitchen floor in front of the refrigerator.

"Two, three weeks, maybe longer. I'm not sure," she says.

"Why?"

I can't believe she's leaving me alone with Dad. I haven't had a big spasm since fourth grade, but the fear of my unpredictable hand spasms going big whenever they want—at home, at school, or in the middle of the night—is constant. Dad can't hear me if I yell for help, especially at night, when his hearing aids are sitting on his dresser. If my sixth-grade teacher calls him at work, Dad can't hear over the phone either. If my school even knows where he works. I am not aware of any backup plan on my behalf.

"I'm going to Philadelphia," Mom says. "I need a break."

A break from what—housework? My spasms? Dad? But she doesn't elaborate.

I think Mom would move back to Philly if she could. "I'm a *city* girl," she announces when driving around Greendale, creating an identity barrier between her and her present life, refusing to read a map or drive the highways and getting repeatedly confused at the four-way stop sign two hundred yards from our house, a turn she's made a thousand times. "Which way are we?" she asks.

"Still left, Mom," I say, annoyed.

But she can rattle off the names of every one of her first-grade class-mates from her tiny elementary school nearly five decades earlier. "My people," she says, which never seem to be us.

But something has changed in Mom.

"With all due respect, Father Barton is smoking pot," she says one night at supper about a priest at St. Alphonsus. Mom doesn't say how she knows this for sure. Father Barton isn't just a priest, however. He's the cool, avid bicycler "hippie priest," at St. Al's, with slick curly hair, big round glasses, and bare feet in leather sandals poking out from beneath his clergy robe, no matter the season or temperature. A living Jesus, I think.

Mom has taken to adding "with all due respect" to the front of her opinions and conclusions about many people, usually after return-ing from the grocery store. "With all due respect, Mrs. Lewandowski looks *terrible*," she'll say about a random acquaintance, as if the prefix absolves her of the insult.

"And the Dolinskis are dealing drugs" she adds about our next-door neighbors after an unfamiliar car pulled into their driveway in the middle of the night. Why she's awake to be watching, I don't ask.

"It's probably their doctor," I offer.

Mrs. Dolinski recently gave birth to a baby at home, which I'd never heard of people doing, but Mom's slow shake of her head and pursed lips tell me she's not convinced.

Another supper, another story.

"Someone's trying to kill me," Mom says, claiming a mysterious liquid was thrown at her windshield from the left side of her car while she was driving one afternoon. By whom she didn't know, but suspected it was the kids she caught smoking marijuana in the church bathroom while I was at Wednesday night religion class. I slip into our garage to look at the station wagon, but I don't see anything amiss.

"I don't think so, Mary," Dad says gently, but it only makes her madder.

As it is, Mom and Dad are fighting a lot. This is new. Mostly when they think us kids are out of earshot, but even in my room with the door closed, I hear their raised voices, if not the exact words. When their shouting gets extra loud, I run down the hallway to the kitchen and plant myself between their face-to-face shouting in front of the sink.

"Stop fighting!" I scream, closing my eyes and covering my ears. "Stop it, stop it, stop it!" It feels good to scream, releasing my helplessness.

They go quiet for a second, then order me back to my room to resume their yelling. I call my best friend, Donna, to meet me on the playground swings at Highland View.

"I think my parents are getting a divorce." I speak my worry into the air, my feet soaring toward the sun, the blacktop empty except for us. Donna is quiet. Neither of us know anyone divorced in Greendale.

⌒

Mom packs a suitcase plus a photocopy of an article she clipped from the *Milwaukee Sentinel* newspaper that had been resting on our kitchen counter.

I read the headline: *Turner Bares Details of CIA Tests.*

The second she first saw the story, she announced to the family that she herself was an "innocent victim of mind control experiments by the CIA." Her ongoing bobble in an ocean of anguish over her Air Force ordeal had reached a culpable shore. At once, she "knew" her electroshock therapy, supposedly for depression, was a part of this secret government operation where innocent people like her were subjected to drugs, electroshock, poisons, and chemicals. The dates of the experiments—1953 to 1964—coincided with her military years and, most specifically, her stay at Walter Reed. Night after night, Mom watched film footage on the evening news, its broadcast triggered by the CIA's admission. Pictures of people in wheelchairs traveled across the screen. "Those people went through what I did and *worse*," Mom said. "They're just *vegetables* today." Then Mom called the National Personnel Records Center in St. Louis to get her Air Force medical records but learned a fire destroyed millions of Army and Air Force files for people discharged September 25, 1947, to January 1, 1964, with names alphabetically after *Hubbard, James*. Mom's maiden name, Sokas, and her 1957 discharge meant her records were gone.

"No duplicates were ever made," the St. Louis people said.

"Maybe your fire wasn't so accidental after all," Mom said back.

⁓

"When is Mom coming home?" I ask Dad. It's been two weeks. She hasn't called, and I'm secretly wondering if she'll come home at all.

"I don't know, honey," he says from his recliner, sounding as sad and confused as I am. The house is quieter, and I feel extra alone. I depend on Mom in a way Tony and George don't, certain the minute she goes to Pick 'n Save for groceries—and now, Philadelphia—will be the exact moment my pinky goes numb, and my spasm goes big.

Three weeks and one day later, Mom comes home.

Without her wedding ring.

"You did *what* with it?" Dad explodes, the two of them standing in the family room after Dad retrieves her from the airport.

"Buried it at my mother's grave site," she repeats, calmly taking his wrath.

"Why in God's name would you do that?" His voice is angry, his face crumpled with shock and hurt. Watching from the kitchen, I can't blame him; I bet he paid a lot of money for her wedding ring, a single round diamond on a dainty silver band. Before she left, I got from eavesdropping that Philadelphia was "thinking time" for her. And while she came home, she left the ring. Maybe she broke up with Dad quietly in her heart, then came home because she felt guilty about us kids not having a mom. She's not saying.

Shortly after, Mom breaks up unquietly with St. Alphonsus.

"I'm done with them!" she declares.

We switch to St. Charles Borremeo, a Catholic church across town, where she quickly joins a bible study with the parish nuns. Then she signs up our family to host the Blessed Virgin Mary—a four-foot resin statue—at our house for seven days.

"Why are we doing this?" I ask from my middle seat of the station wagon as the Blessed Virgin Mary committee carefully loads her headfirst into the back. The Virgin—my namesake—and I stare at one another, her pale serene face angling next to me, her body too long to fit otherwise. I'd seen people haul refrigerators, couches, and lumber in their cars, but never the mother of Jesus.

Mom and Dad carry the Blessed Virgin through our front door and hoist her onto the living room coffee table, newly pushed against our front picture window so people can see her from outside too.

"She's called the Lady of Fatima," Mom explains reverently, "because the Blessed Mother appeared to three shepherd children in the little village of Fatima, Portugal."

St. Charles is apparently a coveted stop on the parish circuit for the traveling statue.

"Maybe we should close the drapes." I say.

"This is an *honor*, Marianne," Mom admonishes. "The Blessed Mother appeared as a vision to the children and promised world peace. And she wants everyone to pray the rosary for protection from evil."

After dinner, Mom disappears down the hallway and comes back holding a variety of rosary beads: clear, wooden, turquoise.

"We're going to start saying the rosary every night," she says, distributing a string to each of us. "Starting tonight."

"Uh, no thanks," George pipes up.

"Yeah, I'm out," adds Tony. What high school boys want to be doing this? But Mom ignores them and herds the three of us plus Dad into the living room.

"Choose a kneeling spot, anywhere you feel comfortable," she says.

We scatter around the room, each draping ourselves over a different chair. Mom makes the sign of the cross, and we follow.

"I believe in God, the Father almighty, Creator of heaven and earth, and in Jesus Christ, his only Son, our Lord..." she launches into the Apostles' Creed, my words joining as automatic as breathing, a second language since birth.

"Our Father, who art in heaven, hallowed be thy name..." Dad moves seamlessly into the next section.

"And lead us not into temptation, but deliver us from evil. Amen," Tony, George, and I mumble in unison while neighborhood kids play kick the can outside.

Ray Clark

I SIT NAKED ON A BENCH in the girls' locker room, crossing my arms over my chest while peeking at the girls to my right and left. While some of my friends are growing breasts and pubic hair, I have nothing. I'm at Intermediate now, the public middle school.

"Sssshowers!" yells Ruth Hardy, our PE teacher, striding through the rows in her matching nylon track suit, a whistle around her neck. A compact, muscular woman with short-cropped blond hair, Ms. Hardy cranks her arm in a circle like a cowgirl lassoing livestock. A facial paralysis pulls her mouth to one side, giving her Ss an airy trill.

"Hardy is *gay*," we whisper in her wake, a brazen seventh-grade rumor that runs unchecked. It's the most dangerous thing we can think to say. Donna and I sometimes hide in the gym lockers to avoid taking a shower, but Ms. Hardy—her sharp gaze taking inventory—notices us missing and bangs on each metal door until we emerge, our heads ringing from her urgent pounding.

"Nice try," she says, her tone victorious. The only acceptable way out is if a girl has her period. Then she lines up to sign her name on a clipboard, verifying the dates of her menstrual cycle. I desperately want to be in the period line, noting the girls who are. *Kimberly has hers? Julie too?* It's just one more thing separating my body from normalcy. I consider lying. How can anyone prove it? But I'd need to remember my lie every twenty-eight days, so I file into the large cement room, arms still crossed, and twirl under the warmish spray long enough to pass inspection: Ms. Hardy standing at the shower exit like a linebacker—legs fixed and apart—holding a stack of small white towels. She doesn't say a word, tracing her finger, slow and precise, down our upper arms to make sure our skin is wet enough to deserve a square of rough terry cloth.

⁓

Middle school sex ed is where I learn about my ovaries, fallopian tubes, and making babies. Class is in the gymnasium, the only space that fits the entire grade, boys and girls. Learning these insights in mixed company makes me fidget, my palms clammy.

Tony reported getting "the talk" in eighth grade at a dad-and-son night at St. Alphonsus, while George curiously missed his talk the following year, the reason a likely combination of the content mixed with Catholicism—and Mom finding out Father Barton was teaching George's session. Besides watching the puberty video together in fifth grade, Mom and I don't talk about boobs or periods, when or how they happen. I'm twelve; she is fifty-four. Does she even have a period anymore? I search the bathroom cabinet for clues—Kotex pads, tampons, anything—and find a couple packs of unopened panty liners.

"When's the last time you went to a doctor?" I ask.

"The only doctor I need is Dr. Schultz," she says.

"Are you in menopause?" I switch tactics, after seeing the word in a magazine ad with "mature" women strolling on a beach.

"Happened after you were born, barely noticed," she says vaguely, brushing off my curiosity.

I haven't started, and she's already paused.

Instead, I escape to my bedroom to read *Are You There God? It's Me, Margaret*, a book about eleven-year-old Margaret waiting on her period. Margaret is my source, informing my parallel question, "Are you there, Mom? It's me, Marianne." I buy a training bra at Southridge Mall with my babysitting money. All my friends have them, and I want the outline on my back too, especially when I wear my pastel-striped turtleneck. It's my favorite shirt because of the way it hugs my shape, undeveloped as it is.

Mornings before school, our group gathers on the sidewalk out front. Like the locker room, the middle school sidewalk is a place for noticing and comparing. Boys circle around us.

"North, south, east, west..." They dart into our group to pull back our bra straps like slingshots, releasing them with a smack. "Equator!" they yell, laughing, my back reverberating with the happy sting of belonging, no matter how fleeting.

On winter weekday nights, the sidewalk group meets at Scout Lake Park, the small lake freezing into an ice-skating rink with a warming house serving hot chocolate and snacks. Tony, George, and their friends go too. Everybody does. "Good clean fun!" Mom calls it. Bra-strap pulling becomes flirty hat and mitten stealing as boys and girls pluck attire off a favorite head or hand, and the surrounding trees witness kissing and vows of romance. Not yet for me though. Boys I like don't like me back. And boys who like me I wish would not. On weekend nights, we hang out in Donna's basement to play spin the bottle, truth or dare, and two minutes in the closet while listening to Bruce Springsteen's *The River* album. Her basement has carpeting, couches, and a bar, unlike mine, with its cold cement floors, cobwebs, and my brothers' beer can collection lining its perimeter. I drink my first beer in Donna's basement too, after we go Christmas caroling and give our tip money to an older brother to buy us a six-pack.

"This is *awesome*," I wince, choking down the bitter liquid. If no one else is saying they don't like it, I won't either.

One Friday night, I find myself stuffed into a coat closet with Troy, a freckly redhead, after the group chooses us to pair up. "What do you want to do?" he asks, his face so close I can smell his spearmint chewing gum.

"I don't know; you decide," I say quickly, afraid to kiss a boy on the lips and unsure what to do with my tongue. So we do nothing and emerge laughing to make everyone else think otherwise.

Footsteps end our night. "Turn on the lights!" Donna's dad yells, marching down the stairs.

When everyone goes home, I stay. Donna and I share the queen-size bed in her chilly basement guest room, burrowing under the covers, hugging our pillows, and reviewing the night.

"Pretend yours is Kevin/Mark/Joe." We kiss or reject our pillows depending on whose name is offered. It's easier to kiss an inanimate rectangle of fluff than a real boy. In the morning, we make chocolate chip cookie dough for breakfast and eat it from the bowl, something Mom won't allow at home because of raw eggs and salmonella.

Donna's house is my respite, a chance to exist in a "normal" family without religion, health food, and conspiracies, though the threat of a spasm continually lurks. I am split into two people—the fun outside Marianne and the anxious inside Marianne, afraid of a big spasm happening in front of my friends. Fear of being found out and disliked if I am. I carry my worries like an invisible backpack. No one can see them, but they weigh heavy no matter how much fun I'm having.

More than ever, I notice the other kids who I assume carry invisible backpacks too. Like Raymond Clark. Ray and I are in homeroom together, our desks side by side. A quiet ginger-haired boy, Ray doesn't have a sidewalk group and walks the halls alone. He might be the nicest kid, but no one gives him a chance. We see only his differences—his ghostly pale skin, too-short pants, and collared shirts buttoned to his neck. "You waiting for a flood, Ray?" ask the athletic boys, my friends, pointing at his exposed ankles. Or they use his name as a synonym for *nerdy*. "That kid? He's so Ray Clark." Ray never fights back, and my stomach clenches at their insults, but I say nothing.

Ray also has something called epilepsy. We know this because every year, Mrs. Clark, his mom, visits Ray's homeroom to talk about it.

"Epilepsy is a disorder in the central nervous system when your brain activity becomes abnormal," Mrs. Clark says. She explains petit mal seizures, where someone loses focus, grand mal seizures, where a person collapses and shakes; and Jacksonian seizures, which begin in one muscle group and progress to other groups nearby.

Sitting next to Ray, I wonder what he thinks about his mom telling everyone about his problem.

"You may notice Ray staring off into space," Mrs. Clark says. "This will be your clue a seizure is starting."

I don't want to notice.

"He may or may not fall onto the ground, but if he does, you'll want to move the desks and chairs, so he doesn't hit his head on anything."

Our worried faces stare at Mrs. Clark, but she promises us our teacher knows what to do.

One afternoon I look at Ray to my right, the clock inching toward 3:00 p.m. While everyone starts stuffing papers into backpacks, Ray stares at the chalkboard.

"Ray," I whisper, tapping his arm. "It's time to go."

But Ray keeps staring.

"RAY." I tap more urgently.

Uh-oh.

Within seconds, Ray topples to his left, bringing his chair and desk with him and toward me. I jump up, and everything, including him, crashes to the floor, his body flopping, his books and papers flying everywhere. Our teacher runs over. Kids cluster into groups like buzz-ing beehives, their frantic chatter rising.

"Children! Quiet, please!" the teacher yells. "Give him space!" She tucks her cardigan under Ray's head to cushion the blows. Kids shove the desks into a circle around him seizing on our classroom floor, his eyes closed, his limbs shaking. I stand in shock, my eyes unblinking, mouth open. But for a different reason than the others.

I am Ray. Ray is me.

My body does *exactly* what his body is doing.

I. Have. Epilepsy.

My face flushes, my head light with the sweaty wooziness of uncov-ering a huge secret.

After school, I run the narrow wooded paths of Scout Lake Park toward home, my thoughts swirling, hope carrying my feet up Laura Lane.

"Mom!" I yell, bursting through the front door. "Mom! I know what's wrong with me!"

Mom is sitting in her makeshift office in the family room, a straight-backed wooden dining room chair pulled up to her manual typewriter on a rickety metal stand pushed against the back wall. After coming home from Philadelphia—"My time in the desert," she's calling it—she and Dad have stopped fighting, and Mom replaced her diamond ring with a cheap gold band from the JCPenney catalog.

And she is now writing in earnest. To her pen pal, Harvey Mackay, an envelope entrepreneur whose business advice column she reads with devotion. Then a short book, a pamphlet really, called, *Vitamins A–Z*, listing every vitamin and its benefits, which she distributes around town. "To keep in your pocket or purse," she instructs to bewildered recipients. If anyone starts a conversation with me at school that starts with, "I saw your mom…" I change the subject.

But lately, and more urgently, she's writing missives to the Veterans Administration and the CIA in Washington, DC. "To demand an apology for what they did to me," she says, her fingers flying 120 words a minute from all her secretary jobs before and during the Air Force. "What they did," of course, is the CIA's mind control experiments.

Mom turns at my voice, giving the carriage lever a decisive zing left, its bell affirming the end of a line.

"I have epilepsy, and it's called Jacksonian epilepsy," I say breathlessly, my book bag and coat at my feet. "It starts in one part of your body and moves to other parts of your body and becomes a full-body seizure." My words tumble over one another. "And this kid in my class has epilepsy, and he had a seizure today, and it was *exactly* what happens to me. He fell on the floor, and his body started shaking, and I knew by looking at him I have it too. And Ray's mom and my teacher called it a seizure, not a spasm. Can you call Dr. A?"

I am breathing heavy, waiting for Mom to catch my enthusiasm like a relay runner grabbing the baton.

"I don't think so, Marianne," she says. "It's your diet, and we're working on that."

My *diet*?

"And we'll keep praying for a miracle," she adds.

Ray Clark is my miracle, as real as any, but Mom isn't seeing it. A gift from one awkward kid to another, it's as if Ray picked me to have a seizure next to in an act of solidarity. "Here," I imagine him saying, "I'm going to help you out."

But I don't have a Mrs. Clark in my corner, and nothing changes for me.

Neither Mom nor I mention the word *epilepsy* again. She keeps buying health food and filling me with vitamins, and I learn more and more I can't trust my own knowing—or her.

High School

HALFWAY THROUGH HIGH SCHOOL, I grow breasts. Big ones, like they are making up for lost time. I get my driver's license and braces too, though Dad agrees to pay for my top teeth only. When I look in the mirror, I don't feel pretty, my self-critique harsh. My body is more soft and round, less skinny and angular. I curl my chin-length mousy-brown hair into two rolls down the side of my head and spray them immobile with Aqua Net, my curling iron brown and sticky with melted hairspray. I am not the girl who gets attention like Sandra, whose white angora dress with the pink satin belt ignites schoolwide buzz before the first bell. My wardrobe, pieced together with babysitting money and from clearance racks, is adequate. Levi's jeans and corduroys. Button-down shirts and striped sweaters. Sneakers.

Every so often, I ask Mom to go to the mall with me because moms and daughters are supposed to laugh and shop together. "You really just need two of everything," she says while I peruse the racks. "One to wear, one to wash." Mom never buys much for herself except health food and magazine subscriptions.

She follows two steps behind me to every store, patiently waiting outside the dressing rooms and paying for a new shirt or lunch. Mom usually orders a plain bagel and a cup of hot water. She likes the endless salad at Olive Garden too, stuffing the buttered bread sticks in her purse for Dad and asking for more before we leave.

"You can't do that!" I scold, looking around for anyone watching.

"Why not?" she says. "They'd go to waste otherwise."

Ours is a forced companionship. I tell her the peripheral stories of my life. Who's dating who. How the football team is doing. But being with her feels like being with someone I know a lot about who doesn't know me back. And being with her is when she talks about Dad.

"I didn't realize your father couldn't hear anything when he took his hearing aids off," she says on our drive home.

Here we go. I keep driving and say nothing, hoping my silence stops her oversharing.

"Then he had trouble keeping an erection, so I masturbated myself to orgasm."

I hit the brakes, jolting us both forward.

"MOM," I say, stunned. This is a new part of her story.

"I do *not* want to know this about you *or* Dad." Something between them must have worked if they had three kids I remind her.

She pivots to her second-favorite topic. "They flew me from Wright-Patterson Air Force Base to Walter Reed Hospital in Washington, DC. Strapped me to a table, put electrodes on my head, and..."

"I know, Mom, you've told me a zillion times," I say more gently. Her expression doesn't change when I shut her down. "I'm sure it was painful."

After a dozen years of hearing the same story, I'm out of empathy. "Get into the present," I want to say. "See your daughter next to you with worries of her own." But Mom is a broken record playing one or two songs, and I want her to listen to the music of my life too.

Greendale High School has groups: jocks, who play sports; freaks, who wear trench coats and smoke cigarettes behind the school; and frocks, who play sports and drink while trying not to get caught. I am closest to a frock: cheerleader by day, drunk cheerleader on the weekends. Before kickoff, I chug sloe gin or blackberry brandy in the girls' bathroom to loosen me up. Drinking is a way I feel free and fun. The intoxicated me is less anxious about my body, my seizures, and my family.

Our parties have moved from Donna's basement to Patricia's basement, where senior guys, the same age as Tony, deliver booze to her lower-level window. Patricia's downstairs has couches and carpeting too, and we dance on the parquet floor under a flashing disco ball. Hours later, with Patricia's parents sitting upstairs, we push back out the booze window anybody too drunk to leave through the front door. These nights I stumble home through the backyards, from the S section to the L, seeing two of everything, then tiptoe to my bedroom through the empty living room, hoping Mom isn't still awake. Dad goes to bed every night after the ten o'clock news.

"Did you have fun?" Mom asks the next morning.

"Lots," I say. And that's that.

I start dating John, a six-foot-tall blond and blue-eyed quarterback. We are a suburban cliché—varsity cheerleader and star athlete, his status making me feel better about mine.

John sees none of my insecurity. He has his own. He scolds me when I talk to other boys. Checks on my whereabouts. One New Year's Eve, I kiss another boy at midnight. John grabs my shoulders and slams me against a wall, my head bouncing against the plaster. I run home at 1:00 a.m., drunken tears and hysteria propelling my feet through the backyards. Mom is awake, and I tell her what happened.

"Do *not* see him again," she says.

"I won't," I agree.

Two days later, John and I are back together. I can't imagine not being half of our popular whole.

When John gets to drive his dad's car, we park on dark and dead-end streets to make out. We take off our clothes after our parents go to sleep. Sometimes we don't wait for that. At my house, we slip in the front door and lie naked under a blanket on the living room carpet, a simple pocket door separating Mom and Dad watching TV on the other side.

"Let's go all the way," John urges, grinding his hips into mine, but I quickly roll to my side, terrified it will hurt. I have finally gotten my period too, and I worry about getting pregnant, though I'm still not certain how the timing works. Sometimes my hand goes numb when John is on top of me. Then I circle my arms around his big body and rub my left pinky behind his back.

"What are you *doing*?" he asks, confused.

"I have a cramp in my hand," I lie, while praying furiously for the numbness to subside, which, so far, it does.

One Friday night, John and I are at a school dance, swaying to "Stairway to Heaven" by Led Zeppelin in the dark and sweaty school cafeteria decorated with crepe paper and balloons. I press my body against his, my arms around his neck, his hands clutching my butt, when I feel it again—the pinch. *Shit*. I snap upright, recoiling my left hand like he's a hot stove.

"What's wrong?" John asks.

"I have to go to the bathroom," I say quickly.

"Can't you wait?" John mumbles, his tongue searching for my mouth.

"I really can't," I insist, twisting out of his embrace and running to the bathroom. Girls crowd the mirror, fixing their hair and lipstick. I rush past their hellos and into an open stall, where I sit on the toilet. If anyone notices my feet, it will look like I'm peeing.

"Please, please, please, God," I pray and rub. Where will I be when my luck runs out? Naked on my living room floor? In a hotel room after prom? Unconscious in a bathroom stall? I let John explore every part of my body, but I don't tell him about my seizures. I don't tell my friends either. And I didn't tell the DMV when I got my driver's license, even though there was a space on the application for reasons I shouldn't drive. If no one can tell me what's wrong with me, I won't tell anyone either.

"You good?" John asks when I return, his hands refinding my hips, his lips my face.

"Great," I say.

⁓

"Your father thinks you're never around," Mom says one afternoon when I am doing math homework at the kitchen table.

He has a point, but what does it matter? I'm not missing anything here. Mom and Dad never have anyone over for dinner, drinks, or card club like other parents. They don't drink alcohol except for Dad's once-a-year Pabst after a hot day of lawn mowing.

Tony and George are gone a lot too, all of us busy with school and jobs. Tony and George play on the golf team, and George does baseball too. They both work as caddies at Tuckaway, a private country club eight minutes from our house. They have since they were twelve years old. Mom lets Tony and George stay out later with the station wagon than I can.

"They're the boys," she says when I ask why, an assurance of their well-being not granted to me.

And yet. It's Tony's antics that have me coming home one night to a scribbled note from Mom pasted to the kitchen cabinet. *At the police station...again.* Turns out Tony's latest underage drinking in the station wagon before a school basketball game had collided with a police officer's curiosity. To this, George claims the advantage of being in the "hidden middle," his description for his friend group doing the same drinking without getting caught.

But Dad's comment stirs up my guilt. Is he saying he misses me? Of anyone in the family, he and I are the most alike, both our bodies holding us hostage—his hearing, my seizures. We both keep diaries, mine under my mattress and Dad's in the family room desk drawer, his brief daily entries summarizing a predictable life cadence. On Sunday afternoons, we play cribbage if I pull a chair over to his recliner and set up the pegboard on a TV tray between us.

A few days later, I find Dad on the couch bench doing a crossword puzzle.

"Want to go to Kopp's for custard?" I ask when he looks up. Kopp's is a popular restaurant close to our house with a different flavor every day. Grasshopper fudge, butter pecan, banana cream pie. Dad furrows his brow like I should know better.

"Why would we spend the gas money when we have ice cream in the freezer?"

"Oh my *God*!" I fume, stomping to my bedroom and slamming the door. Tears jump to my eyes.

"See?" I yell to nobody, "*This* is why I'm never here!" My "this" is a vast and growing feeling of being lonelier at home than anywhere else, part of a family that doesn't feel like a family, more like five individuals fending for themselves.

⌣

December slows time and limits my options. Winter break scatters my friends to their own families and vacations. We have nowhere to go, no one to visit. And Dad and I are the only two who care if we have a Christmas tree.

"Can't put it up too early though," Dad says, "or it'll dry out by the Epiphany." The Epiphany is January 6, the day the Three Kings visited Jesus, and the day Mom allows the tree to come back down, not a minute sooner.

Each year on the second Sunday in December, Dad and I drive to Bluemel's garden center to buy a tree.

"Balsam fir," Dad says, "They're the cheapest."

I look for the tallest tree in Dad's price range to offset the sparsity.

Back home, Dad gets his wooden ladder from the garage to retrieve the decorations from the attic, but not before wrestling the tree into the stand.

"It's straight!" I yell extra loud, his ears buried beneath the branches.

We unwrap each ornament from its tissue-paper holder, spreading them on the living room carpet. I find my favorite pink glass swan from Dad's own childhood tree. For the longest time, we thought it had lost its tail, until one year, I tipped the swan just so, and the brushy strands came poking out a hole in the back.

"Dad, look!" I exclaimed.

"Well, I'll be a monkey's uncle," he said, shaking his head in happy disbelief.

We hang the lights and ornaments; then Dad gingerly lifts the silver icicles from a torn-up box, handing me a bunch too.

"It's not a Christmas tree without 'em," he says. Dad reuses the icicles year after year, some as crumpled and hard as old aluminum foil. Then the two of us stand back to admire our creation, and sure enough, the multicolored lights reflect off the silver tinsel and fill the room with a technicolor glow.

"Looks good," Mom interrupts our reverie with a peek from the kitchen, barely giving the tree a notice, her eyes searching beyond us.

"Working on it, Mary," Dad says, irritation clipping his tone.

He knows she's checking to see if the nativity is up. It goes on the same round table every year, the one holding the Jesus statue and the big thick Bible with gold-edged pages and a red leatherette cover. I hand Dad the fake wood stable with moss and hay bits glued to the top, and we arrange the plastic figurines and animals. Baby Jesus, with his diaper, crossed feet, and permanently outstretched hands, can't be in his manger until closer to his birthday, so Dad rests him in the dirt of a nearby plant. The Three Wise Men aren't in Bethlehem yet either, so we relegate them to a bookshelf across the room.

It's my favorite part of Christmas, decorating with Dad. From there, my emptiness creeps back in.

"I'm not a shopper," Mom announces, absolving herself from gift buying. Underneath the tree stays empty until I tell her exactly what to get me or I buy something myself and give it to her to wrap. It was different when we were little. Dad did the shopping then, choosing one or two things that fit our likings: an erector set for Tony, GI Joes for George, a paint-by-number kit for me. But as we grew, Dad stopped shopping, and Mom didn't start.

On Christmas Eve, I wander into the kitchen, where Mom is standing at her pull-out wooden cutting board slicing peaches to stir into a large bowl of red Jell-O.

"What's for supper?" I ask, secretly hoping for something besides our usual "football meatloaf" or spaghetti. But different isn't in Mom's repertoire, only the recipes from the beginner cookbook she got after getting married, a school folder with a few pages stapled inside. Mom's extra effort is fruit Jell-O versus plain Jell-O, and peaches are better than cherries. Some years, she makes the cranberry marshmallow salad Dad ate as a kid, but only if he asks, because he's the only one who eats it.

After normal dinner in the kitchen, we move into the living room to say the rosary, and Dad transports baby Jesus from the plant to his manger. His curved body fits perfectly into the dented hay. Mom has us saying the "super rosary" now, a shortened version with one decade instead of five. "But with the same power," she assures us.

After a final sign of the cross, I turn on a Christmas radio station on the old stereo to break up the quiet, then divvy up the few presents, one or two for each. We take turns opening, though I already know mine because I bought them. Last, we retrieve our three socks, which Dad hung from the fireplace mantel.

They are real socks from our drawers, versus the big felt and sequined kind from the store. There isn't much room in the seven-inch fabric, so Mom fills them with five lottery tickets each. It's the lightest moment of the evening, Mom watching Tony, George, and I scratching off our tickets with a penny, her eyes expectant. "Anyone a winner?" she says giddily.

The entire celebration takes less than an hour before Tony, George, and I disappear to our bedrooms for the rest of the night. Sometimes I call my friend Troy, who I know isn't doing anything either, the two of us finding consolation in one another's boredom.

Christmas Day is more of just us, except after mass, we eat in the dining room instead of the kitchen. Mom sets the table with the china she got for her wedding from her ma—silver-rimmed white dishes with soft gray flowers in the center. It's supposed to feel special, but even the fancy plates can't stop me from noticing Mom serves the steak and baked potatoes on a china platter, but keeps the canned vegetables and leftover Jell-O in the same old Tupperware containers she stores them in. One Christmas, she simply plopped down the white cartons from a Chinese takeout place on the fancy platter next to a prepackaged turkey roll with stuffing spiraled through like a Hostess snack cake.

Sitting in my hardback dining chair, I know her heart isn't in it. The china says she's trying, but the Tupperware screams, "This is too much work."

Mom takes off her apron and sits down, clutching a white envelope from the Catholic Supply Store.

"Everybody take a piece…" she says, passing around an eight-by-ten pink-colored communion wafer, etched with a scene of Jesus at the Last Supper. We each break off a chunk and hold it between our thumb and index finger.

"*This is my body given for you*," Mom reads from a prayer booklet, closing her eyes. I close mine too and let the thin bland wafer melt on my tongue. Except it transfers to the roof of my mouth and gets stuck, so I covertly scrape it free with my finger.

"*Do this in remembrance of me*," Mom says, as we swallow the wafer body of Jesus, consecrating our insides before eating our steak and Jell-O.

⟍⟋

"What'd you get for Christmas?" ask my friends.

Back at school, we huddle by our lockers. Everybody wears something new—clothes, shoes, perfume, a suntan.

"I got Levi's in blue, cream, and dark green, and a couple shirts and gift cards," I lie to cover up my meager haul. By then, I've gone to Southridge Mall and shopped the after-Christmas sales, pretending my new clothes are gifts.

"Cool," everyone nods before heading to class, the conversation already forgotten in the hallway chatter, shame lingering in my hot cheeks.

Cerebral Allergies

I MADE YOU AN APPOINTMENT WITH a Dr. Arya," Mom says, casually, one morning.

"Who and why?" I ask, confused.

"For your spasms," she says, explaining Dr. Rathna Arya is a homeopath in Madison she read about in a magazine, a doctor who heals people naturally. "Without *drugs*," she adds, saying this part louder than her other words.

"Seizures, Mom," I correct her. Then, "No, thanks, I'm good."

I didn't ask her to do this. I'm a junior in high school. I haven't seen a doctor for my seizures since Dr. Strassburg in fourth grade, and I stopped talking to Mom about them after Ray Clark. I want Mom to be my confidant and advocate, but I can't manufacture this connection.

Mom keeps the appointment with Dr. Arya and tells Dad to take off work to drive because she doesn't do highways. I know I can refuse to go, but I also know when Mom has a plan, I'll use more of my energy to convince her otherwise than to just go along.

The night before, Dr. Arya instructs Mom to have me take a bath in vinegar.

"To clean out your toxins," she explains, dumping two cups of apple cider vinegar into the warm water.

"You're both crazy," I tell her, shielding myself with a towel while lowering myself into the smelly tub. Sitting and soaking, I think about John and my friends. Whatever they are doing tonight, it isn't this. My eyes take in the wallpaper border Dad pasted just below the ceiling line. The continuous ivy pattern is interrupted by a piece that doesn't match the rest, Dad using a random scrap to fill the gap instead of spending money on a new roll.

The next morning, I stay home from school and take a second vinegar bath to chase away any last poisons. Then the three of us get into Dad's Corolla, make our way out of Greendale, and merge onto Highway 94 toward Madison.

"Left lane, Jerry...LEFT!" Mom yells into his right ear.

"For God's sake, Mary, I know," he snaps back.

"*Highway 47. Detour ahead. Thru traffic, stay left,*" Mom announces to no one. She has a habit of reading highway signs aloud while we drive.

Ninety minutes later, we pull up to a one-story brick building that reminds me of Dr. Schultz's beige cube. Why are all mom's doctors in bland one-story buildings? Pulling into the parking lot, I notice we're the only car here, and I don't feel surprised. A sign out front reads:

Sai Health Clinic

Dr. Rathna Arya, FICAN, MRCP, FTM&H

Rathna has a lot of initials after her name I don't recognize.

Outside our car, Mom flips open a small notebook she brought from home and reads aloud. "*FICAN: Fellow of the International College of Applied Nutrition. MRCP: member of the Royal College of Physicians. FTM and H: fellow in Tropical Medicine and Hygiene.*"

"Tropical Medicine?" I repeat, imagining a pina colada with herbs.

Inside, the three of us sit in the small waiting room that looks like it used to be something else, a hair salon or bakery maybe. It smells like incense and spices. A mixture of cinnamon and curry perhaps. A tall skinny gentleman wearing a white turban comes around the corner, his hand extended to shake ours.

"Hello," he says, offering us a clipboard of paperwork. "I'm Rajesh Arya, Rathna's son and a Certified Master Hypnotist."

Maybe he'll hypnotize me, so I forget I'm here.

A short and plump Indian woman with fuzzy black hair pulled into a topknot soon joins Rajesh. A colorful sari covers her, neck to ankles. She looks grandmotherly, like a wooden nested doll.

"I'm Dr. Arrrr-ya," she says, trilling the R and motioning for us to follow. Dad doesn't move, happy with his *Reader's Digest* while Mom jumps on command. I reluctantly follow.

I sit on a long padded bench in an exam room, Dr. Arya perched on a round stool across from me. Mom stands quietly in the corner. Dr. Arya asks about my seizures, my diet, the regularity of my poop, and scribbles notes about my answers. Then she rests her paperwork on a small table.

"Here. Hold this," she says, handing me a small metal cylinder. It is attached by wires to a rectangular machine with dials, gauges, and lights. Picking up a second tube that looks like an electronic pencil, Dr. Arya presses it into the back of my right hand, which holds the first tube. The gauges vibrate on contact.

"What are you doing?" I ask.

"Checking your energetic outputs," she says. "This is an EAV machine. It's for electroacupuncture diagnosis. I can tell the health of your organs by how much energy they output. Points on your hands and feet correspond to your insides."

Okaaaay, I think, watching her needles jump around as she presses different points on the back of my hand.

"Anything over sixty means potential inflammation and irritation."

After a few minutes, she leans back, gathering her breath.

"You have severe cerebral allergies affecting your whole nervous system," she says. "Brain stem. Cerebrum. Your adrenals, gonads, and pituitary glands are irritated. And you're hypoglycemic."

"Wow," I say sarcastically.

"Indeed," she goes on, ignoring my adolescent cynicism. "You have congestion in your sinuses too, especially the tube to your ear. Stagnation in your ear, jaw, larynx. Your pancreas is very irritated and not adapting well. Not digesting proteins, carbohydrates, and fats."

Is she for real?

"Lastly," she sums up. "Your spleen, colon, liver, and large intestine are very irritated and congested. Annnd we need to detoxify your bowels."

She is not getting near my bowels.

"Could these allergies be causing her spasms?" Mom asks, lapping up every word.

"It is quite possible and *very* likely," Dr. Arya says, adding that I also have two chemicals in my body—autopolymerisat and vinylpolymerisat—the root cause of my cerebral allergies. "We will detoxify them, too," she says forcefully, like an exterminator ousting rats. While I mentally check out, the two of them make a homeopathic plan for me.

Driving home, Mom reads signs aloud and hums along to her Patsy Cline cassette tape, her mood lifted by Dr. Arya's diagnosis. Dad focuses on the road. He isn't a part of this except for transportation. Hasn't been since fourth grade; why start now?

Mom ups my vitamin regime with new and more supplements, and three times a day, I squeeze a few drops of liquid under my tongue from a small dropper bottle. It feels thick and slippery in my mouth, like dish soap.

A tincture, Mom calls it. To get rid of my chemicals.

Dad drives us back to Madison two more times.

"You're better," says Dr. Arya, "but still congested."

More supplements. More tincture dish soap. And a new giant vitamin called Super Stress. *To relieve it or cause it?* I wonder.

After months of my homeopathic routine, my insides feel exactly the same, except for more annoyance at Mom for making me do this. I already know what's wrong with me—I have epilepsy—and I don't believe this regime is going to fix it. Sure enough, my hand goes numb as usual. One afternoon, Mom sees me rubbing my fingers. She calls Dr. Arya right away, who tells her to give me three potassium vitamins, some B6, and to bring me in for acupuncture.

"I'm done with her," I say, like Mom said about St. Alphonsus. "You can go back yourself."

‿◡

My body isn't my own, more an entity to be assessed and guessed about, and my brother Tony joins the chorus.

"You're getting fat," he says, barely through the front door from college, in Greendale for a visit. Tony is a sophomore at UW-Madison, working and living there for the summer. I am five feet four inches and 118 pounds, the same as I've been for a few years.

"Missed you too," I respond, pretending I'm unaffected, while my insides reel with self-consciousness. It's the first thing he's seeing after being gone for months, and instead of ignoring him or telling him to go to hell, I hear his opinion as fact.

My body is wrong in yet one more way.

Retreating to my bedroom, I stand in front of my mirror and lift my shirt. *My waist could be smaller,* I think. I pinch the fat on my stomach, then turn to see my belly from the side. It protrudes, more round than flat. I can't control my seizures and messed-up insides, but I *can* control how much my body weighs, and this makes me feel powerful.

I eat one carton of yogurt and an apple a day. It's easy to starve myself during summer. School is out, and Mom is working at a new secretary job for Wisconsin Crane and Hoist, a home-based business. From 9:00 a.m. to 4:00 p.m., she is in a basement office, ordering crane parts, processing invoices, and managing payroll. She went back to work, she says, because she misses making money and wants to help us kids with extra expenses. College for Tony and George and soon me. The owner doesn't seem to notice Mom's rising salary, though she is giving herself frequent raises.

"My goal before I die is to give you each the same amount," she says. "To the penny." Mom starts a ledger in a spiral notebook to keep track. *Marianne: People magazine and Chapstick: $6.49.*

I step on the bathroom scale. Five pounds disappear in seven days. This is easy.

"You look great," people notice, so I keep going, motivated by a new feeling of authority over my body. I clamp down on my food intake like a vise on wood and start looking at food labels. Anything with too many calories or fat grams doesn't pass my lips. I eat carrots, rice cakes, fruit. I drink water to quell my stomach pangs. Beer and Boone's Farm are still allowed because skinny means I get drunk faster. When I'm out to dinner with friends, I move my food around my plate to make it look like I'm eating. Or I take two bites of pizza, then hide the rest in a napkin on my lap.

This isn't normal, I know. An obsessive fortitude takes over my psyche, and I push away the worry I have crossed the line between me controlling my food and my food controlling me. I've heard of anorexia nervosa, the eating disorder, but I won't let myself use these words to describe what I'm doing.

"You look too thin," Mom notices one morning, pausing by the garage door on her way out to her job.

"I'll eat at work," I promise. I am working as a waitress at The Onion Crock restaurant, a soup and sandwich place at the mall. Mom doesn't push the issue, but my friends start talking.

"You're too skinny," they say, but I hear their words as a casual complaint versus an alarm bell. They don't know I run around my neighborhood when I think I ate too much.

"Maybe," I deflect. I'm achieving what I set out to do—lose weight—so their noticing is fuel to keep going.

"It's not that bad," I tell myself, because at least I'm not throwing up.

By senior year, I weigh 105 pounds. My sharp hip bones flank my concave stomach, my blue jeans bag around my skinny butt, and my biceps protrude on stick arms. My head looks big for my body. I stop getting my period, the one I waited forever to get. When more time passes without it, I get a sinking feeling I have gone too far, with a double sinking feeling it might be too late to fix it. What if I can never have babies? Mom is my obvious link between me and getting help, so one day I ask her to take me to a normal doctor who knows about periods and how to get them back after they disappear. She doesn't pry beyond a surprising willingness to get a name from her church friend.

Dr. Edward Lathers, the gynecologist, looks older than Dad. His name, Lathers, reminds me of soap. He is tall with a pale oblong face and sparse gray hair parted to the side.

"Nice to meet you," he says, shaking my hand and smiling. His voice is smooth and gentle like soap too. I figure he's taking time to look at my face before my lower parts. He leaves briefly, and I disrobe, then sit on the exam table in a blue gown, my stomach nervous looking at the metal stirrups.

"Let's see what's going on." Dr. Lathers reenters, then washes his hands. I count ceiling tiles while he explores my vagina.

"What's your favorite subject in school?" he asks, trying to distract me from his probing, which I feel all the way up to my abdomen. A few more pokes and tugs, and he sits back on his stool. I close my legs and prop myself on my elbows.

"Marianne, you need more fat on your body to menstruate," he says. "Your hormones can't do their job without it, and your bones are more susceptible to fractures. Add more protein to your diet, an extra glass of milk, yogurt, ice cream." He also prescribes a birth control pill to "kick-start" my cycle.

"Your body'll know what to do once you gain a few pounds," he reassures me, patting my arm. I stopped trusting my body a long time ago. And I'm not very nice to it, withholding the calories it needs to function.

Mom and I drive to Walgreens.

"I don't know why these doctors think they have to solve everything with pills," she says, but doesn't talk me out of filling the prescription.

As much as I want my period back, I throw the birth control pills in my desk drawer and decide to not decide about taking them. I am stuck between two fears: the fear of ruining my reproductive abilities forever and the fear of gaining weight.

My invisible backpack is getting heavier.

I have other things to worry about too, like where I'm going to college, and right now, my need to control my body is winning over my need to menstruate.

The Nunnery

I SIT CROSS-LEGGED IN A "GET to know you" circle in Murray Hall, an all-girl dorm known as "The Nunnery" at the University of Wisconsin-Eau Claire, a smallish college four hours north of Milwaukee. Twelve of us squeeze into a room. My still-skinny frame easily makes space for others around me.

"Check this out!" says a girl lying on the top bunk. She holds up the centerfold of a *Playgirl* magazine, moving it side to side like a kindergarten teacher during story time to make sure we all can see his large flaccid penis.

"Enough, enough!" claps a young woman, walking into the room. Her name is Carol, she says, our RA and "caring big sister" for the year. After dispensing a few rules about how she will assess a twenty-five-dollar fine for any unaccompanied boys in the dorm, she invites us to go around the room and introduce ourselves. And tell everyone why we chose Eau Claire.

When it's my turn, I hear myself say, "I'm Marianne, and I've always loved Eau Claire."

This is a lie. I am here because John said we should go to different colleges "to have different experiences," and I let myself be talked into this. My friend Julie was going to Eau Claire, so I tagged along on a campus visit with her and her parents. I convinced myself I liked it too, while John went to UW-Madison, where I really want to be. Julie and I are roommates, and we have matching striped bedspreads. And now, instead of sitting at a Badger football game in loud Camp Randall Stadium, I am sitting in the quiet Nunnery looking at a *Playgirl* spread.

UW-Eau Claire feels small like Greendale. Nestled on the banks of the Chippewa River, it is a quaint, tree-filled campus. It's location on the river makes it particularly frigid, another reason I shouldn't be here. I hate being cold. Every morning, I walk down a steep hill to my classes and pass the same people at the same time coming up the hill. Boy with Plaid Jacket at 10:01 a.m. Girl with High Ponytail at 11:15 a.m. I am undeclared, which means I don't know who or what I want to be, which seems reasonable for an eighteen-year-old. My first semester is filled with much of what I did in high school—English, math, chemistry. And economics, which is new.

"Do you have micro or macro?" a friend asks.

"I don't know the teacher's name," I reply.

⟋⟍

One Friday in December, my alarm rings me awake at 6:00 a.m. for an 8:00 a.m. lab. The sky is dark, my comforter warm. I tiptoe down the ladder from the top bunk, trying not wake Julie, then gently push open my closet door to grab my shower caddy.

And that's when it happens—the pinch in my left pinky.

What the hell? I drop my caddy and bolt upright. *No. Fucking. Way.* I haven't had a hand seizure in months, and it's been eight years since my last big one. Why now? Why today? Any hope I had of outgrowing them—gone.

Julie stirs and rolls over, now facing me.

This can't be happening.

But it is, the numbness quickly traveling through my fingers.

Something feels different, though. Bigger. More intense. I grab my left hand and start rubbing, trying to push the sensation out through my fingertips. "Fuck. Fuck. Fuck," I breathe, my chest tightening with fear. I rub harder and more urgently, my right thumb digging in and blistering the skin of my left palm. It isn't working. "Why, why, why" I whimper, my mouth dry, panic rising. "God, you gotta stop this," I plead. This can't happen here and now. It *can't*. But it is. And in a way I haven't felt before, the sensation more demanding, more insistent, like huge ocean waves slamming into shore. I back away from my closet to give myself space to fall. My left arm is straight up by now, coming over the top of my head, tipping me off-balance. This part is the worst. As much as I attempt to crouch lower to cushion the blow, I will awkwardly fall to the floor, and it will hurt when I do.

I look at Julie still sleeping. We've known each other since fifth grade, but none of my friends know about this. Today is coming-out day.

"Julie!" I yell, landing on our thin carpet remnant laid over cement. "Call nine-one-one!"

She jumps out of bed, eyes wide, hair askew.

"What's *wrong* with you?" she yells.

I can't answer, already on my way to unconsciousness. The last thing I see is her reaching for the telephone, which we cleverly attached to the side of our wooden bunk bed.

My limbs extend rigid, my fists tight. *Thump, thump, thump,* my head keeps time on the floor, my neurons misfiring. I disconnect from my dorm room, hearing my voice in the tunnel of nothingness, my yells bouncing off the walls. "Help me, me, me, me..." they echo.

The storm courses through my body, shaking every part for what seems too long before subsiding like a hurricane finding land. Limp and exhausted, I can't move. Can't talk either. But I'm still alive. Is it safe now? I open my eyes into a ring of faces, every girl on my dorm floor staring down at me, whispering to one another. When did they get here? Who let them in? How long have they been watching while I didn't know? *Go away*, I shout in my head. My RA stares down at me too, stunned with the rest of them.

"Marianne," says a voice. "The paramedics are on their way."

My short yellow nightie with a cartoon character on its front gathers around my waist, my Hanes bikini underwear and unshaven legs in full view. I feel damp between my legs. Sliding my hand over my crotch, I press to confirm I've peed on myself, the first time I've done this. I taste blood on my lips. *Let me sink into the floor and keep going*, I think, *away from the stares.*

Let me sink, sink, sink into the ground away from being me. No one will find me in my deep dark hole.

The EMTs make their way into the room.

"Girls, girls!" My RA finally snaps into action. "Everyone out."

Julie, still in her pajamas, stands off to the side, watching quietly as two big men fill our small room. One covers my body with a wool blanket, a welcome shield. He wipes the blood from my chin.

"We're gonna put you on this stretcher," he says kindly.

I nod.

"One, two, three," he counts, and up I go. They tuck more blankets around me and click a seat belt around my waist. Julie packs clothes for me. They ferry me down the hallway and stairs and out the front door of The Nunnery, past students beginning their day, backpacks slung over shoulders. Staring up at the sky, I feel eyes on me, certain the story is spreading. "Did you hear what happened in Murray Hall?" I imagine the buzz in the hallways and group showers. "This girl had a seizure." The ambulance doors open. Up and in I go, the doors closing behind me, the scene all too reminiscent of my first seizure on Laura Lane.

It is a short ride to Sacred Heart Hospital, my mind reeling. There is something still very wrong with me. I spend the morning in the emergency room being examined, giving my history, getting a CT scan and EEG. Dr. Bounds, the ER doctor, meets with me later that morning.

"Your EEG and CT scan are normal," he says. "Everything you describe tells me you have a seizure disorder. I find it hard to believe you've never been treated thus far."

Me too.

"I talked to your mother," he continues, "told her I'm starting you on Tegretol, an anticonvulsant."

Did Mom try to talk him out of it?

"Will this stop me from having another seizure?" I ask.

"That's what we hope, but there are no guarantees," Dr. Bounds says. "It's all about finding the best drug and dosage for you." He talks about side effects and testing my blood to monitor the drug in my system. But I am not listening. I am absorbing that I am eighteen years old now. An adult. And I can take the damn pills if I want to, no matter what Mom thinks.

⁓

I don't remember how I got back to The Nunnery. If I walked or took the bus. Julie is gone at class. Our room is quiet, a stark contrast to the morning's chaos. *I should call Mom,* I think, though it's more obligation than desire.

"Hello?" she answers.

"Mom?" I squeak out. "I had a bad seizure this morning." My tears pour out with the words. Sitting on Julie's bottom bunk, I curl over myself, forehead in my left hand, phone in my right. I've been holding in the morning's emotions for hours.

"I'm going to call Dr. Lathers to see if that hormone pill he gave you could have caused a spasm," Mom says first thing.

"Seizure," I interrupt, my energy for this exchange quickly waning. "Because you know how drug sensitive I am…"

I tune out as she talks on. What did I expect? Empathy? I yearn for her to think of me first. To acknowledge the fear and awfulness of my morning. To drop everything and drive to Eau Claire. Or hop the Greyhound bus at first chance. It doesn't register for her to feel my feelings. Instead, she blames. This time Dr. Lathers's hormone pill, which I started taking a few weeks earlier to bring back the period I still don't have. Because I'm still starving myself.

"Whatever, Mom," I say, cutting her off. "I'm taking the Tegretol. I can't *wait* to take the Tegretol. Especially if I never *ever* have to go through this again."

We hang up, and I climb to my top bunk to take a nap.

Mom calls back a couple hours later.

"Dr. Lathers thinks it's unlikely the Ovulen caused your spasm, but it's *possible* if you have some brain swelling from it."

Right now, I don't care about the why. Dr. Lathers's hypothesis is a poor substitute for a mom who should be a soft place to land. It's up to me to figure out how to help myself. And right now, this means taking Tegretol and leaving Eau Claire. Cut and run. Just like from St. Alphonsus to Highland View. Leave when it's too uncomfortable to stay.

Will I always run when things get hard?

Or am I running toward something better?

I can't feel the difference inside.

No one in my dorm asks about my seizure. Julie and I don't talk about it. And Mom and I don't mention it again either. We all pretend it never happened. But I know what everyone saw, and I carry the humiliation in my cells. What am I doing in The Nunnery anyway? How the hell did I get here? But I know. By listening to my boyfriend instead of myself. John and I have seen each other just twice since starting college. Visiting Madison reminds me of everything I'm missing, and with four hours between us, I simply start forgetting about him and us, while trying to act otherwise during our weekly phone conversations.

"I miss you too," I lie.

I start my five-month countdown to May, sending away for information from every school in the Big Ten Conference. Spreading the glossy brochures on my dorm floor, I imagine myself in the photographs. I want to sit in the stately vine-covered buildings at The Ohio State University with fifty-two thousand other students, playing Frisbee in my swimsuit with cute boys on the Oval, the big grassy spot in front of the student union. I want to cheer at football games in Ohio Stadium, just like the happy—and likely drunk—kids in the pictures. I don't know what I want to do when I grow up, but I know I want fun. And Ohio State looks fun.

"I don't understand why you have to go *all* the way to Ohio," Dad says from his recliner when I'm home for spring break. "Madison is a fine school."

He is right. Madison is more than fine. But I am practicing choosing for me.

"I'll take out loans to cover the extra," I assure him.

Mom is supportive. "The greatest gift I can give you is the gift of independence," she interjects in her breezy, detached tone. If independence feels like a ship with no anchor and a fuzzy destination, she is succeeding.

⌒

To bide my time, I go out with Julie and her new friends, who love punk rock music. I'm taking four pills a day now.

"Abstain from drinking," the doctor says, but this would make me more separate than I already feel, so I drink my usual amount, three or four beers, and fall asleep at the bar, my head resting on the table while my friends party around me.

"Wake up, Marianne," they say. "It's last call."

Every few weeks, I ride the campus bus to the hospital lab to make sure there's enough Tegretol in my blood. I haven't had another seizure, small or big.

"Are seizures the same as having epilepsy?" I ask the doctor.

"Yes, epilepsy is having two or more unprovoked seizures," he says. "And you've clearly had many more than that."

Clearly. I met the criteria in one week of fourth grade alone. I think of Ray Clark, and how I witnessed his seizure in seventh grade. How he and I were different on the outside but alike on the inside. And how it took six more years to know for sure what I already knew then.

"Marianne. Epilepsy," I say aloud when I'm alone in my dorm room.

I want to hear the sound of my name next to my diagnosis. Like putting on a coat, an identity layer between me and the world.

I picture conversations.

"Oh, Marianne?" says Imaginary Person.

"Yes, she has epilepsy," says Second Imaginary Person.

I am relieved to finally have an explanation, but I don't fully accept it either. And tell anyone? No, thank you.

～

George picks me up in May, and we throw all my stuff into the back of the station wagon. George has switched schools too, from UW-Whitewater, a small college west of Milwaukee to the University of Texas in Austin, after deciding he wanted to study commercial real estate in Texas more than accounting in Wisconsin.

"Let's get the hell out of here," I say to my brother, feeling lighter and lighter as The Nunnery gets smaller and smaller in the rearview mirror.

Ohio

THREE MONTHS LATER, MOM, DAD, and I drive the ten hours to Columbus, Ohio. It's supposed to be a seven-hour drive, but Dad needs to stop every two hours to stretch. "Oh, my achin' back," he mutters, walking stiffly in a loop around the station wagon, hands on hips. Mom sits patiently in the front seat, humming "Ave Maria." By midafternoon, we pull into the parking lot of The Ohio State University's Ohio Stadium. It's a horseshoe structure, way bigger in person, and my new home. I got a spot in the Stadium Scholarship Dorm, an ancient coed residence hall built into the west side of the football stadium. Living here is a form of financial aid; each resident works five to seven hours a week in a housekeeping or cafeteria job to offset the cost of room and board.

"She's already come and gone," says a random girl as I stand at the threshold of my new room, holding a box of clothes. "Jennifer," she adds with a smile, extending her hand. I am assigned to Unit K, the dorm divided into sections like Greendale, and paired up with a freshman named Tracy from a tiny town in southern Ohio. Tracy's lower bunk bed is made, stuffed animals resting against her pillow. The college brochure described Stadium Dorm living as no frills, and it is accurate. Eight rooms make up Unit K, four on each side. On one end of the short and dark hallway is a single pay phone and the only windows, overlooking the parking lot. On the other end is a huge shared bathroom. I peek inside at the long row of sinks, cement floors, and peeling wall paint. A cockroach skitters across the counter.

Thirty minutes later, I'm moved in. "Your dad wants to get on the road," Mom says, the three of us standing back in the lot next to our car. "Before it gets dark."

I nod, knowing their plan is to stay at a hotel somewhere in Indiana.

"Good luck, kiddo," Dad says, leaning in for a hug. Mom kisses my cheek. And just like that, they snap themselves back into their seats and drive away.

⌣

I want to be a TV reporter.

Sitting in my first journalism class, I watch my professor draw a large inverted pyramid on his whiteboard. *Pertinent facts*, he writes in the widest section at the top. The part I care about—the emotional backstory—is the teeny tiny point at the bottom.

I approach him after class.

"What about people's feelings?" I ask.

"No room for the fluff, just the facts," he says.

No fluff? I swim in fluff. Ruminate in all its moody permutations.

I walk out, drop my journalism classes, and ditch my career plan. It's a familiar strategy, my cut-and-run, quitting the whole if one part isn't working. I don't know how to live in the confusing place of ups and downs coexisting, believing I'm being guided by God or a higher power or anyone for that matter. All I know is figuring things out is up to me, and today this means I'm at college, and I need to be going to class for something.

Lying on my upper bunk, I revisit my OSU brochure and scan the list of majors, ruling out finance or anything medical. And I seek hallway guidance.

"What should I do now?" I ask my new Unit K friends.

Slumped against my doorframe, my tears loom. I can't listen to John this time. He and I are no longer. Two weeks before leaving for Ohio, I flew to Florida to tell him in person. His family had moved from Wisconsin to Florida, and John was bulking up to play football for the University of Miami. His head looked small next to his massive shoulders and growing biceps. He had traded his tight faded Levi's and baggy sweatshirts for thigh-hugging white shorts and pink polo shirts, and it made breaking up easier.

"What else do you like to do?"

"Baking!" I say.

The next day, I enroll in home economics, which lasts a week longer than journalism. Within hours of hearing about the curriculum, I decide I don't want to learn about cooking or children, and I switch to the College of Business.

Everything is business, I reason. And I can bake chocolate chip cookies on the side.

⟳

I trade Eau Claire humiliation for a freer spirit and weight gain. Unit K girls find Unit L guys. We hang out at the bars on High Street and bond over 2:00 a.m. gyros and pizza. Living inside the stadium means twenty-four-hour access to the football field, where we run the track and stargaze from the fifty-yard line. On football Saturdays, we access the game through secret tunnels and back stairways, mixing drinks in C Deck—the cheap upper-level seats—from the miniature vodka bottles and lemonade cans hidden in our pockets. I keep my epilepsy a secret, sharing a newly curated version of me.

Every few weeks, I disappear to the campus medical center for a check-in.

"Get adequate rest, and be mindful in your lifestyle," says Dr. Paulson, my new neurologist.

I nod and ignore his advice, swallowing my pills with beer, spit, or whatever liquid is handy. I haven't had a big seizure since my dorm room in Eau Claire. My left hand tingles from time to time, and when it does, I take a few extra pills, thinking the more the better, never mind my dizziness and nausea from the mild overdose. From the outside, I look solid and put together. On the inside, I'm anxious and uncertain. Like a hard candy with a gooey middle.

My first visit back to Wisconsin is winter break. My friends are counting down the days to be with their families. To eat, play games, and be merry! None of this is waiting for me. Nonetheless, I find transportation on a ride board in the student union, where strangers with cars advertise to those without. Halfway home, I call Mom to tell her where in Milwaukee to pick me up.

"It'd be great if you can stop by," she says.

"Stop by?" I repeat. "Where else am I going for Christmas if not to my house where you and Dad live too?"

"You know what I mean," she insists.

Actually, I don't. I don't know other moms who welcome their off-spring with the same excitement as seeing an estranged third cousin at a funeral. I move 450 miles away, find new people and possibilities, but I can't shake my deep longing for home where home is a familial place of belonging with a mom visibly happy to have me there.

⁓

Over time, I move into off-campus housing, ending up with five girls I know from Unit K. We each have our own bedroom, and we dumpster dive for furniture to fill it. I have Tony's old waterbed I retrieved from home. I pick up odd jobs to help pay my bills: cleaning houses, working for Belinda in the engineering school office, and being the Gatorade Girl for six summer weeks. Quaker Oats had come to campus interviewing for one coed team to mix Gatorade each morning, drive around in a white van, and hand out samples at the park, softball games, or anywhere else we could find hot and sweaty people to "quench their deep-down body thirst." I trade phone numbers with a few of the cute boys we meet along our routes, much to Ed's—the Gatorade Guy—disappointment, as I learn he wants our brand partnership to be a romantic one.

To advance my future, I join the campus chapter of the American Marketing Association. "It'll look good on your resume," our professor tells us. A businessperson shows up at our biweekly meetings to teach us about the real world. I like afterward better, when we head to the bars. I also pledge a coed business fraternity called Delta Sigma Pi that becomes a place of deep friendship with my "brothers": Parties and formals. Road trips and romance. A dating foursome emerges: Todd and Jackie, and Rob and me. We're inseparable. Rob is an aspiring DJ at a local radio station, and he works the overnight shift, midnight to 5:00 a.m. We talk on the phone into the wee hours. Rob lets me win his frequent donut giveaways, and he dedicates songs to "a special girl who should be sleeping." For the first time in a long while, I am exactly where I want to be.

⁓

One afternoon, Patti, the marketing club president, pulls me aside at a meeting and hands me an envelope.

"You should apply for this," she says. "You have better grades than me."

"*This*" is a scholarship, and the award is an all-expenses-paid trip to New York City to attend a conference sponsored by the Direct Marketing Association. It's an effort to get college kids interested in the direct marketing industry—aka junk mail. I send off the twelve-page application with my made-up goals and dreams and real teacher recommendations, and a couple weeks later, a fat envelope arrives in my mailbox, bestowing me a spot with twenty-four other kids from around the country.

I've never been to New York City, and it's only my second time on an airplane, the first a high school spring break trip to Florida, when my friends convinced me the emergency oxygen mask was a necessary part of takeoff. Landing at LaGuardia is landing on another planet, the diverse people and languages mesmerizing my Midwestern senses. I sit in the back of the shuttle bus, clutching my suitcase, and look up at the buildings, straining my neck to see the tops. The air smells like exhaust, urine, and grilled hot dogs. Small cities of people crowd street corners to cross. Eyes down, toting briefcases, bumping shoulders. No time for pleasantries, impatient taxicabs honking an urgent soundtrack. I watch a man snatch a purse from an elderly woman walking down the street. She turns. Shakes her umbrella. He runs. Two guys appear from nowhere and tackle the thief. There is more action here in five minutes than in a year in Ohio.

"Is this my stop yet?" I shout at the driver, afraid he'll forget to drop me at the Sheraton.

"Shut up already," scolds a ragged-looking dude slumped in the seat behind me.

For five days, I sit in an over-air-conditioned ballroom to learn about copywriting, A/B testing, and open rates. At night, two dozen of us explore the city, see *Cats* on Broadway, and eat pizza, corned beef sandwiches, and giant soft pretzels from street corner vendors. By the end of my trip, I know New York City and Manhattan are the same thing. Boroughs aren't suburbs. I like cappuccino. And the junk mail industry can use a smart kid like me.

Back on campus, college graduation looms. A parade of companies visit the career center, and I interview with Carnation, Caterpillar, Hormel, and Procter and Gamble.

"Why do you want to sell milk/tractors/chili/Tide?" the recruiters ask me in my one blue suit and pastel plaid silk bow tie, an empty briefcase at my high-heeled feet.

I don't, I think, but say, "I can't imagine loving anything more."

No job offers come.

"Ask the good Lord where he wants you to go," Mom says over the phone. We talk once or twice a month; she mostly wants to know if I'm going to church.

"The good Lord needs to speak up," I say, increasingly anxious. "Because I need a plan."

I try Mom's idea.

"God, show me where you want me to go," I plead with the clouds while sitting near Mirror Lake, the smallish pond in the center of campus where couples kiss and stressed-out college seniors like me contemplate their future. Then I close my eyes and listen. Nothing, just birds. It's hard to trust an invisible being who is supposedly everywhere and seemingly nowhere.

In early May, my phone rings. It's Jack Fink, one of the speakers from the conference. Would I be interested in working for a direct marketing company in Stamford, Connecticut? Does God have the same voice as Jack Fink? He flies me to an interview, where everyone is nice, and the work sounds as interesting as junk mail can be and more creative than tractors or chili.

I'll start in July, we agree.

"A girl named Lydia Helfrich in accounting is looking for a roommate," Jack says. Helf and Helfrich? Yes, God is Jack today.

On my last day of college, I shower with a beer keg left in the bathtub from my graduation party the night before. Ice chunks clog the drain, and yellowed water collects around my ankles. Mom and Dad have driven from Wisconsin and will be here in thirty minutes for the ceremony. I am happy and sad. I don't want to shower with beer kegs anymore, but I don't want to leave my safe and happy college cocoon either.

Weeks later, I stand on my rickety porch with Todd, Jackie, and Rob.

"Well, this is it," I say.

"This is it," Todd repeats.

Jackie hands me a brown paper lunch bag for my upcoming road trip. I peek inside at two granola bars, a package of peanuts and a bottle of water. Then we fall into a group hug.

"We'll always love each other," we promise.

Walking to my new used Honda I bought with Dad's cosignature, I don't look back at my porch. "The car payment is all yours," Dad assured me. The drive is all mine too, though Dad mailed me a TripTik from AAA, a step-by-step direction packet outlining my route from Ohio to Connecticut. My clothes and belongings fill the trunk and back seat. I leave my waterbed for my roommate. Lifting my door handle, I feel something soft jammed underneath—a folded-up white paper napkin covered in Todd's penmanship:

Marianne, it's not very often I meet someone like you. No matter how long it takes anyone to get to know you, they'll be glad they did. Anyway, I will truly miss you. One more thing...no matter how bad it gets, you always have us. Don't ever hesitate to call, ever... Goodbye, Marianne. I love you.

Todd.

Tears blur my vision, and I blink away my emotion. But slipping into my front seat, I rest my forehead on the steering wheel and sob big hyperventilating sobs. What am I doing? This is a cut-and-run I don't want. To stay where I'm loved seems kinder to my heart, but I don't know a way of being in which self-kindness trumps self-sufficiency. Turning on the ignition, I wipe my eyes with my hands to preserve my napkin and inch down Thirteenth Avenue. I imagine my friends standing arm in arm, waving at my taillights, but I don't want to know for sure.

Connecticut

OHIO BECOMES PENNSYLVANIA, MY DASHBOARD clock glowing 1:00 a.m. I need to pee, but where? No McDonald's, no rest stops, no nothing on this desolate stretch of rural blackness. Finally, a run-down tavern with a neon *open* sign beckons in the misty distance. I pull in, push open a heavy door, and come face-to-face with an obese greasy-haired man perched on a barstool, cigarette hanging from his lips.

"Heya, beautiful," he purrs, stroking his long tangled beard.

"Restroom?" I ask.

He points left. While I use the broom-closet bathroom, I envision Hairy Man blocking my exit with his flannel-clad chest and having his way with me. Nobody knows where I am. Mom and Dad don't. My friends don't either. How long will it take somebody to notice I'm miss-ing? Who will my new company call when I don't show up for work?

But Hairy Man doesn't budge.

"G'night, princess," he slurs as I run back to my car.

Bleary-eyed, I find a cheap motel and double-lock the door. A queen-sized bed with a faded floral quilt fills the dark-paneled room. It smells like a grandma's closet. This is not the "hooray for my first job" feeling I envisioned. I find a Bible in the bedside drawer and slide it under my pillow to help me fall asleep.

The next day, just after noon, I drive into the exact-change toll line of the George Washington Bridge without exact change. *Shit*. I consider backing up, but my rearview mirror shows dozens of cars zooming in behind me. Sweat pricks my temples. Inching closer to the gate, I shove my car into park, fling open my door, and jump out, jog-walking toward the automatic arms while desperately searching for a human being. Cars blare their horns, my Wisconsin license plate a billboard for my naivete.

"Excuse me!" I wave to a worker a couple of lanes over. He looks my way. "Excuse me, but I don't have exact change!"

"Oh, for God's sake," he frowns, walking toward me. "Whadda ya got?"

I hold out my palm.

"A dime and a twenty."

"Give me the dime and get the fuck out of here!" he says, dismissing me with his middle finger.

An hour later, I walk through double glass doors into my new office, quiet and sterile like a hospital. Cubicles, the exam rooms, line the wall.

A tall and wispy woman emerges from my right.

"Marianne?" she says.

I nod.

"Jessica," she confirms coolly, looking me over.

Jessica's khaki pencil skirt, blue oxford shirt, and penny loafers are a world away from my baggy sweatpants, wrinkly T-shirt, and sneakers.

"Follow me," she commands, clutching her car keys in a manicured hand, pinky up. Jessica is renting me a bedroom in her house because the day before I left Ohio, Lydia called. Her grandmother is dying, she said, and she needs to take care of her instead of being my roommate. I called Jack Fink in a panic, and he hatched the Jessica plan.

Trailing her cute VW bug, we wind through the twisty Connecticut roads with vague street signs to a house in the woods. It feels like camping, with dirt roads and plentiful trees, a short wilderness trek to borrow sugar from a neighbor. Can I find my way back to work?

"You're in here," she says, pushing open a bedroom door to a tiny space. "Oh, and you're not paying enough to use the kitchen."

What the hell? This bedroom is $250 a *week*. Is the bathroom included?

I unpack my car, then drive from Jessica's campground to buy bread and peanut butter for dinner in my bedroom kitchen.

"Welcome, welcome," Jack enthuses the next morning, leading me to my very own exam-room cubicle. The office colors are crimson and dark gray, an homage to the company's Harvard-educated founders. A magnetic name sign announces my occupancy; a desk and computer await my productivity. Jessica sits directly across from me, tight-lipped and glaring; my direct supervisor, Chris, occupies an adjacent square. A ringing phone and clicking computer keys are the only sounds. Three days ago, I stood laughing on my beloved porch with my best friends. Now I am in a strange office wearing a skirt and silk blouse, pantyhose and heels, a confining grown-up uniform.

I want to run back to Ohio, where I have too many friends to count. Instead, I'm one of three women in my department, and the other two ignore me. We all have the same job—account executive—but I'm five years younger, and my breasts are bigger. Is this the problem? Days in, Cindy, the secretary, tells me both women are complaining about me already. "Why does *she* get to travel?'" they whine to Jack after he brags I will be visiting my first "real clients" in California. Being the one who hired me, he has a certain pride of ownership.

"This place is *weird*," I whisper to my brother George on my private desk phone. George is now in grad school at UW-Madison, and I call him to hear a familiar voice.

"And I'm not making enough money to live," I add, my bedroom, food, and car payment quickly depleting my meager checking account. "I'll move back to Wisconsin in the middle of the night," I whisper. "Jack will find my chair empty, but I'll be in Chicago by then."

George laughs, but I am serious. Cut and run.

"Or you can ask for a raise," he says.

I walk the fifteen feet to Jack's office, rapping quietly on the doorjamb.

"Marianne," he looks up with surprise, "what can I do for you?"

Crossing the industrial carpeting, I settle into the comfy chair facing him. *So this is success,* I think, eyeing his expansive wooden desk and window overlooking Summer Street, a poor excuse for a real down-town like Chicago's or New York's.

"I know I just got here, but I can't stay," I say quickly. "Everyone is nice, but I can't afford it." I exhale, my stomach excited about packing up and going back to the Midwest.

"Then we'll give you a five-thousand-dollar raise," he says. "Immediately." *Shit.* Money and kindness persuade me back into my cubicle.

⤺

From eight to five, I write copy to convince Citibank credit card hold-ers to join our *incredible* shopping, dining, and travel clubs, which offer *amazing* discounts and cash back to members! All for *only* twenty-nine dollars per month! Problem is, I feel like a crook. We automatically charge people *unless* they read the fine print about how to cancel. *Negative option billing* we call it, which sounds to me like a fancy name for stealing. Confused and pissed-off people hound our customer service reps, who read one of umpteen scripts convincing them to stay.

"Just give 'em back their money," I tell Chris. "They clearly don't want our service."

"Your job, Marianne," Chris says, "is to talk people into our products, not out of them."

⁓

Two weeks later, I happily move out of Jessica's house because one week after I arrived, Lydia's grandmother died, and the two of us are back on as roommates. While we look for our own place, we move into her dead grandma's apartment in Yonkers, New York, a mostly older people's high-rise twenty minutes outside Manhattan with a view of the Brooklyn Bridge from our living room window.

"How was work today, girls?" the sweet residents greet us from their rocking chairs out front. It is oddly comforting to live here, surrounded by her beloved grandma's spirit, well-loved furniture, and delicate dishes. The smell of cinnamon potpourri permeates every room. Many nights, I stare out my bedroom window, New York City glimmering in the distance. I'm awed by how far I've come yet plagued with a familiar emptiness of being alone in the big world, rooted to nothing and no one. The longing, I recognize, is a maternal one, a deep desire for a mother's care and guidance.

A month later, Lydia and I find a cute two-story townhouse in Stamford at the end of a quiet cul-de-sac and ten minutes from our office. She calls me "Mare," which sounds like *meh* in her nasal East Coast accent, but I'll take it—a nickname! I start air-kissing people's cheeks with my hellos and goodbyes, and with her, I settle into the single working girl's life: weekly happy hours at the Rusty Scupper and dating a string of eager and hopeful men, including one sexy Aries named Chad, who works as a headhunter one floor above me. We meet in the elevator midday, stopping between floors to make out until he shares one night over dinner that he already has a girlfriend in Atlanta.

My first Thanksgiving in Connecticut, Lydia takes me to her family's house in Upstate New York.

"*So* glad you're here!" enthuses her short Italian mom, wrapping me in a warm hug, while her tall, angular dad strides into the living room in tight bicycle shorts.

"Sure you're ready for us?" he jokes. He rides sixty miles a weekend, Lydia says, rolling her eyes at his *very* snug attire. Sitting at their festive and abundant table, I listen more than I talk, captivated by what looks like a typical family life with a mom who appears to like being a mom and wife, and three daughters who interrupt one another because there's so much to say. They embrace me as the fourth daughter/sister, and it's my first visit of many.

People in Connecticut want to be my friend and date me and give me a raise, which is why Mom's detachment confounds me so. The person I expect to love me most seemingly wants the least to do with me.

"Why don't you ever call me?" I ask.

"I don't want to be an itch," she says.

"An itch?"

"I don't want to interrupt your life," she clarifies.

"Aren't you part of my life?"

Jim

I SIP MY COLD BEER, WHICH tastes like summer.

"That's Jim, who lives in Connecticut," says Chris, my childhood friend who still remembers my Pepsi shirt. I flew to Wisconsin with Lydia over the Fourth of July weekend for Summerfest, the annual lakefront music festival. The three of us are sitting at a crowded picnic table listening to the Bodeans, a popular Milwaukee band. The breeze off Lake Michigan cools the humid night air, which smells like falafel and corn dogs. Chris is dating Patrick, a guy from the F section in Greendale who I've known since kindergarten. Jim is his older brother, out of high school before I got there.

I look where she gestures. He's cute, his face tan, jawline chiseled. And almost too perfect in his white sleeveless tank, faded jean jacket, and gelled-up hair. A gold loop hangs from his left ear.

"He's probably taken," I say, but later I wander over.

"I know your brother Tony," he says, smiling a wide smile with nice teeth. "You came to one of his parties in Madison."

I cringe. I know the party, the one where I clung to the wall drinking a beer while wearing my favorite blue and green striped shirt, its collar flipped up like Elvis Presley.

We agree to meet up for a bike ride back in Connecticut and swap phone numbers. Two days later, coming down the escalator in New

York's LaGuardia airport, I see Jim by the luggage carousel and regret my ponytail and makeup-free face.

"Here we are again," we marvel and reagree to get together.

He doesn't call.

A month later at a crowded street fair in Norwalk, the city next to Stamford, Lydia and I see Jim again, standing with three guys, drinking a beer. Jim lives in Danbury, an hour north, so it's an unexpected sighting. We catch eyes, and he walks over. He's been playing tennis, he says, his hair disheveled, his shirt wet with sweat. I'm unnerved by his good looks.

"Lydia, this is..." I blank. "My brother's friend from Greendale."

"It's Jim," he says, extending his hand.

"Yes, Jim," I remind myself out loud. Payback for not calling.

"What are you doing next weekend?" he asks. Jim is going to the Newport Jazz Festival, and do we want to meet there? "We can check out Block Island," a small island off the Rhode Island coast.

A *jazz* festival? It sounds so sophisticated. Is he inviting Lydia and me to join him and a girlfriend he hasn't mentioned yet?

"Call me," I say, doubtful he'll follow through.

But eight days later, Jim rings me out of sleep at 7:00 a.m.

"Looks like it's just me," I say. Lydia made other plans, and my stomach flutters at the thought. I throw on jeans and a T-shirt and drive forty-five minutes north to the ferry crossing in New London, a small coastal city. Jim's black Honda Prelude waits in the parking lot, a newer model than mine because he's an important-sounding engineer for Hughes Aircraft.

His door pops open.

"Glad you made it," he says, walking toward me in all his tan and boyish-grinning glory. Before I can respond, he takes off his T-shirt to put on a white sleeveless tank, a fashion theme of his. My breath sucks in at his muscular half naked body, and I'm suddenly shy. Opening his passenger door, he motions me in and turns the radio to a smooth jazz station, orchestrating the exact sequence of events I need to fall in love.

We rent a moped and explore the seven-mile-long island. I hold his torso from behind, wondering what the right amount of tightness is. Too tight, and he'll know I like him. Not tight enough, and I'll career off the back. But I *do* like him. He's friendly and funny. Kind and handsome. We trade life stories on a rooftop bar overlooking the Atlantic Ocean. His gaze on me through dark sunglasses excites my insides as my alcohol buzz settles in. I tell him everything about my childhood seizures and epilepsy diagnosis—the first time I openly offer this part of me—and brace myself to be less of a possibility. But it's nary a blip in our easy talking. And a destined segue to Jim sharing how his best friend in middle school had seizures on the playground, and Jim was the one to consistently find a teacher to help.

"I'm sorry you went through that," he says.

Six compassionate words, and I feel more cared for than a lifetime with Mom. Later we get ice cream, him strawberry and me chocolate chip. He pays. And on the ferry ride back to New London, I close my eyes and rest my head on his shoulder, knowing we've moved from casual meetup to something more, and I'm not going back to the Midwest after all.

Labor Day weekend I move into a new house with new roommates, Katherine and Lori, after Lydia buys a condo in Yonkers near her grandmother's old apartment. I got a new job too, at a corporate events company in New York City, a forty-five-minute commute by Metro-North.

"Hi," I say on my day one as a train rider, sliding into an open seat next to a guy in a suit reading the *Wall Street Journal*.

He looks up with an audible sigh and eye roll.

"You're not from around here, are you?" he says, condescension in his tone.

"I am not," I reply, checking my outfit for clues to my Wisconsin roots.

"Because no one talks on the train." he instructs.

Sure enough, every head is bent into reading or sleep.

"Right," I say and extract my *People* magazine from my briefcase, tucking it into a *Businessweek* for cover.

Five days a week, I pull into Grand Central Terminal and spill onto the platform with hundreds of thousands of others. Balancing coffee and briefcase, I jostle toward the exit, then jog four blocks down Forty-Second Street, past mountains of black garbage bags and disheveled panhandlers, to my new old high-rise office in Times Square.

Simply getting to work is exhausting.

My "exciting opportunity," says Josh Wood, my boss, is writing new business proposals, video scripts, and collateral. What he didn't mention in our interview is how his "damn bipolar disorder" makes him highly erratic and that the senior vice president would kiss me at Friday happy hour. On the upside, Josh offers me his studio apartment on the Upper West Side whenever he's out of town, and Jim and I make love for the first time in Josh Wood's Murphy bed. *Something more* with Jim has become *us, together, as often as possible.*

Then one Monday, I show up for work, and Josh Wood doesn't. His office is dark, his furniture gone. Frank, the president, summons me over the company intercom.

"Josh quit to go to art school in Oregon," Frank says, sitting behind his big oak desk. "You still have a job, in case you're wondering."

I am wondering.

"You're going to be Ken's secretary." Ken is a sales guy and one of Frank's favorites. Cocky and chauvinistic like Frank too.

Hell no, I think. But it's all I have, so I drag my desk from outside Josh's office to outside Ken's office to fetch his coffee and make photocopies. I need another new job. But I need a new neurologist more. My Tegretol refills from Dr. Paulson, my Ohio State doctor, are expired, and he wants me to get someone local.

⌒

Dr. Louise Reese is a petite woman with wire-rimmed glasses and a cute pixie cut. I sit on her exam table on a Friday afternoon and tell her my history while she does the usual looking, poking, and listening.

"Your cognitive functions are excellent, and your sensory exam is normal," she says. "And you've never had an MRI?"

I shake my head no; I've never heard the term. While MRI technology was first developed in the 1970s, it wasn't until the early 1980s that MRI machines became commercially available for widespread clinical use.

"MRI is short for *magnetic resonance imaging*." Dr. Reese explains a newish diagnostic tool that gives a detailed image of the body's soft tissues without using ionizing radiation. In my case, the brain.

I nod, zoning out as she talks about checking my medication levels and updating my scans.

"Sure," I agree, eager to start my weekend with Jim. We have plans to go biking and see the early fall colors.

"My nurses will be in touch," says Dr. Reese, handing me a new prescription. Five pills a day now. "And I'll see you in six months."

A week into the new year, Jim and I drive to an imaging center in Westchester, New York, for my MRI.

"Are you sure you want to come with me?" I verify. It's new to have someone with me, physically and emotionally. He squeezes my hand yes.

A male technician fetches me from the waiting room, and I change into a blue gown and matching booties before he leads me to a bright white room with a huge round machine in it.

"Do you have trouble in closed spaces?" he asks.

I don't think so until this very moment when I might.

"You'll want these," he says, handing me earplugs, then gestures toward a dark window. "We'll be in there, talking to you through a microphone in the machine."

I nod, feeling less certain and more alone. I am twenty-three years old, an adult, but I feel like a little girl too, afraid of what's coming and whether it'll hurt. It's moments like these I want a mom versus my boyfriend of five months. I don't tell Mom much about my health because she doesn't ask. It feels one-sided to keep telling her without feeling like she cares.

For sixty minutes, I lie like a corpse as the machine whirs and bangs and clunks—loudly. But there's no pain.

"See anything?" I ask on my way out, trying to sound casual.

"Your doctor will be in touch," the guy says. "We're not allowed to share results."

Two days later, my phone rings at my desk. Dr. Reese is on the line.

"Are you sitting down?" she says.

"I am," I say, lowering my head for privacy.

"We got your MRI results back..."

"And...?"

"And..." says Dr. Reese. "You have something in your brain that shouldn't be there."

"What? Like what?" I press.

"Well, we don't know exactly. A lesion of some kind. I want you to get a second MRI with contrast."

"Contrast?" I squeak out, my mind spinning.

"They'll inject a dye into your body that will give us a more detailed picture of your brain," she says. "It doesn't hurt; it's just a little uncomfortable."

I nod as tears threaten.

Her nurse will call me, she says, and we hang up. I don't move. The phone call lasted less than a minute.

"Are you okay?" asks my coworker, but I don't answer, sliding from my chair and speed walking to the hallway bathroom, where I deep breathe, fear somersaulting through me.

What the hell is in my brain?

The question dominates my every thought until Jim and I go back for the second MRI, which shows, without a doubt, a round spot on the left side of my brain the size of a dime.

How long has it been there? Is it growing? Am I going to die?

I throw my wondering at Dr. Reese at our follow-up visit, sooner than the original six-month plan.

"Let's get your CT scan, EEG, and blood work done," she says, "and we'll meet to discuss everything in two weeks."

"Two weeks?" I repeat. Everything is suddenly urgent.

"Marianne," she assures me, "two weeks isn't going to make a difference in the big picture. You're well controlled on medication right now."

Or not.

Opinions

T O PASS TIME AND QUELL my anxiety, I sign up for a class, How to Start a Greeting Card Company. It's at the Learning Annex, a community education program at an old warehouse building in the city, and I go to aerobics class at a health club that's a six-minute walk from work down Broadway.

"Are those yours?" asks a girl. Well-endowed herself, she is staring at my naked chest as I change into my sports bra in the locker room.

"Original."

"Hot damn," she whistles, and we walk into the studio together, fast friends thanks to my breasts.

"Jog in place, jog in place," the teacher says, a thumping beat filling the room.

I jog.

"Windshield wipers!" She shouts a new move.

Back and forth I'm waving my hands over my head when midwave, I feel it. The pinch in my left pinky.

Are you fucking kidding me? Here? Now? This can't happen. I'm on medication. But it is happening, the numbness quickly spreading through my left hand. I haven't felt this kind of pulsing since my dorm room in Eau Claire six years ago. I bolt from the front row into the empty locker room, frantically searching for the bathroom stalls. *Shit,*

shit, shit. I sit on the toilet, doubling over with my left hand cradled in my right while it curls into the claw. I rub harder and deeper, trying to push out the numbness, blistering my skin in the process. IT. ISN'T. WORKING. Dear God, no. *Please, please, please,* I beg. I can*not* have a seizure in the bathroom stall at a health club in New York City. I don't know *anyone* here.

Numbness crosses my wrist, the usual point of no return. I sit and rub and pray. "C'mon, God," I whimper. "I'll do anything you want. Please not here." My arm is raising. Should I get on the floor now? No. I need to find someone who looks friendly and tell her I'm having a seizure and to call Jim.

And just as I get up, I feel a shift. A subtle but real subsiding. Can it be?

The numbness is miraculously stopping its march and receding toward my wrist. Did God hear me? I slump on the toilet, sweaty and limp with relief. When I'm sure it's over, I peek through the stall. The locker room is still empty. I grab my stuff and call Jim to meet me at the train station in Norwalk. Between the spot in my brain and this—what is happening to me?

The train pulls into the Norwalk station, and I see Jim's silhouette waiting on the platform. I slump into his embrace, tears releasing my fear.

In the morning, I call Dr. Reese. She ups my meds by one pill, and I go to work on a Tegretol high—shaky, drowsy, and pale.

"You don't look good," says Ken and sends me home, where I have another hand seizure. Two seizures in two days. I am back in fourth grade, desperate and hollow. Dr. Reese prescribes a second pill to calm my nerves.

By early afternoon, I am heading to Stamford Hospital for blood work and an EEG. Then to St. Joe's for a CT scan. Sitting alone in the waiting room, my head down in a magazine, I see familiar shoes toe-to-toe with mine. Jim. An angel in human form. This is what presence feels like, I think, when someone shows up in solidarity. Not to fix or doubt, but to simply be.

"I think you should sit tight," Dr. Reese says. We are back in her office after my tests. "And keep getting an MRI every six months."

"So you're telling me," I reiterate, "that I have what feels like a ticking time bomb in my head, and we should wait a half a year to check on it? What if we look in month one, and it starts growing on month one plus one day?"

She smiles at my exaggeration, but I am serious.

"Marianne," she says gently, "Your Tegretol levels are good, your CT and EEG are normal, and the lesion is likely slow growing if it's growing at all."

She bases her opinion on my long history, but all I can hear is: *Lesion. Likely. Growing.* My stomach tightens with annoyance, resistance, and impatience. This scene is familiar, doctors telling me things that don't make sense to me, while I try to connect with my own truth inside.

"Send me somewhere else," I say.

A month later, Jim and I drive to the VA Medical Center in West New Haven to meet with doctors from Yale's Comprehensive Epilepsy Center. It's an hour from my house and one of only two such centers in the U.S. pioneering new treatments for epilepsy. I carry my MRI scans in a gigantic brown envelope. Sitting in the waiting room, my eyes lock on a young girl wearing a helmet. Empathy floods my chest, thinking of myself at her age. I can't imagine wearing such a blatant advertisement of my disorder. And yet, I take solace in someone caring enough to protect her brain.

⌢

A nurse calls my name, and Jim follows, my second eyes and ears. Two doctors in suits walk in, and we shake hands. Drs. Dennis Spencer and Richard Mattson are the head neurological team. Dr. Spencer looks like

Father Time, tall with a long gray beard and small round glasses. Dr. Mattson is shorter and younger, and both have kind, wrinkled eyes. We trade friendly banter before up goes my scan onto their light box, and I steady myself for their opinion.

"You're fortunate," Dr. Spencer says, pointing at the spot in my brain, "to have what appears to be a clear origin for your seizures."

Fortunate? This is a new twist in perspective.

"Otherwise," he explains, "we'd need to surgically implant electrodes into your brain, then induce a seizure to see where it's coming from."

My breathing stops. I can't imagine someone making me have a seizure on purpose.

"You've likely got an abnormal blood vessel, scar tissue, or possibly a tumor here," interjects Dr. Mattson. They'll map its location on the MRI to know exactly which part of the brain to remove.

"With surgery?" I quietly voice the obvious.

"No other way," says Dr. Spencer.

I left Dr. Reese for a different answer, but I'm not sure I like this one either.

A week after my Yale appointment, I find a handwritten note on my desk at work. I have found a new job at a video production company in the city. *Come see me*, it says and is signed *Bill*. Bill is the owner, and I know what's coming.

I sit on his small green couch opposite his desk. "We're not a good fit, Marianne," he says, handing me a packet of paperwork. Up close Bill looks boyish with his side part and mock turtleneck. But his wall of windows overlooking Midtown Manhattan underscores his importance.

No shit, I think. My latest boss, a redheaded whirlwind named Marcy Flanagan, hired me after one interview because she is so busy. From the start, she's juggled a thousand to-dos while I sit at my desk looking out my tiny window, calling friends, and thinking up ideas for my greeting card class.

"Okay," I say and walk out his door in a haze of disbelief. I've never been fired before, and my shoulders sag with disgrace. I shut down my computer, quickly stuffing my few belongings into my backpack, tears forming. Marcy is nowhere, and Bill's note is still on my desk. *Thanks for the opportunity*, I scribble and bolt from the building, wondering why I feel the need to say I'm grateful when I'm not.

How will I pay for health insurance to cover my surgery? I take the subway to the unemployment office in a rough part of the city and wait in line with hundreds of others. "No more applications today," grumbles the helper lady when I finally get to the window.

I lean on the counter sobbing, "Please," I beg, but she won't budge.

"I'm closed," she says, snapping her window shut near my fingertips.

The guy behind me asks if I want a job selling insurance. I don't.

On the quiet late afternoon train, I slump in a seat. Rush hour hasn't started yet. The only thing I know for sure is I can't recuperate from brain surgery in my house. My roommate Lori and I discovered Katherine is struggling with an eating disorder called bulimia. In addition to her taking my food, I find my clothes and credit cards hidden in her bedroom. I don't yet understand the complexity of her illness, and my capacity to deal with my problems and hers is minimal. Her new boyfriend, Joel, a manager at the General Nutrition Center, is living with us now too, the two of them cooking nonstop to fuel their macrobiotic diet.

"Clean up after yourselves," I yell. "And I'm tired of Joel in our bathroom when I need to pee!"

Katherine is unmoved.

"I pay rent too," she says calmly, saliva stretching in the corners of her mouth.

A week later, I come home from errands to a long note taped to my bedroom door. To me, from Joel.

You have serious issues and need to find Jesus, it says, among other suggestions. Joel has a point. I do have serious issues—in my brain. And in addition to Jesus, I need to find one more opinion on what to do about it.

Back to the city I go with my MRI envelope and catch the subway to Columbia Presbyterian on the Upper West Side, a world-renowned hospital recommended by friends. I had signed up for short-term health coverage called COBRA through my ex-employer, a big monthly amount from my small unemployment income.

The neurologist, another older man in a white medical coat, clips my films to his light box. His office is like a fancy living room; sturdy bookshelves line one wall, a dark mahogany desk in the middle. I sit in a deep upholstered chair with armrests. My legs dangle.

"You gotta get this out *now!*" he says, tapping urgently with his right index finger on the dark circle in my lit-up skull. I flinch at his insistence while he explains how they'll use a CT scan to locate the lesion.

"But it's never showed up on a CT scan," I say calmly. His eyebrows raise like an annoyed parent.

"Then we'll give you a double dose of contrast and *make* it show up," he counters.

"Yale is operating off the MRI," I say, feeling suddenly knowledgeable— and impatient again. How can this smart doctor in a big important hospital not know this?

"They can't be doing that," he says, his mood seemingly switching to jealous rival. "We don't have that capability."

"Well, they do."

I stand up, opening my envelope to signal I want my scans back from his light box. His eyes widen at my sudden departure.

"Thank you for your time," I say. And for my clarity. My inner knowing is talking again, this time with an urge to get the hell out of his living room and take my brain back to Yale.

⌒

Amid my searching, Mom comes for weekend visit, a first to Connecticut. I've been inviting her since I moved here nearly two years ago, but she's reluctant to leave Dad alone. I assure her he'll be fine for three days. Jim and I pick her up at the airport in his car because I sold mine to save money. Waiting outside LaGuardia, Mom clutches a small dusty suitcase older than me. I take in her familiarity—short brown hair teased to fullness, large plastic-rimmed glasses, zip-up white sweatshirt with "*Proud to Be a Veteran*" silk-screened across her large bosom. Mom is losing height, but her round face and high cheekbones belie her sixty-five years.

"Hi, dear," she says, and we hug. The term of affection heartens me. Hosting her is less excitement, more tentative hope. Hope our visit will be easy and light. Hope we'll find common ground. Hope I'll shorten the emotional distance I feel.

For two days, Jim and I show Mom around Connecticut and take her to the Statue of Liberty and a Broadway show.

"He's a good catch," she says about Jim. "And cute."

Her schoolgirl comments and happy energy for sightseeing bring a levity and welcome distraction from the pressing matters of my health.

On Sunday morning, Mom and sit at my kitchen table before heading back to the airport. I retrieve my MRI scans from my bedroom.

"Here it is," I say, circling my finger around the dark spot, explaining with my new vocabulary: *contrast, lesion, right parietal lobe, Yale, resection.*

Sipping from a mug of hot water with lemon, Mom is quiet. This is where I'm expecting parental inquisition. "Are you sure? What do you know about this doctor? How complicated is this surgery? What are the potential side effects? When do I need to arrive? How can I help?"

But no questions come. She sips more water.

Is she confused? Over her head? Disinterested?

"Well…?" I prompt to fill the space.

"I'll keep praying," she says finally, and it's clear: I'm on my own with this one.

A few days later, I call Dr. Spencer's office at Yale. My MRI still sits on the table amid unopened bills and Katherine's cookbooks. I'm torn between listening to doctors, myself, and Mom's unspoken opinion that makes me second-guess.

"I'll put you through," says the nurse. My sweaty palm grips the receiver; I'm not used to talking on the phone with a world-renowned neurosurgeon.

"Marianne, how can I help you?" Dr. Spencer says kindly.

What a beautiful question.

"Does anyone really know what they're doing?" I ask. "Dr. Reese wants to wait and see while Columbia is ready to go on a treasure hunt."

Dr. Spencer chuckles, but I hear more comradery than condescension.

"That's why I want to do a brain biopsy, Marianne," he says gently, "To find out exactly what we're dealing with. He explains how they do pathology in real time during surgery. Testing tissue while I'm on the operating table. And how if they find something bad, they take it out ASAP.

"If you were my daughter, this is what I'd recommend."

My eyes water. *This is it.* The five words my heart needs: *If you were my daughter.*

Someone who sees me for me—a scared and overwhelmed young woman in need of compassionate guidance. What I've been seeking from Mom is coming from this kind doctor, a near stranger and just one of many I've held at arm's length, defenses up.

"Okay," I exhale, "Let's do it."

I call Mom next.

"I decided to have brain surgery," I say when she picks up.

"I don't know, Marianne, I just don't know," she replies after a few seconds. "I'm going to bring this to my bible study, and we'll pray for a miracle. We'll pray for that spot to disappear, so you don't need surgery."

It is an honest and earnest reply, yet my insides bristle.

"I appreciate that, Mom," I say, "and while you're praying, I'm going to have the surgery. I hope you'll come, but if you don't want to...."

I sound bitter, and I can't help myself. I've been driving to doctors and collecting opinions for months. Oh hell, for *fifteen years*. I've ruminated, worried, listened, stressed, and clawed my way to fledgling certainty, and I want a decision medal in the form of her immediate and audible support.

But I cannot receive what she cannot give.

I'm not against prayer. I talk to God too, though I'm not sure it matters, and I can't see that prayer *is* Mom's language of support.

"Think about what you want to do and let me know..." I say more calmly. "And can you let Dad know too?" She assures me she will.

Yale schedules me for mid-July, a month away and a week before my twenty-fourth birthday.

I move out of my house and into Jim's in Danbury. Closing my back door for the final time, I see Katherine's pots and pans in our sink, ants meandering through the dish tower.

Mom decides to book a flight. She's coming alone, she tells me, and I'm surprised—and softened—by her verdict, given my impatience with

her reluctance. Two trips in two months is uncharacteristically atten-
tive for her, even if one is medically induced.

I am ready, ready, ready.

Blue Cross Blue Shield is not.

⁓

Three days before my surgery, my phone rings.

"You haven't had your health insurance long enough to cover your
preexisting condition," says a voice from Yale's billing department. "So
you'll need to wait six months," she says indifferently, "or pay ninety-
two thousand dollars out of pocket."

I collapse onto Jim's couch, my sobs mingling with his commisera-
tion. Mom cancels her flight, and Dr. Spencer, my surgeon dad, assures
me six months won't make a big difference in the big picture. Here is
this message again: the big picture. As much as I want to believe his
consolation, I cannot see a grander view where this disappointment
makes sense. It simply feels like a big ol' "just kidding" from a bully
universe, one more disappointment in a line of many. "I'm going to get
you so close to an answer," it dangles, "and make you wait some more."

Jim and I drive five hours north to Maine to put some distance
between me and my distress.

"No need to grow," I tell my lesion. "Just chill out."

Surely my brain knows I am close to a mental collapse.

Answers

JANUARY FINDS ME IN A different place: less alone.

I take a freelance writing job in Norwalk, where I write new business proposals and sales copy for corporate clients. My temporary gig becomes a welcome place of belonging with coworkers-turned-friends. On my last day before surgery, the company hosts a goodbye party for the "spot in my brain" at a local bar. Christopher, my usually surly boss, dons a bald cap in solidarity.

"We'll be here when you're ready to come back!" he promises, raising his drink in my direction. A dozen people join the hoist, and I lift my glass in return. Dim lighting lessens my self-consciousness at being seen and supported, a new and welcome feeling. Not lost on me is how my first surgery getting canceled is the very thing that allowed this beautiful gesture and gift. The bigger picture, perhaps.

I pack my suitcase with my favorite flannel pajamas and toiletries, and Jim and I retrieve Mom again from LaGuardia.

"Your dad is going to church every morning you're in the hospital," she says, preempting my wondering why he didn't join her. I can't be sure what information Dad gets from Mom or whether Tony and George know I'm having surgery. I haven't told them; we don't have a habit of regularly being in each other's lives. George is working and living in Columbus, Ohio, now with his new wife, Linda, originally from the S section in Greendale. I last saw them a year ago at their wedding. I was a bridesmaid. Tony is in California, getting his MBA at Pepperdine University in Malibu. Happily single, I assume, as I haven't heard otherwise.

Mom, if anyone, is my family point of contact, but I want to hear from Dad too. To tell him things and have him tell me things back. To leave out the Mom middle. A few weeks earlier, I had given Dad a TDD telephone for Christmas that I won from a radio station granting holiday wishes. *My wish,* I wrote in late November, *is for two TDD phones so I can talk with my hard-of-hearing dad.* A TDD, short for *telecommunications device for the deaf,* resembles a typewriter with a keyboard and display screen. One person—me—types a message, and the letters convert into electrical signals that travel over the phone line. When the message reaches its destination—Dad—the signals convert back into letters that appear on the receiving TDD. But Dad and I hadn't figured out how to use our TDDs yet, and he needs the Mom middle to help him figure it out.

⌒

"I'll take the couch," Mom says at Jim's house. She is staying with us, but she won't go upstairs. "I can't sleep up there knowing you two are in the same bedroom." Which admittedly sounds gentler than, "You're living in sin."

The next morning, the three of us check me into Yale New Haven Hospital. After taking ten tubes of blood, an EKG, and a chest X-ray, the nurse puts me in a room for the night with two other women. I move my bed into an L shape to look around. The lady next to me is out cold, surrounded by a half a dozen people.

"What's wrong with her?" I ask, overly curious why everyone else is here too.

"FUO—fever of unknown origin," a guy answers. "Doctors sliced her down the middle, looking for the reason." I close the curtain between us. Now that I know, I don't want to know, my heart heavy for this woman.

Later, my neurology team stops by to brief me on my surgery, an anesthesiologist in tow.

"We can clearly see the lesion," Dr. Spencer says, "but what we *can't* see is if it's in the sensory part of your brain or the motor part."

"Soooo…" I prompt, feeling uneasy.

"So you'll wake up with no feeling in your hand or no movement, but we can't tell you which," says Dr. Mattson.

Could they have mentioned this before? The surgery is tomorrow morning. Maybe this "oh by the way" is on purpose so I don't overthink it. No feeling or movement. Either will suck, but I know it's a worthwhile trade-off to be done, hopefully, with seizures forever.

Dr. Spencer hands me a clipboard.

Things can go wrong. There are no guarantees, says the tiny type.

Inhaling courage, I sign my permission, regardless of the outcome.

⌒

At exactly seven the next morning, a nurse strides through the door pushing a gurney. Mom and Jim are back too, after leaving Danbury at 5:00 a.m.

"We'll take her now," the nurse says cheerfully, as if we're off to coffee. I scooch from my bed to hers. She covers my bare legs with a blanket, then holds up a syringe.

"For anxiety," she says, giving my inside elbow a two-finger tap. This is it. I'm really doing this, my fear softening into warm relaxation.

"I'll be in the waiting room, saying the rosary," Mom says.

Out my door we roll, down hallways, and into elevators to a basement corridor where Dr. Insurni, a fourth member of my brain team, is waiting. I am a passive participant in a well-orchestrated dance, one person handing me to the next. It is oddly comforting, this being waited on and cared for, even if I'm paying them to do so.

"We need to shave your head," Dr. Insurni says after a kind hello, magically extracting a privacy curtain from a pole attached to my gurney. There is no *we* about this. He has the blade; I am on Valium. Propping me upright, he flicks on his razor and meets the tender skin of my neck, the buzz bringing me back to Dad's driveway haircuts for Tony and George on Laura Lane.

"Can you at least leave my bangs?" I ask. "So if I wear a hat or scarf, it'll look like I have hair."

Dr. Insurni chuckles.

"That's a first, Marianne," he says, quickly shaving up and around my skull, my hair falling in chunks around me. In twenty seconds, he is done, and I feel my scalp, soft and pokey like a guinea pig, my bangs a fringe on my forehead. There is no turning back.

Next, Dr. Insurni places a heavy ring on my head.

"An iron halo," he says. "Attaches to your skull."

He means literally—with screws.

The Novocain needle pierces my tight forehead skin, the sting releasing ready tears.

"Pain or pressure?" he asks, tightening a small knob.

"Pressure," I whimper. "Pressure, pressure...pain!"

More Novocain, four shots in all. Last, he places a grid over the ring, a cross between a catcher's mask and an upside-down flowerpot, close to my eyes and fanning out near my mouth.

"This helps us map the exact spot of your lesion in the MRI," Dr. Insurni says, adding, "So Dr. Spencer doesn't need to go fishing."

Their desire for precision is comforting.

We are on the move, racing down a hallway. Why the sudden hurry?

Dr. Insurni drapes fabric over my head to hide me and my hardware from nosy people like me as we travel through the corridors. On my back under a cloth, an iron bar screwed into my forehead, my tears stream down my temples. What was I *thinking* choosing this?

A mystery hand, soft and smooth, grabs my right hand.

"Hey..." Jim says. "I'm here."

"Where is Mom?" I ask, my voice muffled.

"Trying to keep up."

"How did you find me?" I ask. No answer. No time to chat. Run, run, run. I reach behind with my left hand, hoping to bridge the distance for Mom, but I get a stranger's instead, thick and calloused.

"We'll see you when you're done," Jim says, releasing me to go where they cannot.

I roll into the operating suite headfirst, the intense light brightening the space underneath my fabric. Hands remove the cloth; my eyes flinch. Doctors and nurses move with purpose in the white and chilly space, lighthearted banter mixing with the watery sounds of hand washing and the clinks of surgical instruments being readied on trays. Soft music plays, smooth jazz like Jim's and my first date. A masked nurse looks down with smiling eyes.

"Everything will be okay," she says.

"Ready, Marianne?" the anesthesiologist asks.

It's the last thing I remember before the IV goes in, and I go out.

Minutes, hours, or three days later, I feel my breathing tube being tugged from my throat, scraping my esophagus on its way out.

"What was it?" I ask groggily, squinting into the lights.

"Shhhhhh," a nurse says, but Dr. Spencer overrules her shushing.

"A tumor, Marianne," he says gently. "And it's all gone."

A tumor? I had a brain tumor? But before I can ask more questions, I fall asleep again.

I wake up in the ICU. Needles fill my arms, tubes up my nose. My calves float up and down in alternate succession, powered by two balloons encircling my legs.

"To prevent blood clots," says a nurse.

A turban of bandages covers my skull. Mom and Jim lean against the far wall, looking at me. They tell me it was a nine-hour surgery.

"Can you believe it was a tumor?" I say.

"You look good," Mom says. "Your cheeks are nice and pink."

⌒

Nurses wake me every hour.

"Who is the president? Can you count backward from ten?" they ask.

Tethered in place, I mumble answers. Medicine drips into my veins. Machines buzz, beep, and hum. Fluorescent lights illuminate the hallways around the clock, with no door to shut them out. But it's all a worthwhile trade-off for the truth. After fifteen years, I know the secret my body kept so very long. The struggle to figure it out is blessedly lifted.

At 3:00 a.m., I buzz the nurse.

"Yes?" she says.

"I have to pee."

"No, sweetheart. You don't have to worry about that," she answers. "You have a catheter."

The pain in my belly disagrees. I buzz again.

"No, you *really* need to come in here," I say. "I'm gonna bust."

Two nurses appear at the foot of my bed and peek under my gown. "Oh wow, your catheter is kinked!" one says.

"Sorry about that, honey."

"Me too," I say as two gallons of pee pour out of me.

These invitations to trust myself are showing up in all kinds of ways.

The next morning, Dr. Spencer appears. He's doing rounds and sits on the edge of my bed.

"You had a low-grade astrocytoma," he says calmly.

"Is that bad?" I ask.

"It's a type of glioma that develops from star-shaped cells called astrocytes that support nerve cells."

His words, in doctor speak, sound foreign, but I like the idea of my brain cells being star shaped.

"How'd it get there anyway?" I ask.

"No one really knows." Dr. Spencer adds some thoughts on the mystery of human development and how it's a miracle more people don't have cells going rogue when one considers how many there are.

"You surprised us," he continues.

"But it was benign?" I confirm.

Dr. Spencer nods. "But those type of tumors can grow and change, so it's good it's gone."

It is good.

I won't need radiation, he adds, confident my pathology showed clear margins.

I stare at my left hand in my lap, a numb lump, and will my pinky and thumb to touch, but they won't budge. I can't feel *or* move my hand.

"Your brain's been jarred," Dr. Spencer says, sensing my unasked question. He reaches into his coat pocket.

"Close your eyes," he says. My palm is pressed downward. "Feel anything?"

"No," I say, discouraged, opening my eyes. A quarter rests in my hand. Less than twenty-four hours after surgery, and I expect my body to be back to normal.

"You'll get some feeling back," he assures me, "but not all. And the movement will improve over time."

A commotion erupts on the other side of my curtain. A guy is being moved in next door.

"Oh, my fucking head!" he screams while a woman begins wailing. Instantly alert, my adrenaline doubles my heart rate and shortens my breath.

"I want to move rooms!" I frantically plead with Dr. Spencer, certain this guy's pain is going to make my head explode too.

"He'll calm down; don't worry," says Dr. Spencer, patting my arm.

⌒

Three days later, I move to a private room, free of machines and free of nurse overinvolvement too. It's unsettling after every-fifteen-minute check-ins. Jim and Mom visit every day, their company a comfort. They sit and read. We watch TV. I sleep. They sleep too. I walk laps around my floor with Jim or a nurse. There's not much else to do in the early days of mending.

"How do you feel?" Mom asks.

"Fine," I say, because I do. My head doesn't hurt. I'm mobile. My appetite is good. My insides, however, are restless and reflective. I am grateful my tumor is out. So grateful. But my gratitude is tinged with sadness for having had it in the first place. Sorry that my childhood was plagued by fear and trauma and insecurity, with a mom who rejected the medical help that may have lightened my physical and mental load. I know many people carry bigger challenges than me, and in my short time in this hospital, I meet three.

Down-the-hall Jake, a teenager from Atlanta, takes fifteen pills a day and underwent what he calls Phase 3 testing, where doctors took away his meds and put electrodes on his head to map the origin of his seizures. Eric, the screamer next to me in ICU, is missing a chunk of his temporal lobe and needs to relearn his words. And Carol. Dear Carol. A woman my age, Carol came to Yale in status epilepticus, which means a single seizure lasting at least thirty minutes. Dr. Spencer rewired her brain, and Carol is relearning to walk. My well-controlled seizures and small tumor look easy next to their stuff, though they didn't feel easy.

One night, the three of us gather in Jake's room.

"Do you ever feel different and lonely?" Eric asks. The three of us nod. These strangers know something about me that few do, and it doesn't make me less than; it makes me feel understood and welcome.

On day six, an entourage of residents shows up in my room, the sun barely up.

"We're here to take off your bandage," they say, all men in their matching white coats, holding clipboards.

"Right now?" I ask. Still groggy, I'm not ready to see my bald and stapled head. But before I can object, the chief resident grabs the end of my gauze and unwinds it, dropping the bandage pile on my bed, crusty, yellow tinged with dried blood. Cool air tingles my naked scalp, and I reach to shield it from their stares.

"Looks good, Marianne," he says, pulling a white paper hat from his pocket and lofting it on the bed. "Here, wear this."

It looks like something a McDonald's trainee would wear or a paper boat a kid sends down a river.

"No, thanks," I say. I'll wait for the hat Jim promises to bring.

After they leave, I go to my bathroom and stand at the sink, head down. Lifting my gaze, I take in who I see, expecting to be repulsed. Instead, I feel curiously accepting and intrigued. What little hair I have looks dark compared my usual fake blond. My jagged bangs cover the open sores on my forehead. Turning my head, I check out my incision, an eight-inch wound curved over my right ear. It is red and swollen, heavy staples pulling the skin taut. But they are evenly spaced, like the person who did it cared.

I have a nice-shaped head, I think, moving my palm over its even roundness. My eyes look big and bright on my face, and Mom is right: my cheeks are smooth and pink. I look like me despite my new hairstyle. But the girl in the mirror feels different. Relieved and affirmed. Light and safe. People came alongside me, and instead of feeling judged, I feel loved. What was scary and shameful to reveal brought more kindness and support than I've ever known. Do some people feel this seen and accepted all the time?

A steady parade of people visits. Friends and coworkers. Even my boss shows up, though I'm extra conscious of being in my pajamas with the company vice president. We talk and eat ice cream, watch movies, and share office gossip. It gives Mom and Jim some needed time off too.

But when darkness comes and the floor quiets, darkness revisits my brain. I imagine the worst. *What if I still have seizures? What if I never get any feeling back in my hand? What if? What then?* One night I take a shower, holding the sprayer in my right hand while trying to grasp the wet soap bar in my left. It slips to the floor and skitters across the tiles.

"Dammit," I mutter. Though missing a piece, my brain hasn't lost its knack to scold my body's performance. Later that night, the hospital floor hushed, my fear talks loudly. I call Jim.

"I'm scared," I whisper.

"Want me to come down?" he asks.

I smile on my side of the phone, touched by his willingness.

"Can't," I say. "Visiting hours are over. And it's late."

But sixty-five minutes later, Jim appears in my doorway.

"The nurses looked the other way," he laughs.

Jim motions me to scooch over. I'm in a hospital twin bed with guard rails, hardly cozy for two. But he climbs in anyway, holding me until I fall asleep and disappearing sometime before morning.

"If you don't want him, we'll take him," the nurses tease. I want him.

Eight days after surgery, Dr. Spencer and the residents come by my room to take out my staples. Gingerly pressing his scissors against my scalp, he tugs and clips, the metallic snipping sending tingles through my body.

"You're good to go," he says, the metal bits falling onto my bedsheets. I check myself in the mirror to make sure blood isn't squirting out of my skull. The incision looks friendlier without the metal tracks, and the skin is sticking together. Brain surgery one week, back to life the next.

Packing my clothes and gifts, I walk my balloons and flowers to Hazel, my elderly neighbor next door. She is sitting in her wheelchair in the hallway as usual.

"For you," I smile.

"Leaving so soon?" She smiles back, her usual blah mood lifting.

Back in my room, I am brushing my teeth when my left hand tightens. Shit. I bolt into the hallway, frantically searching for Dr. Spencer, who's in the next room.

"My left hand!" I stammer, barging in, his surprised patient gracious at the interruption. "It's numb!"

Dr. Spencer doesn't react.

"Your brain's been traumatized, remember?" he says gently. "Prickles are normal."

Normal maybe, but they take me from zero to terror in a split second.

Jim is waiting in my room when I return. He reaches out his arms, and I rest against him.

"You ready?" he asks.

I need to be. They aren't offering more time at the Yale Hotel. Sitting in the passenger seat, I watch trees and buildings speed by. The highway feels extra fast, the day overly bright. I feel like a different person, my nine days at the hospital a transformative divider from my "preknowing" life.

Through our front door, I walk directly to my MRI scans and press the film against the dining room window.

"So that's what you were," I say to the dark spot. "Do you have any idea how much hell you caused?"

⌒

The next morning, Jim goes back to work. He's missed a lot the past two weeks. It's just after nine, and I'm sitting on the couch. Mom emerges from the kitchen, cereal bowl in hand.

"I want to go home," she says matter-of-factly.

"Why?" I ask, confused. It is my first full day home from the hospital. She is supposed to stay one more week, two total.

"I'm not needed here," she explains. "You and Jim have it covered."

Whatever "it" is. Likely the caretaking, but perhaps the relationship too. Whatever I need—comfort, conversation, a glass of water—is, in her mind, being handled by someone else. She's off the hook. Free to go. She showed up for the surgery out of duty, desire, or guilt, I'm not sure, and is resolute in her decision—no remorse, explanation, or second-guessing in her voice.

I tip my head back on the cushion and close my eyes. Hurt and rejection course through me, lumping in my stomach. Unbeknownst to her, I had been quietly holding hope that this—her daughter's long-awaited brain surgery—would spark the sudden appearance of a relationship that has never been, filling our physical and emotional distance with talking, reading, walking, laughing. Didn't she want this too?

How can she not want to be my mom? What is it about me? About her?

"Okay," I relent, my acquiescence sending her into motion.

I watch her pack up her few things and listen to her call the airline to rebook her ticket.

Less than twenty-four hours later, she is gone.

Whatever the real reason, I take away this: I am not worth her time.

Marianne and her mother at her wedding, 1991.

Marianne and her four children, 2010.

PART II

Garden of Thanks

I HAVE NOTHING BUT TIME.

"Low-key activities for eight weeks," says Dr. Spencer at my first follow-up visit two weeks after my surgery. "And no driving."

His to-dos sound simple enough. I'm tired, and my head itches from new hair growth. Other than that, I feel fine. No headaches, dizziness, or pain. My deeper wonderings are less straightforward.

"Do I still have epilepsy without my tumor?" I ask.

"It's all about seizure frequency," says Dr. Spencer. "No recurrent seizures, no epilepsy."

"Will my tumor grow back?"

"Possible, but unlikely," he replies and recommends a yearly MRI to make sure.

"And how long do I have to keep taking my pills?" I'm still at five a day.

"What's your comfort level without them?" he counters, reminding me how scar tissue in the brain can still cause a seizure. He first plopped this surprising—and distressing—news at my bedside shortly after the surgery. All this, and I end up with the same seizure fears? On the upside, my neuropsychological testing showed minimal impact on my brain function. I'm the same smartness I was before surgery.

"Zero comfort," I say.

With ten hours a day to fill, I watch TV. Talk to friends. Walk around my neighborhood. Hang out on my front step and savor the winter sun. I check out library books on self-healing and lie in bed, taking deep breaths and visualizing brilliant white light filling my brain and mending my incision from the inside out.

"Where'd you get your cute haircut?" asks the reference desk librarian.

"Yale New Haven Hospital," I reply, turning my head to reveal my scar. "Ninety-two grand."

My shaved head tells one story of healing, but my insides are talking too. They thank me for listening to myself and ask if they can finally exhale because they don't have to hide anymore. They feel freer than they have in a very, very long time.

Freer but not free.

Mom's sudden departure reinforces my belief that, brain tumor or no, I'm not enough to reshuffle myself on her priority list and secure her presence when I want it most.

To piece together the whole of our journey, I request my medical records from every doctor along the way, starting with my first ER visit. Within weeks, they trickle into my mailbox, folded into thick envelopes. Coffee in hand, I read them like a novel, main-character me ping-ponging through misdiagnoses and dashed hopes. Acute strain brachial plexus, wayward vertebrae, and cerebral allergies. It's the first time I'm seeing the doctors' side of the story in their words. I open the envelope from Dr. Strassburg, my first neurologist in Milwaukee, and smooth his typewritten verbosity on my lap.

His four-page summary describes a nine-year-old me explaining my "spells." His conclusion:

"I am inclined to feel that the symptoms are most likely on the basis of a psychosomatic disorder. This is probably a form of conversion reaction, and the youngster may indeed be using this for her own secondary gain. Certainly, I can find no evidence of any organic central nervous system disorder to account for the symptoms. I think the possibility that this represents a focal seizure disorder is a remote one. However, since that possibility is even remotely present, I think that we should take steps to rule it out further."

I read and reread his summary.

Her own secondary gain?

I sat in his office chair dying inside, earnestly hoping and praying he was the one who could and would fix me. Hiding behind playground trees and in bathroom stalls, I was hardly seeking attention. Anger riles my insides. He, like Dr. A, suggested it was my mind's doing. And though he was willing to take a closer look, Mom put an end to seeing him after I started taking the medication he prescribed.

I get up to grab a notebook on the kitchen counter.

I wasn't making it up, I write in a summary of my own. *I had a brain tumor.*

Dr. Strassburg will not remember me. If he's even still practicing. Thousands of patients have sat in the chair across from his desk since.

Why is this so important to me—decades later—to tell him how he affected me?

I want to divvy up responsibility for my pain. To have him own a sliver of the suffering I experienced, a wound much deeper and more lasting than the one on my head. I want to believe I'll get him to think for a second. To realize the weight of his skepticism on a hurting kid. It's the same slivers I want Mom to own, shards that pierced my heart with feelings of aloneness and abandonment.

And, frankly, still do.

"I did the best I could with what I had...under the circumstances," she tells me repeatedly, banging her fist on the nearest flat surface for emphasis.

When will I believe her?

Fixed physically doesn't mean fixed emotionally.

One Saturday, I ask Jim to drive me to the art store to buy watercolor paints and paper. It's been a year since my greeting card class, and I'm wanting to make thank-you cards for everyone who gave me gifts during my hospital stay. I like the idea of doing something creative with my time while personalizing my appreciation. By Monday morning, my dining-room-table art studio is ready. Sitting in my pajamas, I drip color onto my paper and watch the paint pool and spread, mesmerized by its freedom, fluidity, and beautiful imperfection, a new concept for my like-to-control self.

With beginner strokes, I create what comes through me, simple daisies with one-line stems and petals. Blobby blue flowers with golden brown middles. Coffee cups filled with sepia lattes. I draw letters and messages. *Thank you so much. With gratitude.* I'm hardly a natural compared to long-ago classmates whose inherent knack for proportion, shading, and perspective earned them As in art class. When I mess up, I start over, scattering my cards on the floor to dry, a garden of thanks sprouting around me.

This feels better than reading my medical history.

One afternoon, my friend Evan comes over. He and I met when I bought his brother's Volkswagen from a for-sale board at Jim's work. No more train commute meant I needed a car again.

"Whatcha doing, Mare?" he asks.

"Just painting these silly little cards." I downplay it, self-conscious about my new hobby.

"I can sell those," he says, scooping up a few. Evan is an interior designer in town and my most frequent visitor. So far, he's rearranged my furniture, wallpapered my kitchen in Waverly English Ivy and convinced me to buy a blue chair-and-a-half—much trendier, he says, than my ordinary-width beige chair. He also knows all the gift shop owners in town.

"Trust me, no one will want them," I say.

But Evan ignores me and comes back a few days later with orders: Six pink stick flowers. Six blobby blue flowers. A dozen sepia lattes.

"Seriously?" I look at him in disbelief.

"They're sweet, Mare," he says. "Told you people love this handmade stuff."

But *my* handmade stuff? Soon my card making takes over the entire dining room. Flower, flower, flower. Tree, butterfly, sun. Words, words, words. A dozen birthday cards. Two dozen sympathy. Thirty baby shower invitations. I create, and Evan delivers. It is fun until it isn't, the joy of self-expression quickly kidnapped by quantity and repetition—and my need to return to my paying job.

I call Susan, my greeting card teacher, for advice. She invited us to use her as a resource.

"Choose twenty of your favorite designs and make cards for all occasions," she says. "Oh, and do a catalog too," she adds, assuring me a simple black and white photocopy is enough. "Then find yourself some sales reps, people in the business of selling to the gift shops."

"Got it," I say, and Jim agrees to help.

I name my tiny business Watercolor Works and register it as a partnership with the Secretary of State. One night at 3:00 a.m., the crunch of a car hitting mine out front shocks me awake, a drunk teenager behind the wheel. We use the insurance money to fund our first printing, dozens of cardboard boxes arriving at our doorstep.

I place a small advertisement in the back of *Greetings* magazine, the industry trade publication, and find two sales reps, one in Minnesota and the other in Colorado. We buy a fax machine and connect a toll-free number to our home phone. And we ship one or two orders every few weeks at the post office on our way to our real jobs.

Our small enterprise is a happy diversion matching the brightness of being on the other side of my surgery, something new and good and joyful blooming from something hard. Blooming, too, are Jim and I together, a blissful cadence of being in love: Brunches and dinners. Bike rides, picnics, and tennis. Movies and concerts and road trips. Conversations about forever.

On a Friday afternoon in late April, Jim picks me up from work. He won't tell me where we're going, and I'm quietly hoping. An hour later, we pull up to a bed-and-breakfast in New Milford, a small historic town north of Danbury. It's nearly dark when we arrive at the large house with white clapboard siding, black shutters, and a wraparound porch exuding romantic charm. Inside, I plop down on our queen-sized canopied bed covered in a patchwork quilt.

"Can we move in here?" I ask, Jim kissing my forehead.

"Don't get too comfortable," he teases. "Dinner at eight."

As the waiter clears our dishes from the candlelit table, Jim pushes a small black velvet box toward me, flipping open its hinged top to reveal a sparkling princess-cut diamond ring resting on white satin.

"Will you marry me?" he asks, getting down on one knee.

Though I had quietly suspected this moment was coming, his

proposal is surprising and tender. Reaching down to hug him, I nod, happy tears confirming my yes, grateful for this guy who has already done so much for me, arriving in the nick of time to share a journey I would have faced alone or with Mom, which would have felt the same as alone.

"Your dad's a yes too," Jim says, reaching into his pocket to give me a long and narrow printout from my TDD phone. Jim had called Dad to ask for his blessing, their word-for-word exchange recorded on the thermal paper.

⌒

Months later, we fly back to Greendale for the holidays. Donna, my childhood friend, throws an engagement party for us at her parents' house in the S section, my middle-school refuge. Mom and Dad come too, a meaningful effort given their penchant for staying home. They stand together in the kitchen, surrounded by the din of overlapping conversation. Mom takes in the frivolity, holding a plate of appetizers while tapping her foot to the holiday music. Dad holds a plastic cup of red punch, his face affixed with forced pleasantness. I recognize the look. He can't hear a thing while trying to project otherwise.

"You can leave, Dad," I say gently touching his sleeve and making eye contact, so he can read my lips. His shoulders release at the permission, a genuine smile replacing the fake one. He hands me a small wrapped box. The party invitation told guests to bring a Christmas ornament for Jim's and my eventual first tree. Admittedly, I didn't think they would, Mom not a shopper and all. But Dad came through.

"Can I open it now?" I say, curious.

He nods, his eyes expectant.

Inside, resting on red tissue paper, is our swan, its bushy silver tail proudly resting on the delicate paper.

Earth Angels

TWENTY-FOUR HOURS BEFORE THE WEDDING, Mom calls me from their hotel. I am in my kitchen-turned-makeshift-beauty-salon. My dress hangs from the window's drapery rod, its ivory beaded bodice sparkling in the midday sun.

"I have good news and bad news," she says, her voice oddly upbeat for half-bad news.

I lower into a chair, my senses on high alert. "What?"

"The good news is we're here," she continues. Our Wisconsin family flew in the night before, except for Mom and Dad, who drove the four-teen hours to Connecticut, Dad refusing to get on an airplane.

"The bad news is we got in a car accident on the way."

I hold my breath as she details how a semitrailer in Pennsylvania changed lanes into Dad, bulldozing their Buick off the road and into a ditch, their car crumpled but drivable.

"Oh my God, Mom," I exhale, my stomach dropping.

"We're fine, we're fine," she confirms, remarkably detached.

What if they had died on their way to our wedding? Or were in comas? Paralyzed? *Keep breathing*, I tell myself. Is this the jolt of gratitude I need to offset my recent disappointment about Mom not being a part of my wedding planning? No dress shopping together. No check-in phone calls. None of the "normal" stuff I saw my friends' moms doing with their bride-to-be daughters. Her justification is the same as her departure after my surgery: "You have it covered," she said. "I have nothing to contribute." I am looking for presence, not performance. Togetherness versus being a to-do. My rational brain keeps working to believe it isn't me. That she doesn't know what she doesn't know and how lucky am I to have amazing friends to fill in the gaps.

But my daughter brain feels ripped off.

"How's Dad?" I ask. Being the sole driver is heroic enough given his bad ears.

"He cried when it happened," Mom says. "But he's better now."

We hang up, and compassion fills my insides. I picture Dad weeping in a ditch on the side of the road, his beloved car smashed in. I'm guessing he didn't sense the semitruck nearing them until it was too late. Months earlier, Mom told me Dad went to the ear doctor and learned he had only ten percent hearing left.

"How does he feel about that?" I asked.

"You'd have to ask him," she said.

So I did, with an eight-page letter. I wrote that while I knew him, I didn't really *know* him. *Forgive me*, I said, *This is going to be a bunch of questions about your life pre-Marianne that made you who you are today.* I asked about his childhood home, siblings, school, friendships, and whether he played sports. What he did on the weekends and whether he ever went to prom. I asked why he feared spending money and whether he was mad at God about his hearing. I invited him to write back *and introduce me to your history, thoughts, and feelings.* Then I signed off with *I love you, Marianne-o.* Using my nickname to let him know this was just between us. For weeks, I eagerly checked my mailbox for a lengthy and loving reply. But nothing came.

Finally, I called Mom. "Did Dad get my letter?" I asked.

"He slipped it into his desk drawer," she said, knowing because she went snooping. "Said something about you being nosy."

I keep knocking on the parental door of wanting to know and be known with no answer.

⁓

Our wedding day arrives like a New England postcard, maple trees ablaze in red and orange, a warm October breeze dropping leaves like confetti. Our wedding is now doubling as a going-away party—for us. A month earlier, Jim moved to Minneapolis to take a new job, and we agreed I'd join him after our honeymoon.

Fiftyish friends and our families fill the seventeen pews of Sacred Heart, a quaint white clapboard Catholic church tucked at the end of a narrow wooded lane. Jim and I considered eloping. Easier, cheaper, a tad rebellious. But I couldn't let go of the traditional wedding vision— white dress, veil, maid of honor, and matching bridesmaids. Would I go to hell for getting married in a Catholic church while living together, having sex, and using birth control? Maybe, but I didn't know how *not* to be Catholic either. I went to mass because I should and to make sure Father George saw us in the pew and our money in the offering basket, so he'd agree to marry us in his cute little church. We didn't mention in our premarriage classes that Jim and I shared the same address, and we hoped our teaching Sunday School to first graders—its own kind of penance—balanced things out in God's eyes.

Standing face-to-face at the altar, we clasp sweaty hands. Jim is the most for-sure thing in my life.

"Till death do us part," he repeats after the priest, slipping a ring on my finger, his watery eyes matching mine. It's the first time I've seen Jim cry.

After mass and outside photos, Evan chauffeurs us in his dad's antique Chrysler Imperial to the Cobb's Mill Inn, a historic restaurant and lodge with a huge wraparound deck, nestled on the Saugatuck River. Puffy white clouds float across an azure sky. Sipping champagne, I gaze at the water, flanked by a dazzling autumn. Dozens of guests mingle, many coming from afar to celebrate us. I am buoyed by this beginning: no tumor in my brain and a man who loves me whom I love back. After dinner, the inn fills with live music and the unexpected: Mom and Dad on the dance floor. In her salmon-colored dress and white Naturalizer sandals, Mom holds Dad's outstretched hands, the two of them smiling and bouncing to the music. Never have I witnessed the two of them having fun together, and I'm riveted. Mom's face is flush with excitement, and I wonder if I'm catching a glimpse of who she was before marriage and motherhood.

Two weeks later, I land in Minneapolis after a surprise Halloween blizzard dumps thirty-two inches of snow on the city. I was supposed to fly on the thirty-first until Jim called. "You can't come," he said. "The city's shut down." *Surely, he is joking,* I thought, as I looked outside at a glorious fall-colored Connecticut to which I'd returned to oversee the move. I flipped on the TV. Parka-clad newscasters stood along clogged highways, holding microphones in puffy-mittened hands.

"What kind of crazy place is this?" I say as we drive thirty minutes south to Jim's one-bedroom apartment in Burnsville, which feels like the middle of nowhere, cold white flatness stretching in every direction.

Jim's new job is working as a production manager for a boss who wants him to manage production around the clock. He is out the door every day at 6:00 a.m., back at 3:00 a.m. I don't leave the apartment, trapped inside by relentless snow and bitter cold. Watercolor Works is with us too, in numerous cardboard boxes piled around our apartment.

Our new marital bliss quickly deteriorates.

"I wouldn't have come if you were never going to be home!" I complain as Jim collapses on our bed, my loneliness for friends and familiarity translating into anger and blame toward him.

"Remember...we decided *together* to move here?" Jim says. "Connecticut was expensive. We want to buy a house. We wanted this." *This* is us learning—me learning—to be a *we*. The give-and-take. Better or worse. For much of our three-year relationship, I had health issues. Jim supported me, and I received it.

I am not as adept in reverse.

Slowly, I acclimate. We learn how to divide chores and paychecks. We move out of the apartment and into a small rental house in a south Minneapolis suburb. I find a job at a small public relations agency in downtown St. Paul, and we make new friends who add the fun and camaraderie I am missing.

Three years into Minnesota, we build our first house in White Bear Lake, a northeast suburb of St. Paul. Jim switches jobs, and I find a new one too, at a corporate communications company in downtown Minneapolis. And after dinner, when most child-free couples go out or watch TV, we tend to our growing business. I paint new cards in a spare bedroom upstairs, and Jim packs orders downstairs. Our marketing plan is simple: paint more designs, find more sales reps, add more accounts. It works well enough, and soon we qualify for UPS home pickup, a true business milestone.

One June weekend, Mom and Dad agree to drive to Minnesota to see our new home. I proudly give them a tour of our downstairs world headquarters, which is basically gray metal shelving full of cards, plus a couple folding tables for order filling.

"I don't know where you get all those ideas," Mom says admiringly, shaking her head at our shelves in disbelief.

"What will you do when you run out of them?" Dad counters, his forehead furrowed.

"There's enough in my head for now," I reassure him.

"Just don't quit your real jobs," he adds. "Then you won't have health insurance." Dad gives me things to worry about I haven't yet considered.

On Friday evening, I buy us tickets to a minor league baseball game in St. Paul. The four of us sit in the bleachers eating popcorn while dark clouds gather in the distance, the air thick with humidity.

"Looks like rain," Dad says in the fourth inning. "We should go."

"C'mon, Dad, try to relax," I say playfully, but he fidgets and sky watches, so we leave.

The next morning, I attempt the local parade, an annual kickoff-to-summer event.

"Where are you taking us?" Dad pipes up from my back seat. I watch in my rearview mirror as Mom pats his knee.

"This'll be fun," I say before two raindrops hit my windshield.

"I want to go home," Dad says, his voice an anxious waver.

Oh, forget it, I think and make a U-turn back to my house.

A couple hours later, Mom comes up from downstairs. I am on our couch, flipping through a magazine.

"Your dad wants to go home," she says, pausing. "To Greendale."

"Really?" I look up, surprised and not surprised.

"He's bored," she says. "And he misses his bed."

Bored? Tears sting my eyes, and my mouth opens to object, but I close it, resigned. Could he have chosen a different word? I'm not enough to keep his interest either, his bed more appealing than time with his daughter. I'm unable to see I'm pushing him too far beyond his seventy-two-year-old comfort zone. They ferry their small duffel bags across the family room and out to the car. Jim and I stand arm in arm on our front walkway while Dad revs up his Corolla. Before we turn to go back inside, Mom's passenger window rolls down, and her head pokes out. Tears are sliding down her cheeks. I walk closer.

"Be glad you have a normal marriage," she says quietly as Dad backs them out of the driveway. Her tone is different from what I've heard before, resigned and sorrowful, and her truth pierces my disappointment. Dad can't hear what she said, sitting behind the wheel, oblivious to her pain, both oblivious to mine. It is a waterfall of emotions, each of us stuck in our own flow.

⁓

"They don't want to be part of my life," I say.

I am sitting on a couch across from Gail, a therapist I find close to my downtown work. I've never been to therapy before, but after years of feeling rejected, I decide to let a professional weigh in. Do my feelings make sense?

"Your mom, for one, is incapable of relationship," Gail says from her floral upholstered chair, handing me a tissue. "She never had it modeled for her."

I get this, Mom's parents were immigrants who barely spoke English, and her dad died young. Her own mother wasn't planning shopping dates and spa getaways. And yet, I have a hard time accepting it. Mom knows the name of every vitamin in existence and who to keep pursuing at the VA and the CIA.

I tell her exactly what I need: time, connection, presence.

She can choose me if she wants to.

"You have every right to grieve," Gail says. Grief. It's an option I hadn't considered, and it fits. Mourning the loss of what's missing and may never be.

"But what do I *do* with the feelings?" I ask. I'm tired of lugging them around.

"Maybe writing will help," she suggests.

This isn't a new idea. I have been writing my way through life for as long as I can remember. A locked diary under my elementary school mattress. Secret thoughts written in spiral notebooks in middle and high school to chronicle feelings, friendships, and thwarted romance. And in college, I captured my daily life in a series of matching diaries that I bought via mail order, giving myself five lines per day. Getting my thoughts from the inside to the outside helped me make sense of them. Now my journal is a growing document in my laptop computer, pages upon pages of my ramblings—password protected.

I take Gail's advice, but instead of journaling, I finish a book I had started in the wake of my surgery, inspired by Jim, Dr. Spencer, and the others who helped carry me through. My earth angels, I called them. For all my divine doubts, I received guidance, protection, and care in ways I couldn't have orchestrated myself.

Forty rhyming stanzas later, *The Gift of an Angel* recounts God's careful choosing of a guardian angel for every new child.

Gathering his host of angels,
God considered them one by one.
"I need a volunteer," he said,
"to watch over this daughter or son.
Your role in a child's life
will gently unfold with the days.
You'll be a protector, keeper, friend...
and wise teacher of life's ways.
There will be frightening times for sure,
when danger stirs alarm.
It's then you must forget all else
and protect this child from harm."

Transforming my experience into a story of hope for others sparks excitement I'm eager to share. I bring my writing to work and read it to my coworker Scott. He and I are friends outside the office too. When I look up from my desk, his eyes are red and teary.

"You *have* to publish that," he says.

I don't know how to make or illustrate a book, but I'll figure it out. Just like I'm trying to figure out how to get my cards in front of the holiday buyer at Dayton Hudson, a regional department store chain headquartered four blocks from my office.

I eye my envelope of greeting card samples sitting on the corner of my desk. Same as it has for weeks. My clock reads noon. *What the hell,* I think and grab it.

Motivated by Scott's encouragement, I jog-walk to Fifth and Nicollet, weaving through crowds of workers on congested side-walks, and flow into the revolving-door entrance of Dayton Hudson. I wind past perfume counters and men's shoes to the reputed hidden back elevator—sure enough, it's there—and press 6 for the buying offices. No one checks my ID or verifies an appointment. In fact, no one is here at all, just empty couches, tired carpeting, and a display of Andes mints, likely stale. A handmade sign taped next to a dark receptionist's window points to a telephone on a small table. I tiptoe over, my eyes finding her name on a list of extensions: Mary Joseph. Besides wondering if her name helped her secure the Christmas buying job, I wonder if her reputation is accurate—terse and hard to please.

Sweat dampens my forehead.

"Don't answer, don't answer," I silently implore after punching in her number.

"Mary Joseph," she says curtly.

"Uh, hi," I stammer. "I'm Marianne Richmond, and you don't know me, and I'm standing in your lobby, and I make greeting cards and want to know if you want to buy some."

I sound like an idiot. Two seconds pass, a silent eternity.

"Leave 'em at the front desk," she orders; then *click*, we are done.

Setting my envelope on the counter, I sprint back to the elevator.

Three hours later, my desk phone rings.

"This is Marianne," I answer, my usual greeting.

"And this is Mary Joseph," declares a more congenial voice.

Tightening my grip on the receiver, I straighten my posture.

"I got your cards..." the voice continues. "And I like them. Very much."

"That's great," I squeak out, then listen to her explain how, if she is going to "merchandise" a four-foot section of my holiday cards, I need a lot more designs to choose from.

"*Dozens* more," she says.

A four-foot section of my cards in sixty-seven Dayton Hudson stores around the country?

"I can do that."

Looking for
the Same Thing

THINK YOU'LL HAVE KIDS?" ASKS Donna over lunch, retucking a picture of her one-year-old into her wallet.

Donna and I both live in Minnesota now, though we don't see each other much. For years, I wanted to *be* Donna. To live in her beautifully furnished two-story house with a mom who breezed into the kitchen in a cute tennis dress instead of selling Shaklee products door-to-door, ingesting blue-green algae, writing letters to the *Village Life* editor, and power walking around Greendale with ski poles. I wanted to eat family dinner at her round retro kitchen table with the space-age chairs as if plucked from a 1950s movie set. As kids, Donna also had a pet rabbit she kept in a weathered wooden cage in her backyard through which we pushed lettuce leaves and carrot bits. I was desperate for a pet after Mom gave away our dog, Flip, when I was six. Flip the beagle was George's birthday gift he named after Flip Wilson, the comedian. But when George stopped picking up Flip's poop and Mom didn't want to start, she put an ad for a free dog in the newspaper, and we watched Flip bound out the front door into the arms and minivan of his new family. Soon after, to console my sadness, I bought myself a hamster I named Butch and replenished his cedar chip carpeting and food pellets with beloved consistency. Until one day Butch mysteriously disappeared from his cage, and we never found him.

"I want to feel what you feel," I say between bites of salad. "You seem really happy. But I don't, and I'm not sure I ever will." A lot of my friends are having babies. George and Linda too, who live in Illinois now with their two little girls.

After six years of marriage, people want to know if Jim and I are having kids.

"Are you waiting?" they ask.

"No, we're just living," I say.

I don't have enough reasons to want children of my own. Mom and Dad didn't make it look very fun. When we visit Jim's family for the holidays, a dozen toddlers run wild, their parents unable to eat a meal. *Who'd want that?* I think. I like our little family of two. We work and travel and grow our business. After the big Dayton Hudson order, Jim quit his corporate job and found us a small downtown Minneapolis office space in an old warehouse building.

But as more and more people procreate around me, I start to second-guess myself. Do they all know something I don't?

⟳

My period is late.

We are using the diaphragm for birth control except for one November night in front of the fireplace with the diaphragm in an upstairs drawer. I didn't want to add "the pill" to the five Tegretol pills I'm still taking after Dr. Spencer's warning about scar tissue causing a seizure. My only other physical reminder of my surgery is the permanent loss of feeling in three fingers of my left hand—the movement came back—and I get my annual MRIs to check on my brain. So far, no suspicious areas and no seizures, little or big.

"Do you think...?" I say to Jim, then answer for him. "I really hope not."

But the pee stick from Walgreens says yes, and I'm dizzy with panic, my body growing a tiny human I don't want to be growing. *I'm gonna get rid of it,* I tell myself. Cut and run. I consider everything that will change, our freedom gone. But when I consider abortion, I also tell myself God doesn't approve. Somewhere in the Bible, it says children are a gift from the Lord and blessed is the person whose quiver is full of them. How can I throw away God's gift in my quiver? I'll go to hell for that too; I'm already on the list for premarital sex and contraception.

For weeks, I wrestle with what to do.

"Having a baby will be great," Jim says. Mr. Optimistically Flexible.

"Yeah, maybe this is happening for a reason." I eventually come around. "A chance to do family our way." It's this thought—this invitation—that moves my angst to cautious excitement, and by January, I'm all in.

⌒

"My stomach hurts," I say one Sunday night, lying on the couch with a book, Jim watching football on TV.

"You're probably just tired," he offers. He and I spent the winter day cross-country skiing in a nearby park.

Hand on my belly, I go upstairs to use the bathroom. Turning to flush, the toilet bowl is bright red.

"Jim!" I scream.

His footsteps bound up the stairs.

"There's blood," I stammer, my voice high and panicked. "A *lot* of blood!"

What do I do? The doctor's office is closed.

I hobble into my bedroom. From my nightstand I grab my *What to Expect When You're Expecting* book and flip to the index. *B for blood.*

See Miscarriage, it says. What's a miscarriage? I remember Mom saying she had a couple of them, and all I know is it meant she lost the baby.

I dial the emergency room, Jim watching me, helpless.

"Are you still bleeding?" they ask.

I check the Kleenex I stuffed in my underwear.

"A little."

"Unless you are hemorrhaging," the voice tells me, "You can call your doctor in the morning."

I don't sleep. All night I tell God how I want this baby, hoping he isn't punishing me for having doubts. "I've totally changed my mind," I whisper. "It just took me awhile. Please let everything be okay."

⌒

The next morning, I drive to the medical clinic.

"Hop on the table," says Dr. Walton. She's been my doctor for two years, and I haven't needed her for much beyond an annual physical. Her perfume overwhelms the room, the same Jessica McClintock scent I wore for eighth-grade graduation.

"We'll get a quick listen of the baby's heartbeat."

I look at the ceiling, my shirt up, leggings down.

"There's *your* heartbeat," she says, moving her stethoscope back and forth over my belly.

More moving and listening.

"Still yours."

"How about now?" I urge.

"Well..." she hedges. "I'm going to send you to the hospital for an ultrasound. That'll give us the best look."

I know she knows, and she isn't telling me.

Jim meets me at the doctor's office, and we drive together to St. Joe's. The day is cold and gray, my mind the same.

A female technician calls us to a room. Again, I lie down. She squeezes cold jelly on my stomach and starts scanning with her wand.

"Well?" I ask.

She doesn't answer me, her wand still searching.

"Do you *see* anything?" I press, annoyed by everyone's silence.

"The doctor will be in," she says.

Five seconds later, a man in a white coat rushes through the door and peeks at the screen. "Not viable," he says briskly and disappears.

"What does *that* mean?" I look at the technician, tears springing to my eyes.

"It means the baby's heart stopped beating," she says gently. "It's not alive anymore. I'm so sorry." Setting down her wand, she leaves the room too.

I erupt, sobs racking my body. Jim envelops me until I'm spent.

There is a dead baby inside my stomach. What am I supposed to do now?

From the hospital lobby, I call Dr. Walton.

"Your body will expel it naturally," she says.

"Will it hurt?" I ask.

"You'll have cramps for sure. Like a bad period, but you can handle it."

"What if I can't?"

Monday, Tuesday, Friday. For days I wait, and nothing.

Confused, I go back to work.

"I was pregnant," I tell my coworker Angela, "but I'm not anymore. It's still in me."

"What are you *doing* here?" she says, shocked.

"What else am I supposed to do?"

The only guidance I have is to handle it on my own. I'm familiar with this. While no one can help me miscarry a baby, the solitude of the endeavor triggers a physical and emotional aloneness I've known since childhood. And while Jim is willing to support me as best as he can, I crave a motherly comfort beyond his reach.

"Get a D and C," Angela says. "They knock you out, get rid of everything, and you wake up on the other side of it."

Simple, I think. Like cleaning out the garage.

But the next morning, all hell breaks loose. Bad period, my ass. I curl into a ball on the floor. Sprawl out on the stairway. Sweat and cry and curse. I lock myself in the downstairs bathroom while Jim bangs on the door.

"What can I do?" he implores.

"Nothing!" I yell, doubled over, clammy, nauseated. There isn't room in here for two people and my agonizing pain.

After umpteen hours of writhing, I feel a *whoosh* of something come out, and with it, the pain subsiding. Afraid to look, I do. A tiny fetus floats in the middle of the toilet, about two inches long. Shaped like a comma, it has an eyeball, teeny hands and feet, and a bumpy spine. I cannot flush my baby comma down the toilet. Horrified and frantic, I hop into the kitchen, my pants at my ankles, look for Tupperware, and scoop it—him? her?—up with a plastic cooking spoon.

Jim reappears.

"Our baby is in the refrigerator," I say stoically, rebuffing his hug. My husband is offering me comfort, and I—numb, exhausted, empty, and sad—want to be untouched. My expertise in self-reliance needlessly perpetuates my sense of isolation.

Monday morning, I deliver my Tupperware to Dr. Walton, who promises to run some tests.

"To see if we can get some answers," she says.

Answers are good, but they won't bring back our baby.

I sit on the couch in our empty house and stare at the wall. Jim is at work. Overseeing a business comes with a conviction of indispensability. He didn't ask permission to go to work, and I didn't request otherwise.

No one else knows I was pregnant, so no one knows I'm hurting.

I call a few friends for support. Mom too.

"I'm sorry," they say.

"You can try again," they encourage.

"God works in mysterious ways," they explain.

I find little solace in a phrase that chalks up my circumstances to God's higher maneuverings at a divine control booth. As if he purposely orchestrates disappointment so he can look like a hero later.

My friend Julia brings over chocolate chip cookies and sits close to me on the couch. Julia was my first friend in Minnesota. We met when I was looking for a job.

"What if I can never be pregnant?" I say. My body has been disappointing me for years in one way or another.

"It'll all work out." She consoles me, and I want to believe her.

Over the next weeks, flowers arrive at my doorstep and sympathy cards in my mailbox, including one from Mom. After a few lines of genuine-sounding condolences, she pivots. *See?* she writes in her loopy penmanship, *I told you those drugs were a bad idea.* I absorb her words, anger burning through me. Slamming her card on the kitchen table, I pick up the phone.

"How can you *say* that to me?" I demand when she answers. "I take those pills so I don't have to live every second of every day in fear of having a seizure like I did for *ten years* because of you not letting me *take* any pills!"

Tears are mixing with my words now.

"How could you hang me out to dry like that?" I implore, terrified nine-year-old me speaking through grieving thirty-year-old me.

It's quiet on her side of the phone.

"Well?" I push, my trembling voice verging on hysterical.

This would be an excellent time for a long overdue apology.

"You don't know what it's like to live with a hard-of-hearing husband," she says, finally.

"Oh. My. GOD," I say, my exasperation palpable. "What the *hell* does that have to do with me?"

Nothing and everything.

Will she ever see what I went through because of her decisions?

But in this heated moment, I see our sameness too. Mom wants an apology from the CIA, and I want one from her.

We are looking for the same thing—a desire for who and what hurt us to see how much.

But the real kicker? Mom's comment rouses my self-doubt like a stick does a sleeping bear. I throw my Tegretol in the garbage and quit cold turkey.

No checking with Dr. Spencer.

No weaning off it slowly over time.

Cut and run and done.

⟳

I can't sleep, thinking about my tiny fetus with miniature body parts. Two, three, four in the morning, I watch the hours tick by. I move to the guest bed for a change of scenery. Onto the basement couch. I take Benadryl and Tylenol PM, but sleep won't come. I call Dr. Walton, who prescribes Elavil, an antidepressant that makes me see double. I visit a hypnotist in an old two-story house in south Minneapolis who swings a crystal in front of my nose to unsuccessfully help me forget my trauma. And I order a sleeping program off the internet, three cassette tapes of a man's soothing voice telling me to imagine sparkly golden light enveloping me into slumber. But the rhythmic *click-click-click* of the cassette circling in my tape player keeps me awake.

Increasingly desperate, I call Gail, my therapist.

"Perhaps you should see a psychiatrist," she says. "A medical doctor who does therapy and can prescribe medication."

Exhausted, I drive to a mint-green building in a run-down part of St. Paul and sit across from a stoic man wearing a blue sweater vest who looks diminutive behind his expansive desk. Always the giant desk between doctors and me. Power and knowing on their side, anxious seeking on mine.

"You. Are. Chemically. Depressed," he says in a monotone cadence, punching each word for importance. "Your miscarriage has retraumatized you."

The loss of my pregnancy is triggering the same out-of-control body issues my seizures provoked, he explains, and he prescribes Paxil, another antidepressant, and trazodone, a sleeping pill.

More pills to replace the Tegretol and Elavil I just threw away.

For weeks, I exist in a haze of new side effects. Dry mouth, grogginess, and dizziness, while Mom's words tap at my conscience: "You know how drug sensitive I am." Do we have this in common too?

Gail urges me to pause, reset, and reassess what Jim and I truly want. I don't know what I truly want, and what Jim wants is to see me happy. Replacing what I lost as soon as possible seems to be the quickest way.

To prove to myself my body can cooperate.

Nothing solid or truthful is informing my frantic choices, and three months later—I'm pregnant again.

Upon This Rock

MONICA LEWINSKY HAD ORAL SEX *with the president*," Mom reads aloud from the *Milwaukee Journal* newspaper. It's early June, and I am sitting at the kitchen table on Laura Lane after driving to Greendale to see our house one last time before Mom and Dad move to Maple Meadows, a senior apartment complex built by the nuns in Mom's bible study. Mom is their hero after she intervened with the bank to help convince reluctant loan officers to lend money to nuns with no credit history.

"What's *oral* sex?" she asks, moving her paper to look at me.

I pause midsip of my Sanka instant decaf coffee, the only option available because Dad doesn't own a coffee maker.

"Do you *really* want me to tell you?" I ask, setting down my cup.

"Yes," she assures me, so I detail the nuances of oral versus regular sex.

"Egaaaad," she says, the *gad* stretching two full seconds. "Who'd wanna do *that*?"

Poor Dad, I think. As it is, he is not happy. "I feel like I have to move to save the marriage," he confided earlier, sidling up next to me on the couch bench. "Your mother has become very…supervisory."

He is just seeing this? Dad doesn't want to leave his grass, garden, or basement woodshop. He is miffed too, about Mom's latest diet, called

Fit for Life, which has her eating the equivalent of an entire farmers market in fruit until noon, then dividing the remainder of her daily intake into proteins and carbs.

"If you eat foods in the wrong combination, they will rot in your stomach," Mom explains, quoting the diet's founder, who is making the talk show rounds. Dairy isn't technically allowed, but Mom justifies ice cream for dinner because it's all one food group and has calcium. All this means Dad is on his own for cooking, which isn't sitting well with him. His repertoire is slim, mostly fish sticks and french fries or a frozen Hungry-Man dinner, the branding accurate. When I relayed Dad's complaints, Mom was unyielding.

"Sister Cecelia gave us first dibs on a *luxurious* ground-level two-bedroom apartment," she said. "This move is good for him; he just doesn't know it yet."

Mom abruptly stands and disappears down the hallway, and I follow her to my childhood bedroom turned *her* bedroom and office. My once beloved decor hasn't changed. The bright green carpeting and blue butterfly wallpaper clash with her navy and red wool Air Force blanket she's using for a bedspread.

"Does Dad care you don't sleep in the same room anymore?" I ask.

She doesn't answer, her reply superseded by her loading colorful file folders into her arms from the bottom desk drawer. I follow her out.

"My rejection letters," she says, plopping the folders on the kitchen table. She's been filing claims with Milwaukee's Department of Veteran Affairs since I was in seventh grade to receive disability compensation for three issues she says are "service connected" to her electroshock therapy: back pain, anxiety, and right-hand-ring- and middle-finger fractures, the latter two I haven't heard her mention before. The VA isn't believing it though, claiming Mom's Air Force discharge papers showed no such issues.

"Good," I say, my hand moving to my newly growing middle. "Maybe now you can focus on something else."

⌒

My belly expands as the weeks pass, but I can't relax, terrified of seeing blood when I pee. Every time I flush, I brace myself to see red, exhaling when I don't. Pregnancy after miscarriage is a dance between hope and fear, and I envy the women who blissfully sail through nine months, unaware it can be any other way. Still, I buy matching nursery decor. My friends throw me a baby shower, and Jim and I go to birthing classes, where I watch videos of laboring women writhing in pain. Giving birth looks highly unpleasant and the opposite of modest.

It is too late to cut and run.

On the coldest day in January, after thirty hours of labor and a last-minute vacuum extraction, Cole James Richmond arrives, seven pounds, seven ounces of perfection, and I am a mother, the very word brimming with possibility—and trepidation. What will my version be? I am starting from scratch, my *What to Expect* book as my motherhood mentor versus my real-life one.

The nurse whisks Cole away to be cleaned and weighed, and Jim helps give him his first bath. We call friends and family. I save Mom for last, not wanting her to say anything that dims the high of this moment. But she is audibly moved, offering earnest congratulations through quiet sniffling. I feel her caring. Maybe this is finally our time, I hope, grandmotherhood more her calling.

Two days later, I am discharged, and Jim goes to work. Weeks earlier, I quit my full-time job to focus on our business too, after my self-imposed maternity leave.

"He left you home alone?" Julia says, aghast. It is not ideal. Our company needs someone running it, and I'm used to being on my own.

"Have your mom come up," she says. "That's what moms do."

This is a good idea. My breasts are engorged boulders. My butt burns with hemorrhoids and stitches. It hurts to sit and climb stairs.

But when I ask, Mom says she can't leave Dad alone. Her usual.

"What if the doorbell rings while I'm gone?" she says. "Or the telephone?"

Dad is retired now. He spends his time reading and doing crossword puzzles whether Mom is there or not. He's also writing his "memoirs" after deciding, at long last, my letter of questions was more loving than nosy. I email Dad directly, asking if he's okay with Mom coming. It feels sneaky, but I want to know once and for all where the excuse is originating.

"Fine by me," Dad emails back, likely relieved I'm not asking him.

"He doesn't care if you visit," I tell Mom, but I can't persuade her to reconsider. What I'm asking for—time with my new baby and me—shouldn't need this much convincing.

Though Mom says she didn't want to marry Dad, her job as his ears is a deep part of her purpose. Yet the message I internalize is that my and my new baby's place on her care-about hierarchy is below Dad missing a random solicitor.

What is the truth between us? Is it too hard for her to be around me, my bitterness palpable? Do I want too much from her? Perhaps it's me who's not listening. Mom didn't want to be a wife and mother, plain and simple. She's been telling me this for as long as I can remember.

A few days later, I get a card signed, *Grandma Mary*. There's always a card after my disappointment. This is her trying, I know, but it lands a consolation prize on my heart. Like desperately wanting to win the gigantic stuffed monkey at the carnival but getting the plastic harmonica instead. My problem is comparing her to other moms, same as I've been doing since I was a little girl. She is not most moms. Or maybe she is, and I haven't met the other ones.

⌐⌐

Cole sleeps fourteen hours a day. I change his diapers. Feed him. Stare at his tiny fingers and toes. This still leaves me with a lot of downtime.

"What do you *do* all day with a new baby, anyway?" I ask Julia.

"Sleep when he sleeps," she says. "Enjoy this precious time!"

What does this even mean? Before Cole was born, I worked forty-plus hours a week, traveled, and laughed over happy hour with my coworkers. Now I'm home alone, sore, and tired in the middle of a Minnesota winter while Jim goes to (gets to?) work. I need to be productive. To put every minute of the day to use to account for my existence. Self-love and -kindness don't apply to me. Not after a seizure. Not after a miscarriage. And not after successfully birthing a human being. I know being industrious and driven—not rest, recovery, and living in the moment. I ask Mom for her presence because it feels good to receive it, but I don't know how to give mine to myself—and now to my own child. I do not want to perpetuate this pattern.

"I'm bored," I admit to Julia. Just like Dad said to me.

"It can be boring in the beginning," she agrees.

"No one told me that!" I counter, as if I've been duped.

"It gets better, Marianne," she says gently. "Just wait till you get that first smile."

She is right. We find our happy groove, Cole and I, as I allow myself to relax into the baby pace of our days. I push his stroller to the park and meet other neighborhood moms. I shake rattles and sing songs. I play peekaboo behind blankets and read him books in the rocking chair. I lie on the floor next to him, staring at his sweet face and sparkling blue eyes, in awe of this perfect little being, my proudest creation yet. I dress him in cute outfits and tiny shoes and take photos of his every posture and facial expression. I journal his sounds and movements. I am deeply in love, and he is going to know he matters, dammit.

One afternoon, Mom calls.

"When is the baptism?" she asks. "Your Dad and I have been wondering."

This, she eagerly assures me, they will drive up for.

I'd been thinking about the baptism "should," though our Catholic church attendance is now sparse to none. Some Sundays, when I'm feeling especially guilty, Jim drives me to St. Mary's, a Catholic parish a few miles from our house, then goes home to read the newspaper before picking me up an hour later. He doesn't wrestle like I do— conflicted between what I want for myself and what Mom and Dad expect from me.

"I'll schedule it," I say, like making a dental appointment.

I choose godparents—Julia and my brother Tony. My understanding is godparents are tasked with supporting their godchild's spiritual growth. As for qualifications, Julia is a devoted Christian. Tony, not so much, but I figure he knows how to pray. Tony's and I communication has increased of late, us talking on the phone monthly. Julia and I had visited him in California, too, a girls trip to the beach a welcome respite from Minnesota winter.

I buy lasagna and salad and order a chocolate layer cake with a frosting cross. Mom and Dad stay one night. Tony and George come too, and it's a rare family gathering outside of our brief encounters at Mom and Dad's apartment, usually for an hour on early Christmas Eve before we all head to other events. Mom and Dad don't put up a tree, make food, or buy gifts, so it's hard to feel a specialness or purpose for coming together other than the physical sharing of space.

Standing at the baptismal font, Jim and I promise to raise Cole in the Catholic faith, and I know it's a promise I can't keep. I'm lying to this priest, God, and all the people sitting in the pews thinking we'll be back next week with our newly anointed Catholic baby. I cannot pretend to want this anymore, though I know disapproval is coming.

It doesn't take long.

Fifteen months later, we have a second baby boy with deep brown eyes and a tuft of dark hair and name him Adam. Not after biblical Adam, but after a friendly and handsome young waiter Jim and I met while out to dinner one night. And not because I'm certain I want two babies in fifteen months, but because I am afraid of my body *not* being able to make a sibling. "We should start trying in case it takes a while," I said. "In case we have another miscarriage."

In case. What if. The anxiety of a future that may never come to pass.

When it's baptism time again, Jim and I are attending a nondenominational church two minutes from our house and full of former Catholics and Lutherans, among others. *For seekers,* its website says. I qualify.

We drop Cole and Adam off in the Kid Zone before sitting in the large sanctuary for a grown-up service—thirty minutes of rock concert–style worship music and a half-hour sermon where Pastor Rob, a middle-aged husband and dad, mixes biblical teaching with personal stories about fishing and hunting and an occasional movie clip or live skit thrown in. Communion once a month. No kneeling or prayers in unison, and no mention of the Virgin Mary or saints. It's a rockin' party compared to a Catholic mass. Pastor Rob also tells me Jesus is my only path to God. When I was going to confession in fourth grade, the priest's ear was my path to God. Now it's Jesus.

Why can't I just go direct to God without an intermediary?

Instead of infant baptism, the church practices child dedication, a ceremony inviting parents to commit to raising their kids with godly principles while encouraging them to get baptized when they become adults. This having-a-say-in-things-when-you're-older makes sense to me.

But not to Mom and Dad. *Your mom doesn't agree with your decision, and neither do I,* Dad writes in an email. *Looks like Adam is the victim here, in that with his parents denying him a Roman Catholic baptism, he is also being denied a chance of eternal salvation should he suddenly be called home to his Creator…*

The ball is back in your court, Marianne-o, Dad says, encouraging me *to find another Catholic church where Adam can become a member of the mystical body of Christ. What do you think?*

His use of *Marianne-o* tells me he's trying to keep it friendly, but his words sting. What do I think? That this is a big heap of guilt; to him, my choosing differently means sending Adam to hell if he suddenly dies. I don't think God would do that. To Adam or to any baby for that matter. I survey my insides and email him back: I don't feel connected to Catholicism anymore. I'm more excited than ever to explore my faith, and I'd be grateful if they would attend our family celebration for Adam.

I wait two weeks for a reply that doesn't come, and I call Mom.

"I can't step foot in there," she says. Going to Adam's dedication would "endorse" what we're doing, and her "good conscience" won't let her do that.

"Upon this rock I will build My church; and the gates of hell will not prevail against it." She quotes Jesus talking to Peter in Matthew 16:18.

In her mind, this passage proves the Roman Catholic Church was built on the person of Peter, who became the first pope and bishop of Rome and from whom the Catholic Church evolved.

"Mom," I counter, "It doesn't say, 'Upon this rock, I will build my *Catholic* Church.'" *Church* means a group of people. We believe in the same guy, I tell her. I'm just doing it from a different building on Sunday.

She won't budge.

"How about supporting my family and me even when we choose differently than you?" I ask.

"I can't do that," she says.

It is her way or the wrong way. We've been here before.

A few Sundays later, we dedicate Adam with our family of four, my joy again tempered by Mom's rejection. A rejection of my faith this time, but the line has long blurred into rejection of me as a daughter and as a person. Trying to chart my own path feels like walking against a stiff wind named Mary.

A card comes as usual, but this time it's a large envelope with a brochure inside: *Returning to the Catholic Faith*, a thick booklet written by a priest, with a twenty-five-dollar check slipped inside the envelope too.

"To treat yourself to something fun," she says.

Leaky Boat

MY CELL PHONE RINGS FROM a number I don't recognize. It is a sunny morning in late summer, and I'm standing in my family room in mismatched pajamas and my coffee-stained turquoise bathrobe, my unwashed hair askew. Toy cars and wooden blocks decorate the carpet. Cole, eighteen months old, is wrapped around my right leg, wanting me to pull him like a choo-choo train, and Adam, three months, sleeps in his vibrating bouncy seat nearby. I've been working part-time from home, awaiting an infant spot to open at Carla's house, our in-home day care nearby. Cole has been going there since he was ten weeks old. Today is a nonwork day.

"May I please speak to Marianne Richmond?" says the cheery voice.

"This is she."

"This is Kara (pronounced Car-a, not Care-a) from Target," says the voice.

I search my brain for what I left at Target. My driver's license? Credit card? My two children are in front of me.

"I picked up samples of your cards at the stationery show last week," she continues, "and I want to talk to you about putting them in our stores."

The National Stationery Show is the annual trade show in New York City. This year Jim and I sent Carol, our spunky sixty-three-year-old

Minnesota sales rep, to cover our booth because we have two babies at home. Our sales reps are independent contractors paid on commission, different from our three hourly employees.

"I gave your business card and phone number to the cute buyer from Target who stopped by," Carol told me after the show.

"They always stop by, Carol," I assured her. "They've stopped by every year of our seven years going to the show, and nothing ever happens."

Except it is happening right now.

"Uh, okay, great!" I say, switching to my professional voice, running upstairs for privacy while shaking a confused Cole from my leg and hoping Kara can't hear the crying toddler in my wake.

A week later, I drive to the Target headquarters in downtown Minneapolis with Adam strapped in the back seat. I am the majority owner of our business by one percent, and I don't think to ask Jim to work from home today or to find a babysitter. I am a perpetual beginner in self-advocacy.

Sitting in the bustling lobby of the second-largest retailer in the world, I rock Adam's car seat with my high-heeled foot. Employees holding laptops and leather portfolios stream by, talking, laughing, and checking their watches for important meetings, I'm sure. Every person, it seems, is perfectly put together in stylish dresses and heels, skinny jeans and boots, cute hair, and chunky eyeglasses. I shift in my seat, sweaty with nerves, the tight waistband of my skirt pinching my postpartum stomach.

"Marianne?" says an attractive brunette a decade younger than me.

I jump up to shake her hand.

"Kara," she confirms.

"He can't go to day care yet," I say, preempting her wondering why I have an infant with me. "I hope it's okay."

"Not a problem." She winds through a sea of small cubicles in which big decisions are made. Kara's coworkers rotate in and out of her office to *ooh* and *aah* over Adam before Kara tells me she wants to put four of our stationery designs into nine hundred stores and test my greeting card line in thirty-five.

"Great!" I say, enthusiastically, while tempering my urge to hug her.

"I'll be in touch," she promises, before leading us back to the lobby.

"Can you *believe* it?" I ask Adam on the drive home. He is still asleep in his car seat, unaware that his mom and dad's business just doubled in size.

Soon our cards and stationery are in every Target store, twelve hundred nationwide. We move to a bigger office in the same building and change our name from Watercolor Works to Marianne Richmond Studios, Inc., to highlight the creator of the products and the growing scope of our business beyond its watercolor beginnings. Stepping out as the face of the company feels like I'm losing a few layers of insulation protecting my soul from the industry's inevitable criticism.

The Gift of an Angel is selling too, ten thousand copies in its first year. I'm happy enough with my art, even though it's simple. My first attempt at book illustration was aided by me looking at a bunch of Hallmark cards with angels for examples, and my colorful art is childlike in its execution. Customers don't mind. Emails land in my inbox and reviews show up online. *We love this book. A perfect gift.* Most moving are the comments telling me how my words help commemorate a child no longer here, their personal guardian angel. This reflection helps my mending too, giving me an expanded view of my own miscarriage and a comforting recognition of how our stories are both personal and universal.

One morning, I get a call at work from a friend from my previous job. Would I meet with *her* friend who wants to start a card line for grief and loss? "Sure," I say. A few weeks later, Penny sits at my kitchen table and tells me about her little boy, who died at two years old from a rare birth defect. Sipping tea, I am uncomfortably aware of my living children napping upstairs.

"No one knows what to say to you when your child dies, so they don't say anything," she says.

Unfathomable and correct. I am an example of someone wondering what words could offer any solace for such profound grief.

"I'm so afraid everyone will forget my kid."

I don't want anyone to forget Penny's kid.

"Tell me what you want to hear," I say.

And she does. Penny educates me about grief, its long and twisty path. How it doesn't have an end; it is more that one learns to live with it. I take notes. She invites me to a support group for bereaved parents at a church, and I sit and listen in the darkened and somber space. Kids play basketball in an adjacent gymnasium, unaware of the anguish on this side of the wall. The consensus: "This is the unimaginable. A nightmare. Say our child's name. See and be with our pain."

Over time, I feel ready to write and illustrate the book I want Penny and every grieving person to receive:

Some things seemed so usual
on that remembered day.
The sun arose, the birds awoke,
and kids came out to play.
It was not so for you, my friend,
and forever will it be
the day God said to your beloved,
"Come home and dwell with me."

May you sense you loved one's spirit
on a lazy sunshine day
and know the one you miss delights
to watch you laugh and play.
May you feel your loved one's touch
when mild breezes blow
to caress your cheek and whisper soft,
"I still walk with you, you know."

With two books, I honor the start and end of life. More heartfelt emails arrive. More encouraging reviews. Their gratitude lights a compelling purpose within me: to create for others what I crave for myself—to be witnessed—and I continue finding inspiration in the conversations and stories of real life.

One afternoon, I sit at my office desk reading the newspaper. My eyes land on a front-page story and photo: a homeless woman at Sharing and Caring Hands, a Minneapolis shelter, is crying in the arms of Mary Jo, the founder, because, the caption tells me, no one knows it's the woman's birthday. Her anniversary of beingness unnoticed. Here it is again, the innate human desire for acknowledgment of our existence.

I stare at the photo and see myself. Underneath all my busyness and outward success, I too live with the "Do I matter?" question. Even Mom, for all her perceived unavailability, calls me on my birthday at 1:31 p.m., the exact time I was born. But it's fleeting sustenance for an insatiable longing I can't yet dislodge.

I am like a boat with a slow leak in the bottom.

No matter how much love Jim, the kids, and my friends give me, I question my worthiness and significance.

No matter how much proof of my lovability pours into my boat, I am never quite full enough. The photo prompts me to wonder why, exactly, do we love the ones we do? What I conclude is it's the idea of "you-ness," the grand sum of traits, organized just so, that make us who we are. It's a reassuring truth. And validation of the younger me whose epilepsy made her feel more defective than distinctive. *I'm glad you exist,* I want the woman in the shelter to know. *Hooray for You* I write to both of us.

For quite a long time, the world saved a place.
Millions were born, yet none filled your space.
Until the second of a minute of one special day,
you took your first breath and the world said, Hooray!
Perfectly timed, not one minute more.
You suddenly were where you were not before.
But planning preceded your earthly debut
as all was completed in the you-ness of you.

Our family of four fits comfortably in a restaurant booth and one hotel room. It would be easy and logical to stop at two healthy, adorable boys. But I want another baby in my boat. *Two kids is too symmetrical, too perfect,* I tell myself. A third will give each a second sibling to choose from if they aren't getting along with one.

This is a cover-up for the truth I'm ashamed to admit out loud: I want a girl. To create the mother–daughter bond I don't have with Mom. As if I can fill the hole inside me by simply making a new female human.

At night, after the kids are asleep, I research sperm sorting at a lab in Virginia to guarantee a girl, but it is too expensive, so we take a chance. Jim is game—Jim is always game—and we get pregnant quickly.

Weeks later, I bleed.

We get pregnant again.

Weeks later, I bleed.

"Why can't I stay pregnant?" I obsess.

Never mind my body is screaming, *Stop! Take a breath! Be in your abundant life! Sail your full boat!*

One late night at work, I click my way onto the website of a Chicago doctor who specializes in infertility and recurrent miscarriage, treating women whose immunological issues are causing their repeated losses. *I'm sure I have those too*, I tell myself and book an appointment. I can't see how I'm like Mom, chasing promises of a fix, no matter how unconventional. Jim can't talk me out of it. Dr. Walton can't talk me out of it. Nor can the sweet presence of my two children.

I call Mom and ask if I can use their car. I'll fly into Milwaukee, I suggest, then drive the Corolla to northern Chicago, where the renowned reproductive clinic is located. "A pregnancy issue," I tell her, withholding specifics. She puts me on hold while she secures Dad's permission for the use of his vehicle.

"Your dad says he'd like to drive you," Mom relays. Dad wants to drive his thirty-four-year-old daughter to her doctor appointment? Whether he's motivated by fatherly concern for my well-being or fatherly fear for his car's well-being. I am not certain; my gut says the latter. I reluctantly agree. I've asked for presence after all.

Weeks later, I sit in his back seat, the vinyl cushion dusty with unuse. Mom is coming along too, happily strapped in the passenger seat, a pile of orange slices on a napkin in her lap. I am transported back to high school, the three of us driving to Madison to see Dr. Arya. But we are nearly two decades beyond this memory, Dad's hearing and driving skills twenty years worse.

In the exam room, a nurse draws eighteen tubes of blood from my arm, lining them up in a metal crate-like holder, little soldiers aiding the apparent war against pregnancy within my body. The doctor examines my female parts. Two hours later, my labs come back.

"You have natural killer cells in your uterus," the doctor gravely announces, sitting across from me on his stool.

Of course I do.

"Everyone has NK cells," he reassures me. I, however, may have too many, and they're possibly attacking the lining of my uterus and preventing me from maintaining a pregnancy.

I jump onboard his invasive and expensive protocols, trying to repair myself once and for all, my bruised forearms and stomach showcasing the purple-polka-dotted aftermath of three-times-daily heparin injections, a blood thinner.

Amid this chaotic and painful regime, I get pregnant *again* and miscarry at ten weeks this time, an ultrasound confirming an expanding but empty uterus.

"A blighted ovum," the technician says. "I'm sorry."

I'm sorry too. Sad and shattered.

Dr. Walton does a D&C and recounsels me to take a break. The Chicago doctor blames my natural killer cells, and Pastor Rob implores me to embrace God's will for my life.

"When your back is against the wall, DO. YOU. TRUST. GOD?" he shouts from his podium one Sunday.

My still-tender stomach clenches in answer: *Nope. I don't.* I want to be raising my hands with Holy Spirit certainty like everyone else around me, murmuring, "Amen, yes, thank you, Jesus!" But I would be faking it. I am one step forward, two steps back in my belief of a divine and omnipresent overseer.

Once a month or so, Pastor Rob offers up the Salvation Prayer—a chance to guarantee our spot in the ever after. If I invite Jesus to be the Lord and Savior of my life I am saved for all eternity, my sins are forgiven, and I automatically go to heaven.

But sitting in my auditorium chair, my mind wanders. What about people living in Africa who have never heard of Jesus? Are they automatically going to hell because they haven't prayed the prayer? Burning in fire because they are unintentionally unaware? What if there are a couple paths to the higher realms? What if Buddha has some good strategies? And what about gay people? I can't believe they are denied a spot in eternity simply because they're attracted to their own gender. Isn't God supposed to be about love?

"If you said yes to the invitation," Pastor Rob brings me back to the present, "look up at me."

Everybody stands, heads bowed. I open my eyes while still looking down, stretching my eyeballs to see who around me, including my own family, is looking at Pastor Rob as he sprinkles quiet congratulations over the congregation.

"Welcome to the family," he says, nodding. "Hello, hello. Welcome to Jesus's family."

None of us are looking up. We aren't a part of this family without our yes.

For as many years as I've been seeking, for as many churches as I've sat in, and for as earnestly as I want to feel differently, God is still a faraway concept and a last resort. This Christian church tells me I'm a broken sinner. What a sucky lot to be born into. As if I don't have enough issues. I can't draw the parallel between my daily-go-to-work-take-the-kids-to-daycare life and my need for a Savior. Earth and outer space to me. Life feels more like a big Game of Life where everyone sits in their little plastic car with blue or pink peg kids, spins the wheel, and lands on boxes. *You have cancer. Go back three. You got laid off. Miss a turn. You got a new job. Move ahead ten!* While hoping we make it to

Millionaire Acres. Like Donna telling me all about the joys of motherhood, I desperately want to feel others' unshakable enthusiasm about God and Jesus.

Leaving church that day, I switch my prayer to, "Help me believe." If God wants me to believe, He can supernaturally plant that feeling in my heart, I figure. He is God after all. I start reading my *God Calling* book, a gift from Mom, because an actual call would be helpful. I sleep with my Bible under my pillow hoping God's scriptual promise to restore what the locusts have eaten will seep into my mind and life. But none of these efforts counteract my skepticism.

It's only when I have nothing left to give myself, I launch my requests into the Great Beyond and ask for miracles, which maybe annoys God, thinking, *She only comes to me when she's out of options.*

I have one left.

One afternoon, my phone shows a voice mail—a reminder for an appointment I made before going to Chicago, with a local miscarriage specialist whose seven-month wait time made me forget I did.

Two days later, Jim and I sit in two armchairs across from the fertility doctor, me relaying my history and natural killer cell issues.

"Marianne," he counsels kindly, hands folded. "I don't think that's true. You're thirty-five. It's simply harder to get and stay pregnant. That's all." My body knows what to do, he reassures me, as evidenced by our two beautiful, healthy boys. If he thinks I am crazy, he doesn't say it, inviting me instead down the hallway for an ultrasound.

"Great timing," he says, circling the wand on my abdomen. "You're about to ovulate. Go home and make a baby."

And so we do, with zero interventions and injections. Nine months later, Julia Rose is born. Eight pounds at 8:00 p.m., round, pink, and perfect. Holding her in the crook of my arm, I absorb the implausible truth: I have a daughter. Our family of five is complete. Two boys and a girl—nearly the exact same spacing as my brothers and me—with the chance to be the mom and family I wished for growing up.

I am elated and exhausted by the quest.

From my hospital bed, we call family, and again, I save Mom for last.

"I have a daughter, and you have a granddaughter," I say with cautious enthusiasm.

Her chirpy congratulations segue quickly into a graphic tale about her recent bout with diarrhea. I drop the phone, leaving her midsentence, my tears welling. Jim retrieves the phone, Mom's talking still coming through the receiver.

"Mom…Mom…" he says, trying to find space in her ramble. "It's Jim now."

If she wonders where I went, she doesn't ask.

Weeks later, Mom calls our office.

"It's Julia," says Stacy, our new graphic designer, before hanging up. There's eight of us now including Jim and me, and the number swells with extra warehouse help when big orders come through.

"She didn't ask to talk to me?" I say from across the room.

"No," confirms Stacy. "She just wanted to know your baby's name so she can send a card."

Two Worlds

ONE TUESDAY MORNING, I STAND in our new old kitchen. Breakfast dishes clutter the countertops. Plastic tarps hang from the ceiling to contain the remodeling dust in the adjacent living room, the sound of sledgehammers and buzz saws our new daily soundtrack.

With three kids under four, we moved across town to get our home, work, and childcare closer together. And we hire a part-time sitter to come to the house. The end-of-day race from downtown to daycare wasn't sustainable, me needing to leave office at 4:00 p.m. to make the 5:00 p.m. pickup. Often, I'd find the kids parked alone in Carla's mudroom, coats on, backpacks stuffed with art projects, with a digital clock on their laps. One dollar per minute late. As much as I loved Carla's care, my sanity was unraveling.

"Sorry, sorry, sorry," I'd apologize to Carla, the kids, the clock, then scurry with them to my minivan, the engine still running.

I didn't want to like the house when we first found it, a 1957 dark-brown ranch-style with mauve-pink doors and an overgrown yard in Saint Anthony Village, a small community fifteen minutes northeast of Minneapolis.

"We don't need another project in our life," Jim and I agreed, sitting in our car out front.

But Arlene the Realtor stood outside, peeking in Jim's window with her clipboard, and when I stood inside at a huge back window over-looking a small wooded lake, my no became a cautious yes. I imagined an Idyllic Childhood. Hugs and s'mores by firelight. The kids swimming in their underwear and fishing off the dock. Toy dump trucks, buckets, and shovels decorating the tiny beach, the sandy play area begging to be loved again. The longtime homeowners were downsizing, Arlene said, and wanted a young family to continue the memory making. As much as I saw the home's potential, the message of being hand-picked made the opportunity harder to pass up.

Two months in, we are ripping the house apart.

"Let's make a list of what each of us takes care of," I say to Jim. He is dressed and ready for work, computer bag over his shoulder.

"Uh-oh," he replies with the type of husband levity that makes exhausted mothers feel like nagging wives.

Grabbing a notepad and pen from the junk drawer as a prop, *Me*, I write, underlining twice, then list aloud: "Dental and doctor appointments, preschool sign-ups, field trip chaperone, new clothes, birthday parties, playdates, summer camp registration, vacation planning, Christmas gifts, new books, more greeting cards, new art, more ideas."

"You," I point to his column. "Mow the lawn."

"That's not fair," he says, rolling his eyes. "Tell me what you want me to do."

It isn't fair, of course. Jim does a lot too, as the main man at our office, a doting dad, a willing family participator. He pays the bills and fixes things that break. But I want him to magically be in my head and just *know* the bedsheets need washing, the laundry needs doing, the toilet bowl needs scrubbing, and the diapers and wipes need replenishing without me having to divvy out the family chore list—another to-do.

I have one foot in two worlds and can't quit either one, mom to three children and co-boss to nearly a dozen employees counting on

Jim and my commitment to our business and their paychecks. In my mind, everything is up to me, my deeply ingrained life mantra that has me setting up permanent camp in victimhood. Years of not feeling like enough manifest into me striving to be the *most* engaged mom ever and the *most* creative, productive person at work, proving my value in busyness, exhaustion—and sales.

Later that morning, Jim and I sit at a massive conference room table at Target headquarters for the biannual vendor meeting. Surrounded by companies twenty times our size, I read name tags: *VP of this. Director of that.* My self-talk bounces between *Wow, look at me, I'm awesome!* and *What the hell am I doing here?* even though we are a two-million-dollar company now, with products in thousands of retailers around the world.

"This is what's hot right now," says Marjorie, the senior buyer, standing at one end of the table and gesturing toward a dozen giant poster boards propped around the room with ideas gathered from "trending trips" to New York City and China. It doesn't matter if something was original six months ago. A new calendar year, season, or planogram—retail speak for a merchandised store section—is a call for something different from before.

The room breaks into noisy chatter as we all crowd around the boards, politely jostling for a view. I furiously scribble in my notebook and snap photos of Chi Chi La La, a stationery collection featuring bright swirls and shapes, and Pastel Romance, wedding invitations with real lace and rhinestones, to save for later inspiration. A cordial but competitive spirit hangs in the air, each of us with the same goal: to win business. While most of these companies have ample staff and deep pockets, our creative department is just Stacy and me, and my shoulders sag with the pressure I feel to keep coming up with enough new ideas to keep securing the cash flow.

To keep employing our employees.

To keep supporting their families and ours.

Weeks later, we return to the same big conference room to present our opportunities for their guests. It's the buyers, Jim, and me for this meeting, our ideas pasted on our own foam-core boards displayed for evaluation. We take up two of the twenty chairs, and I hold my breath as they eye my creations.

"Cuuuuuute," one says, smiling.

"I don't like that one," the other answers with a scrunchy nose.

I feel small and exposed, our company name my personal identity.

"What do you think of Marianne Richmond?"

"I like Marianne Richmond."

"I don't like Marianne Richmond."

"We want Marianne Richmond."

"We don't want Marianne Richmond."

What we don't have in quantity, I make up for with perseverance and determination to secure face-to-face meetings with buyers from the largest retail chains in the world. Walmart is my farthest effort, me flying to Bentonville, Arkansas, where I wait in the lobby with dozens of other vendors—mostly men in suits—our products stuffed in pull-behind suit-cases. Once I sat next to a guy selling chicken, his frozen samples packed in ice. I register my name, take a number, and hope my sixteen hours of travel and fifteen-minute appointment will end in a yes for us. I tell the personal stories behind my ideas, hoping this vulnerability gives us an edge against the big companies in a David-versus-Goliath kind of way.

The verdict? What they end up buying is not my attempt at trendy, but rather my simple watercolor designs—same as I've been doing since I sat at my dining room table after surgery—perfect for harried moms like me who need to write out a value pack of thank-you notes after her kid's birthday party before she collapses into bed, and not until the dinner, bath, and bedtime routine is complete. I savor my at-home days with the kids. We fill the hours with library story times, playground and zoo visits, art projects, and playdates with friends. Though patience-testing at times, our time together fills my heart with gratitude and joy. Cole and Adam do preschool nearby, giving Julia and me sweet one-on-one time too. My children have ignited in me the biggest love I know.

One night, I lie in Cole's bottom bunk, nose-to-nose with his cherubic four-year-old face, his hair still damp, a fresh Band-Aid covering a new scrape on his nose. I clutch his small hand in mine and close my eyes, inhaling the soft jasmine scent of baby shampoo. Adam is asleep above us, Julia in her crib next door. The house is quiet, the buzz saws recharging.

"I love you, Mama," he says in his high tiny voice.

"I love you back," I reply. "To the moon and stars."

"I love you to the moon and stars, McDonald's, the post office, and grocery store," he continues, and I see where this is going. In giggly whispers, we try to outdo each other's love, our answers traveling further and higher and wider than the one before. I want to swallow these moments whole, a gift to my weary working-mother soul and a sweet balm to the deepest part of me that longs to be mothered herself. Later, I'd turn this conversation into a new book, *I Love You So...* putting into words and art the indescribable quality of boundless, steady, and unconditional love. While our stationery is the cash flow, my books are the purest reflection of my heart, words of worth, and reassurance for anyone who needs them, including me.

"I love you."

"How much?"

"SO much."

"How much is so?"

"WAY, WAY more than you know."

I ache on behalf of my kids now too, wanting them to matter to my mom and dad, but my children are near strangers, less grandchildren and more random little people who belong to their daughter. When we visit, Dad calls Julia "Julie" and shakes hands with Cole and Adam like they are interviewing for jobs. There's nothing to do at Mom and Dad's apartment except look at the giant fish tank in the lobby, which takes ten minutes. Then it's back to the kids jumping on the ratty mini trampoline that fills their tiny family room, a remnant of one of Mom's fitness fads now used as a footstool.

"Look, Grandpa Jerry," Adam says, wanting to hold his hands while he jumps, but Dad ignores him because he can't hear him.

"Dad!" I shout to bridge the awkwardness, "Adam wants you to help him." But the magic is gone, Adam's face twisted into confusion over being ignored by his grandpa, my heart falling.

"Well...we should get going," I say after sitting on the love seat for as long as I can endure before escaping to the home of Nana, Jim's mom, where Matchbox cars, snacks, and affection await. Sometimes I suggest a meetup at a park or McDonald's PlayPlace instead, but the busier the environment, the harder it is for Dad to hear and the more reluctant they are to accept. Deep down, I wonder if they'd prefer we never visit with the kids again and send quiet letters from a distance.

Still, I keep inviting. Us to them, them to us. "You only have to stay a day," I offer.

One Saturday, they accept. I keep an open itinerary, don't talk about church, and witness a momentous scene: Mom stretched out on her side on our family room floor, head in her palm like a girl on the beach, stacking wooden blocks with Julia, the only time I've seen her proactively engage with the kids besides a perfunctory pat on their heads. My hope soars!

Before dinner, Mom and Dad sit at the kitchen table playing Scrabble. I run downstairs to switch out a load of laundry and midstep, I'm stopped by the undeniable smell of...poop. Following my nose to the bathroom, I hold my breath and walk in.

A brown mess covers the wall, the attempted swipes to clean it still visible. Peeking beyond the toilet, I see a small pool of brown in the far corner.

My gut knows this isn't the kids.

I walk upstairs slowly, my mind reeling.

How does a daughter delicately ask about her mother's wayward bodily functions?

"Mom...?" I say quietly after a few minutes.

She looks up from playing her tiles.

"Uh, did you use the bathroom downstairs?"

"I did," she nods, then looks back to the board.

"Everything okay with you?" I persist.

Mom looks back my way, her perplexed expression confirming her confusion.

Or her unknowing.

Or her forgetting.

I stop my asking and grab a bucket, sponge, Pine-Sol, and latex gloves from under the kitchen sink.

On hands and knees, I wipe the dirty walls and tiled floor, wringing out my rag and wiping again. Tears rush down my cheeks, sobs erupting, loss coursing through me. After years of unresolved hurt and disconnection between us, I hoped renewal was still possible.

Today tells me it isn't.

Something new is at play, Mom in the early stages of something yet unnamed.

I cannot be pregnant, I think at 3:00 a.m., wide-awake. Jim and I had sex once the previous month. On day nine. I know this, because I stopped midway to count on my phone the days since my last period, and to make sure I wasn't anywhere near day fourteen. Problem is my cycle is all over the place since Julia was born. Twenty-two days. Thirty-eight days. And now, when I should be sleeping, I can't remember how many days have lapsed since then, only that we hadn't used birth control on day nine, and Jim canceled two vasectomy appointments, one for a golf date and one for a trade show.

I can't wonder anymore. At 6:00 a.m., I get up, Jim already out of bed. An extra Walgreens pregnancy test waits in the bathroom cupboard. I pee on the plastic stick, set it on the counter, then slide to the floor, leaning against the vanity as the result registers above me. How many times have I desperately wanted that plus sign? I have been pregnant seven times in six years. But today, I do not want it.

I reach over my head, slowly bringing the test down in front of my closed eyes. *Here we go,* I think, squinting.

A bold pink plus sign stares back at me.

"Shit, shit, shit," I breathe, my stomach tightening with panic.

Dazed, I find Jim taking a shower in the kids' bathroom, our own bathroom ripped apart.

"We're having another baby!" I yell through the foggy glass, waving the stick in my hand. He wipes away the steam on the door, his soapy face coming into focus.

"We're pregnant," I reiterate more calmly.

"Really? That's awesome, babe," he says, smiling. "Four kids will be fun."

Fun is not the word that comes to mind for me. More *disbelief, shock, fear, overwhelm,* and *exhaustion.*

"The midnight feedings are all yours then," I snap before leaving the bathroom. It's hardly punishment. To his credit, Jim never complains about waking up in the wee hours, able to exist on four hours sleep—inexplicably and happily.

Seven days before Christmas, after making sure Santa will show up for our three other kids, I head to the hospital in the wee hours to welcome Will David into our family.

At thirty years old, I wasn't sure I wanted children.

Eight years later, I have four.

I love my children. I love my family. And I don't recognize my life.

Marianne at her grandmother's grave site, 2018.

Be Brave Little One, 2016.

PART III

Saturday

GO SEE YOUR PARENTS. THE thought persists in my conscience like a mosquito in the bedroom.

It's been nearly a year since our last trip to Wisconsin, and two years since Mom and Dad visited us. I justify our absence as busyness, but a deeper insistence overrules my rationale: I need to get a closer look at Mom, and I need to do it alone.

A few weeks earlier, Dad emailed me. *Our conference with the doctor was a glum one,* he said. A recent physical and CT scan showed Mom's brain function deteriorating. *Alzheimer's dementia,* the doctor called it and drew a graph for Dad to illustrate Mom's five years "of declining and irreversible mental power" before her mind and memory would be "totally gone." He prescribed Namenda, a drug to stabilize and, hopefully, improve her condition, and said nothing else can be done. *Your mom is taking in this news as a royal queen,* Dad wrote. *She blames it all on the U.S. government because of all those tests they did on her when she was in the Air Force. What can you do about it? Pray to our heavenly Father for his help. Won't you? Love, Dad.*

What is Alzheimer's dementia? I asked the internet.

It's an irreversible, progressive brain disorder that slowly destroys memory and thinking skills and, eventually, the ability to carry out the simplest tasks, a website answered. Basically it's a specific disorder under the dementia umbrella. The disease was named after Dr. Alois Alzheimer, a German neurologist, who in 1906 noticed changes in the brain tissue of a woman who had died of an unusual mental illness. After her death, the doctor examined her brain and found extensive atrophy, especially in the cortex, and abnormalities inside and between the nerve cells.

The news wasn't a total shocker after the bathroom mishap, but the Alzheimer's diagnosis is stark. I, too, was seeing the decline in Mom's short-term memory.

"What day is it? Where do you people live?" she asks me over the phone, regathering basic information five minutes after inquiring. She repeats the same five stories from long ago, especially her favorite about finding a fifty-dollar bill in the parking lot of Risky Business, a tavern near their apartment. And while Dad is always showered, tidy, and clean-shaven, Mom is not. She rotates the same few outfits, her hair increasingly unkempt. Last time we hugged, I winced, her smell off-putting.

"Oh, I don't need to get my whole self in the tub," she said without offense. "I just wash up in the sink." Had she not taken a real bath or shower in months? Years?

⌣

I check the family calendar for a break in soccer games, T-ball, and birthday parties.

"Go," Jim encourages me. "We'll be fine." Jim makes everything look easy.

It's a sunny June Saturday for my six-hour drive. I don't bother calling ahead. Dad can't hear the phone, and Mom won't remember me calling. I'll find them home eventually, give or take an hour.

Sure enough, their red Corolla is parked in its spot, a "Proud to be a Catholic" sticker decorating the back bumper, a rosary hanging from the rearview mirror. I peer into the driver's-side window. Dad's seat is covered with a chunky beaded wrap like a NYC taxi driver's.

"It massages my back while I drive," he explains.

Usually, I ignore visitor protocol and walk directly to their back sliding door, a four-foot-high Virgin Mary statue my blessed beacon in the row of identical patios. But today, I follow the rules and dial apartment 131 from the front vestibule.

One ring. Three. Five.

"Hello?" Mom answers groggily.

"Hey, Mom, it's Marianne. I'm out front."

"I'll send your dad," she says automatically and buzzes me in.

Never mind I haven't been here for a while. I could be an alien selling vacuum cleaners, and her mechanical response would be the same. No verbal lilt saved for her daughter. No enthusiastic welcome. She is increasingly impassive.

Groups of gray-haired ladies play bridge in the lobby. Others wait for company, walkers in tow.

Dad emerges from a left-side hallway in an undershirt, baggy slacks, and slippers.

"Hi, sweetums," he smiles, and we hug. His endearments uplift me. "What brings you...?" he begins when Sister Cecilia, Mom's friend and the nun who runs the place, appears out of nowhere. Like a vision.

"Hi, Marianne," she says. "Are you here to take care of your mother?"

How does Sister Cecilia know who I am? I look at Dad. His fake smile tells me he is tuned out.

"What's wrong with her?" I ask. "Did she have a fall?"

"She's declining, Marianne. Has your dad not told you? I've tried talking to him," she continues. "Tell him he needs to tell you kids, but he doesn't hear me or doesn't want to hear me; I can't tell."

I glance Dad's way again. He waits, patiently unengaged.

"They're writing letters to him," she adds. "About your mom."

"Letters," I repeat. "Who is?"

"The residents," says Sister Cecilia, gently touching my forearm. "We love your mom, you know," she says, her ruddy cheeks plumping into a smile. I smile back.

She then walks past us to chat with another resident, and I stand unmoving. Am I here to take care of my mother? I don't think so. I came to check in on them, sure, but I didn't consider my checking leading to anything more. My plan is to hang out today, spend the night, and leave tomorrow afternoon.

Dad opens the door to their apartment. It is hot and stale on an early summer day, an episode of *Murder She Wrote* playing on the TV, the volume low. A brown patch on the ceiling suggests a leak. Mom sits in her usual corner spot, quietly snoring. Her hair is longer than usual, greasy strands delineated on her scalp. A patch of eczema reddens her left wrist, flaky scales freshly scratched.

"Did you hear any of that?" I ask Dad loudly, sliding open the back door for air. "What Sister Cecilia was saying. That people are writing letters about Mom. Is that true?"

He nods and closes the back door.

"Can I *see* them?" I ask, my insides urgent.

For their entire marriage, Mom has taken care of Dad's every need on Maslow's hierarchy, including being his ears. "My husband is hearing-impaired," she's explained countless times to waitresses and store clerks, before repeating the question to him in a tone, volume, and cadence practiced over decades.

The tables of care are turning.

Dad disappears down the hallway and comes back with a small stack of letters. He and Mom sleep in separate rooms. His back. Her bladder. His snoring. Her insomnia. I slump into the love seat and open the first envelope addressed simply to *Jerry*, likely slid under their door.

Dear Jerry,

Look at your wife. Her hair has not been washed in a long time, and her clothes are stained. I sat behind her in the chapel, and her pants are falling down because the elastic in them is gone. She needs a bath. She needs a haircut. She needs new shoes.

Please do these things for her because she is not doing them for herself.

Sincerely,
A Concerned Resident

I read another.

Dear Jerry,

Do you not see what we see? Mary needs help. Her clothes are ripped and stained.

She smells. She needs a haircut.

This is an independent-living apartment building, and I don't think Mary can be here much longer if she doesn't get help from you or someone else.

Sincerely,
A Neighbor

Mom's lack of hygiene is on community display, and she is unaware. Tony, George, and I are unaware too. And Dad is aware but...unmoved? Unable? I know firsthand the humiliation of losing control of bodily functions in public, and I feel embarrassed for her.

"Where does she keep her clothes?" I ask, getting up, the letters falling to the floor.

Mom's pants hang from their shower curtain rod, clothespinned to wire hangers. Made of thin cotton jersey, they are baggy and formless up top and tapered toward the ankle. The elastic waistline, long stretched to capacity, no longer cinches. Large yellowed areas stain the dingy white. I press my nose to the fabric. Pee. Splaying my hand inside the butt area, my flesh is visible through the flimsy fabric. And then I see the rip. Not a mild tear but a split of the entire inseam, midthigh to ankle. Her church attire, the letter writer's dismay. Several shirts hang too. A burgundy polyester top with a rhinestone bodice, several gems missing. An extra-large *Proud to Be a Veteran* T-shirt stained with tomato sauce.

Stunned, I head to Mom's bedroom, the repurposed den. Dad doesn't follow. Her bed hugs one wall, a desk and bureau opposite. Hanging crooked and slipping from its mat is a framed pencil drawing I did in high school of Mom in her wedding dress, my facial proportions way off. Dust balls mingle with rosaries and cheap jewelry on her dresser top, the same fake birchwood dresser I rummaged through as a kid. Novena prayer cards decorate the wall above her desk along with a photo from my wedding reception of her and her brother, Pete. Mom is smiling, flush with joy.

I glance at her, still asleep in her chair, and open her closet. It feels like trespassing, but with a faraway familiarity. Her one fancy dress and one winter coat, both two decades old. Boxes of cards and letters from Tony, George, and me sit atop the shelf next to a Kegel exercise machine still in the package. Going through her clothes, my anxiety escalates. Stained and ripped. Worn out. Yellowed. The smell of urine and sweat nauseate my stomach. Yanking back her bedcovers, I gasp at the sight of her sheets, the pretty yellow print stained deep golden brown. Same as the carpet spot where her feet land every morning. "Oh my God," I exhale, tears pricking my eyes.

I find Dad poking around in his bedroom.

"I need to show you something," I say, waving him to follow. "Look at this," I urge, pointing to her sheets and floor. "The letters are right."

He stands emotionless. They share seven hundred square feet but maintain their own bodies. Is Mom's decline too gradual for him to notice? Is Dad's mind disappearing too?

"Let's go to the mall," I say, "to buy her new things." Like I can remedy this with one trip to Southridge.

"We haven't eaten lunch," Dad objects.

I have detailed the degradation of his wife's well-being, and he is concerned with his stomach.

"We'll eat there." I soften, rousing Mom with a firm pat on her thigh.

She murmurs, slowly looking up through clouded vision. "What day is it?" she asks.

"Saturday, Mom."

"Saturday, Saturday, Saturday," she repeats. The part about me randomly showing up today doesn't register.

It takes us forty minutes to move from the apartment to my van, Mom's pace agonizingly slow. Saturday mall traffic is crazy.

"I'll meet you by Sbarro," I say, dropping them off at the food court.

When I get inside, I spot Dad at a table, sipping his Coke. Then I see Mom. Walking with her tray outstretched like a blind person crossing a street, her eyes big and confused, people nearly toppling her over as they claim the limited seating. Dad left her to fend for herself, likely impatient with her and his rumbling stomach.

"Over here, Mom," I say, rushing to her side. The picture of their existence—him taking care of himself, her failing—is becoming disturbingly clear.

We head to JCPenney, the three of us rocks in a river, shoppers whooshing by on either side. I park Mom and Dad on a ledge in front of two mannequins modeling summer fashions and jog into the bedding and clothing departments. What is the difference between 2X and 3X, really? I hold up pants, shirts, and pajamas, imagining Mom's ample body filling them.

Blue sheets or flowers? Ruffles or plaid? Tan polyester or fake denim? Mom points to her preferences, and our cart overflows.

"How much is this going to cost me?" Dad pipes up, and I show him my credit card to assuage his fear.

"Rosary and chapel are at three p.m.," he adds. "We don't want to miss that."

I am forcing my fixing on them. To Dad, this trip is nothing but an interruption of their routine.

"You're coming to church with us, yes?" Dad says back at Maple Meadows.

"Go ahead without me; I want to make Mom's bed."

He frowns but doesn't insist.

The door closes, and I return to Mom's bedroom, pulling off sheets and pillowcases and clothes from her hangers. I'll wash everything I can in the next twenty-four hours before I head home. I'm sure her body needs washing too, but that's a bridge I cannot cross in this moment. I have only seen my mom naked once, as a young girl when I accidentally interrupted her in the bathtub on Laura Lane. She quickly shielded herself with her hands, but I remember feeling aghast seeing her enormous breasts and ample folds of skin cascading down her front.

In their quiet, hot apartment, I sit atop the growing laundry pile. This isn't about the next twenty-four hours, rather every day that follows.

Will I move past my own hurt to be present for a woman who rarely felt present for me? And who, by diagnosis and disposition, is losing presence, period?

From her unavailability by choice to her unavailability not by choice. And now my choice.

Sure, I could give them both a kiss on the cheek, point to the clean bed and laundry, and say, "You're all set; see you in a year." Get back in my van and back to my life. But my conscience won't let me. Letting them fend for themselves against an unforgiving disease is cruel, and I'm not that. Annoyed scorekeeper, yes. But cruel, no. My empathy for Dad stirs most deeply, childlike in his struggle to make his way in a hearing world where every interaction feels like an obstacle course.

Fumbling in my pocket for my cell phone, I dial George. Though we don't talk often, I'm certain this is about to change.

"Hey, it's me," I say. "We have a problem."

I detail the letters, Mom's clothing, and Dad's seeming unawareness. We need help, we agree.

Hanging up, I wander into the kitchen to search for a phone book. Mom and Dad's cupboards and drawers hold exactly what they need— two forks, two spoons, two knives, two plates, two glasses, and one coffee mug for Dad. I open the fridge, the inside nearly empty except for a quart of milk and one loaf of bread. A package of Chips Ahoy sits on the counter next to a cookie jar adorned with a dancing cartoon pig. This makes me smile. No matter what food regime Mom is on, Dad needs his sweets. I find an outdated Yellow Pages in a drawer and flip to the *H* section, looking for *Home Care, Home Help, Home Health*…anything that sounds like what we need. My eyes land on a bold listing I know costs extra:

Superior Home Health Care: Medical and nonmedical home health care services, companion services, personal care, and medication management.

Perfect. Dialing, I listen to five rings before Kelly invites me to leave a message on what sounds like a home answering machine.

The next morning, halfway back to Minneapolis, my cell phone rings. It's Kelly. She'll gladly meet with Mom and Dad, she says, and tell them George and I sent her to see how she might be of help.

"Can I ask a huge favor?" I say.

"Sure, anything."

"Can you wash my mom's hair while you're there?"

CIA

KELLY STARTS WORKING FIVE HOURS a week, enough time to clean Mom and Dad's apartment, do laundry, and oversee their hygiene and food choices: more protein and veggies, less Taco Bell and Kopp's Frozen Custard. We buy a motorized recliner for Mom, and George takes over their finances as official power of attorney so Dad doesn't have to see himself paying "two hundred dollars a week for strangers in my house."

One night, Mom powers herself upright in her new chair and keeps going forward, landing face down on the floor and wrenching her knee. She can't get up. Instead of dialing 911, Dad covers her with a blanket and leaves her there overnight.

The next morning, Kelly calls George.

"I found your mom on the floor this morning, moaning in pain," she says. "What do you want me to do?"

This is the question. George and I are learning that a trip to the hospital puts into motion a series of events: hospital, rehab, home. And rehab determines whether home is a safe enough place to be. But Mom is hurting, and something might be broken, so George tells Kelly to call an ambulance, and Kelly drives Dad to the hospital in his own car.

After visiting Mom on the sixth floor, Dad walks to the parking lot carrying Mom's blanket and trips over a corner of it dragging on the ground.

Down he goes, nose first, and shatters his eyeglasses. A hospital worker finds Dad bleeding next to his car and admits him two floors below Mom. George drives from Chicago to visit them both. Eight stitches later, Dad is released, and Mom is moved across town to, sure enough, a rehabilitation center that decides Mom needs more hours of supervision.

"Your father is slipping too," the doctors tell us, his hearing, memory, and incontinence getting worse. To save money, Dad is picking up only partial prescriptions from Walgreens. Dad also canceled his long-term health-care insurance policy after twenty-five years of paying premiums, which George learned after calling the insurance company to finally use it for Kelly's services.

"Please, please, please reinstate it," we begged over the phone and in writing, explaining Dad's mental state and frugality, and thankfully, they do.

After rehab, Mom develops sundowner's syndrome, another symptom of Alzheimer's disease. Most nights, she wanders the apartment hallways in the wee hours, randomly pulling the emergency-help cord.

"Residents are complaining again," Sister Cecilia says.

Five hours of weekly care becomes ten, twenty, then overnight surveillance. Our rising costs aren't sustainable.

Rechecking the family calendar for another opening, I fly back to Milwaukee to tour assisted-living places with George.

"Your mom and dad need to be on separate floors," says a senior specialist. Mom in memory care, Dad not yet.

"That's for the birds," Dad says. During a different tour Kelly arranged, Dad refused to get out of the car. When the marketing director finally cajoled him into her office to test his cognitive abilities, she invited him to write a sentence.

I don't want to be here, he composed in his meticulous, slanted penmanship.

One morning, I sit at my kitchen table surrounded by paperwork. One of my tasks is to apply to the Milwaukee Veteran's Administration on Mom's behalf for home health-care services. George and I have become the unofficial parent-care duo, dividing to-dos. Tony is married to Ellen now. They visited us for Christmas a few years back when they first started dating. She's a perfect match for Tony, career-focused and contentedly child-free. We update him by phone. *He could do more*, I think. I have four little kids, a business, and years of baggage.

Our upbringing manifested differently in each of us: George unaffected and compassionate, me begrudgingly dutiful and Tony supportive from afar.

The sixteen-page application asks for Mom's military history and other details I don't know, so Kelly shipped me a bunch of folders from Mom's bedroom desk drawer, the same ones I remember from Laura Lane. I open a red folder. Inside is Mom's original certificate of baptism, yellowed with age and notarized with a watermark, plus a few letters from her ma, typewritten in Lithuanian. Asking Google for help, I attempt to translate the first sentence. *Sweetheart daughter, thanks for money*, it says, more or less. Signed *Motina*—mother.

Next, I open a blue folder. Tucked inside the left pocket are eight pages of loose-leaf paper, the word *Diary* scribbled at the top of page one in Mom's handwriting. Curiosity negates my guilt for reading her private thoughts, and I scan her snippets detailing Air Force life at Wright-Patterson Air Force Base: golf and bowling league, playing on the Kittyhawks basketball team, Halloween parties—she won a prize for her Elvis Presley costume—parades, dinners, meeting Charlton Heston at the first national Girl Scout encampment, and her promotion to captain in 1955. *Handed out candy and cigars to celebrate!* she wrote. Mom handing out cigars. I would have loved to be there.

Her diary ends with meeting Dad.

Jerry picked me up at 10:30. Toured Milwaukee proper, West Allis, dinner at Mader's Restaurant. No emotion, just reporting. This is her last entry, as if her busy, full life stopped abruptly. On paper and in real life.

My mind travels from the kitchen to years earlier when I stayed overnight at their apartment during a business trip. The three of us ate Arby's roast beef sandwiches on TV trays while watching Lawrence Welk and *Mother Angelica Live*, a thirty-minute show hosted by a cloistered Franciscan nun. Compared to my own house, bursting with little-kid activity, theirs felt lonely at night, the two of them in their quiet space. I couldn't remember the last time I had seen Mom and Dad in their pajamas, Dad's matching striped top and drawstring bottoms hanging from his bony skeleton.

Before Dad went to his own bedroom for the night, he walked over to a sleeping Mom in her corner chair and lightly kissed her cheek. Mom had insisted I take her bed, but lying under her blankets, I felt like an intruder, the intimacy of my head on her pillow unnatural. What did she think about before falling asleep? Did she prefer lying on her back or side? I hoped neither of them died while I was there.

"Your father still writes me love letters," Mom told me the next morning, "to thank me for caring for him."

"That's so nice," I said.

"I don't know why he says all that mushy stuff," she replied with a hint of distaste. Nearly five decades of marriage and Dad was still the pursuer.

Last, I open a green pocket folder marked *CIA.* How many other moms have a CIA folder? I rifle through copies of the numerous claims

Mom filed with Milwaukee's VA, some dating as far back as 1977—the year I came running home from middle school to tell her I had epilepsy. She'd been seeking justice for her electroshock therapy for more than twenty years. Stapled blue papers catch my eye, *Rating Decision* across the top of page one in big bold letters. It's a two-page explanation of why the VA declined Mom's last request for compensation.

Evidence #1: Service medical records dated 01-18-52 to 07-08-57.

Reason:
The veteran's military entrance examination was negative for complaints or history of psychiatric problems. Between May and June 1957, the veteran received fifteen treatments of electroshock therapy. She was seen for neurotic depressive reaction, acute, severe, manifested by anxiety, tension, agitation, depression, feelings of inadequacy and self-deprecation, impaired insight and judgment. The records indicated that these symptoms were brought on by the illness of the veteran's mother and an impending marriage. It was stated that the veteran's impairment after treatment was mild and that her condition had improved. At the veteran's military discharge examination, it was noted that the veteran had been treated for depression and that she had recovered.

I read this paragraph a few times to digest its content. Mom was struggling with depression brought on by her impending marriage. Like me reading my doctors' notes after my brain surgery, I absorb this medical assessment about Mom in their words. The military's view: Mom was stressed and depressed. They treated her with electroshock therapy. She improved.

End of their story.

And the beginning of hers and mine.

According to the VA, Mom needed to prove she was still suffering from her alleged ailments to get money. And from what I'm gathering, she didn't show up for any follow-up medical appointments the VA arranged for her.

But I am confused too. The St. Louis personnel center told Mom her medical records were destroyed in a 1973 fire. How, then, did the VA use her records for their evidence and rating decision? I dig through more papers and discover Mom—after this denial—enlisted her attorney nephew, Uncle Peter's son, to re-request her medical records directly from the CIA under the Freedom of Information Act, but that ended in a dead-end denial too. *We were unable to identify any information or record filed under your name.*

Mom's mission to be heard and validated consumed her, the similarity to my own seeking to be seen a poignant irony. Electroshock therapy triggered seizures in Mom's body. Decades later, I have seizures. Though Mom never said it aloud, it's plausible to me she believed she caused them somehow. Passed them from her brain and body into mine. I consider how the egg that became me was already residing in Mom's ovary when she was strapped to the table, her brain zapped. Farfetched, yes, and curious to consider. Perhaps it was guilt guiding her care decisions all along.

Rifling through the rest of the paperwork, I find a lone photocopy of a letter Mom wrote to the adjudication officer at Milwaukee's VA, two days after receiving his final denial.

Contact Walter Reed and see if anyone there will verify mind control experiments were performed there in 1957. You know, as the Bible says, know the truth, and the truth will make you free. I know the truth, and I now feel free. Sincerely, Mary Helf.

As far as I could tell, he didn't write back.

"I know the truth." Mom's truth was hers, regardless of whatever the real truth was. We derive our own, blurring feeling with fact. The formal name for what she was alleging is MK-Ultra, the code name of a top-secret CIA project in which the agency conducted hundreds of clandestine experiments, sometimes on unwitting U.S. citizens, to assess the potential use of LSD and other drugs for mind control, information gathering, and psychological torture. Though Project MK-Ultra lasted from 1953 until about 1973, details of the illicit program didn't become public until 1975, during a congressional investigation into widespread illegal CIA activities within the U.S. and around the world. This coming-out of information was the newspaper article sitting on our Laura Lane counter that first sent Mom on her search.

Was Mom's electroshock therapy experience a common, albeit barbaric, 1950s treatment for depression—or something criminal? I have my opinion, but it doesn't matter. Neither of us will ever know for sure.

Can you bring your video camera to our next visit at Mom and Dad's? I text George. No matter Mom's and my disparities, I have a sudden urge to preserve the memory of her.

⌒

A few months later, George and I sit in George's car on Laura Lane, looking at our childhood home.

"The big maple tree in the front yard is gone," George says. The neighborhood looks older, the houses smaller. Dad's mustard-gold siding is repainted white. We drive slowly up the street and around the cul-de-sac, me poking George's video camera out the window, narrating.

"The fountain is gone!" I say.

George shakes his head in playful disgust.

"They put a pathetic pine tree there instead," he says.

Mr. Bergy's house shows no signs of life. He's either dead or long moved on. With the fountain gone, he likely needed a new hobby.

"Mrs. Zamis never liked me as a kid," I say, passing an old neighbor's house and picturing her scowl as she sized up my mismatched outfits, scraped knees, and crooked bangs. I felt dirty in her presence, unworthy of playing with her daughter, Christine, whose hand-me-downs I got whether I wanted them or not.

We arrive at Mom and Dad's apartment. George opens the freezer while I record its contents. Ding Dongs, Twinkies, frozen mixed vegetables.

"Mom and Dad have more food than they have ever had in their lives," I say, wondering why we're paying Kelly forty dollars an hour to buy Hostess junk food when our goal is better nutrition. Dad sits on his love seat, still in his bathrobe at 11:00 a.m., newspapers scattered next to him and on the floor. Mom is in her usual recliner, her walker parked nearby. She looks clean and cared for in a red plaid shirt and white New Balance sneakers. A string of small wooden beads encircles her neck. Her bottom teeth are missing now, pulled by the dentist for rotting. Her hair is clean and brushed.

"Marianne's feeling nostalgic," George says to Dad, explaining the video camera in my hands.

"So, Mom, how's it going?" I ask, pointing it her way.

"Well, I wish I were a lot younger," she says without missing a beat. I smile at her wit. Tony says Mom has a great sense of humor, but I haven't noticed. Probably too busy being angry.

"What do you remember most about your childhood, Mom?" I ask, and her brain readily accesses street names, long-ago friends, and distant dreams of being a gym teacher.

"I really can't remember how much of my family is living," she says, slowly shaking her head.

"Your brother, Pete, and Sister Nicola are gone," I say gently, "but Julie is still alive."

"Oh, we're the two survivors?" she says, her syllables sticky.

George hands her a glass of water. "To wet your whistle, Mom," he says.

"So, Mom," I continue. "What would you say is your greatest accomplishment in your life?"

"My greatest accomplishment?" she repeats. "Growing up in Philadelphia."

"How about those three beautiful children you have?" I say earnestly, moving the camera aside so I am fully visible.

Up and down her head nods slowly, but she says nothing.

"C'mon, Mom," I prod, "one is standing right here." George has disappeared into the kitchen.

I wait for her recognition, my eye on her through my lens.

Nothing. She stares past me, like she is thinking but can't connect.

I move on, my heart wilting. I've been asking her to see me for a lifetime. She recalls her address at five years old but not her daughter. I know this is Alzheimer's, but it hurts, a cruel continuum of our storyline.

My enthusiasm for my project wanes.

"What's your favorite snack?" I ask instead.

"Banana split," Mom says easily. "I enjoy cutting up the banana and eating it."

I turn off the camera.

A Good Run

S ALES AREN'T GOOD," JIM SAYS.

Five of us—our core staff—sit in our office kitchen for a weekly staff meeting. It is the start of 2010, the country six months beyond the publicized end of the Great Recession. We had made it through what was the supposed worst of it, but our declining sales belie the encouraging news. After years of robust growth, our phones aren't ringing, and gift shops are closing. Target is "vendor reducing," meaning they won't be buying a million dollars of product a year from us anymore. And Walmart returned a hefty number of our books to minimize what they owed us in payables. Couldn't they have picked someone else's?

"If things don't change..." Jim says, his warning hanging in the air. Matt, our sales director, clicks his pen and doodles on his notepad, his face red and eyes glistening. Stacy bites her lip. I read the vintage metal sign hung above the sink: *Drink Coffee. Do Stupid Things Faster and with More Energy.*

Everybody files back to their desks to look busy. I stay back. Some days, I want to be an employee too, able to go home and forget about work. But when I go there, Jim is there too, where we switch to being Mom and Dad.

"Then what?" I ask.

"Then we're done."

"Done?" I repeat, stunned. "And then what?" This is the first I'm hearing of the imminence.

"Then…we get jobs?" he smiles.

He jokes, but it isn't funny to me. Between work and home and my parents, I am maxed out in the doing department. Can't someone else fix this and let me know how it ends?

Back at my desk, I flip on the stereo to lighten the mood, but it doesn't distract from what Jim is saying without saying it: our company is in trouble. How bad and deep, I'm not sure. Our desks are ten feet apart, but I don't know his world. I am writing, art, and product development. He is operations and finance. I sign what is put in front of me—paperwork for loans and credit lines—without reading the fine print, specifically the part where our signatures mean we are personally responsible if the business can't pay. When vendors call looking for money, I transfer them to Sally, our bookkeeper. We haven't missed a payroll as far as I know, and I trust her to pay our bills on time.

A few weeks later, I walk into the office just past 9:00 a.m. Jim and Sally are huddled at her desk, their faces tense.

"What's up?" I ask.

They lock eyes, nervous.

"The bank reduced our credit line," Jim says.

"What does that mean?" I say, leaning on the desk to steady myself.

"It means the company owes them a lot of money…today."

Jim explains we need to pay back the bank for the credit they rescinded, leaving us too little for our daily operations.

"At least we get unemployment," I say weakly, but they both shake their heads.

"Not when you're self-employed," Sally says, referring to Jim and me. The employees fortunately qualify.

The truth closes in on me. What will we do? What will happen to our family?

I turn, walk outside, and sit on the front steps, the bright winter sun countering my fearful thoughts. Two years earlier, we had moved out of our downtown Minneapolis office and bought a building a mile from our house, originally a doctor's clinic we remodeled. I drop my head in my hands and sob, the stress of the past few months—oh hell, years—releasing. Sally sits down next to me, her arm coming around my shoulder.

"You've had a good run," she says, the smell of cigarettes on her breath.

I don't understand. How can we have a business yesterday and not today? How can sixteen years end on a random Tuesday?

⁓

Time loses cadence. I don't know what to do on my usual workdays, so I keep going to the office. Our employees' desks sit frozen in time, computers and notebooks showing the tasks in progress the day the bank called. Forgotten sweaters hang on chairs, favorite candy piled next to staplers. Days earlier, Jim had called a local company known for acquiring smaller cash-strapped entities. "I'll wait to buy your assets from the bank," the owner said.

No, he won't, I think.

I search my inbox for the most recent weekly Target email to its book vendors—more than one hundred of us. Copying the recipients into the *to* field, I write an email of my own. *Dear Publisher,* I say. *I'm Marianne Richmond, and I've shared retail space with many of you for years. We're ending our business, and I'm looking for a new publishing partner going forward. Please contact me if interested. Click.* I send my invitation across the world, then check my email every three seconds to see who wants us.

A few *Good lucks*.

Two phone calls that go nowhere.

Then nothing.

Days and weeks pass. My anxiety escalates. It's eerily quiet before it's not. Creditors begin calling and sending us terse demands for money. A courier delivers a certified letter to Jim, and I read it over his shoulder whether he wants me to or not. The word *foreclosure* swims in front of my eyes.

"Were you going to mention this to me?" I fume, knowing it takes months of not paying a mortgage to get to foreclosure. I am an outsider in our business. Jim and Sally know everything. And what I am starting to know scares the shit out of me.

One morning, two guys in suits from the bank are waiting in their car in our office parking lot.

"Are you Marianne?" they ask.

"No," I say and keep driving.

Another afternoon, a black sedan pulls up in my home driveway. A guy gets out wearing a dark suit, maroon tie, and carrying a briefcase. I meet him at the kitchen door.

"Stuart from the IRS," he says stoically. After some forced chitchat about the weather, he reaches into his briefcase and hands me a stack of papers. "You owe a bunch in back corporate taxes," he says and tells me I can contact him to discuss payment plans.

Get in line, I think, though I imagine the IRS is always first in line.

"Who was that?" the kids ask from the TV room.

"No one," I say and go into the bathroom to cry.

A burly tow-truck driver shows up at my kitchen door next, far less formal than the IRS man. His enormous truck, with a menacing boom and massive silver hook, intrudes on our quiet cul-de-sac. He is here to repossess our car, and do I need anything from its trunk or glove box?

Who in some alternate universe is sending these people to my door in unnerving intervals? Coordinating their timing for maximum anxiety?

"I'll look," I respond numbly, walking to my driveway in my socks to pull maps, coupons, and cheap sunglasses from the front seat storage. I wrestle Will's car seat from the back. Then I watch our Camry ride away, its hoisted front end attached by heavy clinking chains announcing their capture. Are the neighbors watching too? My mind works to problem solve. Where can I get another car?

I call George.

"Is Dad's car still sitting in his parking lot?" Dad hadn't driven in a few years now, his trusty 1997 Toyota Corolla parked in his underground garage.

"Kelly is storing extra gallons of apple juice and Depends in the back seat, but other than that, it's available."

I charge a flight to Milwaukee on my personal credit card. Driving back to Minnesota, I wonder if his car will make it, the rattles and clunks competing with the radio.

"What's up with the red car in our driveway?" Adam asks the next morning. "It's not very cool-looking." At eleven years old, Adam is into cool.

I tell him it is newly ours, that Grandpa Jerry gave us a gift. He disappears out the front door to inspect it close-up.

"I sat in the back seat, and I think we can be friends," he says, coming back inside.

Our building goes up for sale. With no income, we make cash by listing its contents on Craigslist, people arriving in vans and trucks. They walk around our office, wanting more than what they came for.

"The copier isn't available," I say. "But you can have a free box of paper clips."

At home with the kids, I fake normalcy. Sign permission slips. Make

PB&J sandwiches. Kiss cheeks and wave to the bus driver. But once they are out the door, I collapse with uncertainty and fear.

"Can you hear me, God?" I yell in the shower, my tears mixing with the spray. "You need to do something!" A miracle on demand.

After the kids are in bed, Jim and I fight. Or, more accurately, I attack.

"How could you do this to us?" I yell. "You were in charge of the money!"

"I didn't know the economy was going to tank." He defends himself, pointing out how just two years earlier, we had our best year ever, our balance sheet strong, the banks happily loaning us money. But his rationale rings hollow, self-protective, blame-shifting. And does little to allay my constant stomachache, insomnia, and growing hopelessness. It feels like a seizure of a different kind. A life seizure.

I call Dr. Walton for antidepressants, but I can't find the strength to drive to Costco to get them. Instead, I crawl into bed on a Friday afternoon and break open sobbing, envisioning scenes of desperation, our family living on the streets with nothing.

I want to be anywhere but in my life.

How can I disappear in the least painless way?

Fill my prescription and take them all at once?

Jim doesn't know what to do for me.

"It'll be fine," he repeats his usual refrain, sitting on the edge of our bed, but he is the last person I want to hear from. My part of our business was fine; his was not. Me versus him. I know this thinking well, a mental pathway well-worn from a childhood of insecurity and self-sufficiency. His apologies and excuses bounce off my fury.

"I'll kill myself, and you can take care of this mess!" I fire back in my nasally voice, hoarse from crying.

"Don't do that," he says. "The kids and I would miss you terribly."

Dead sounds peaceful and trouble free. I'd find out once and for all if heaven is legit. Jim leaves quietly, and I hear him talking on the phone.

Minutes later, my friend Jane is at my door, then next to my bed, convincing me to pack some clothes. Jane is my best friend in Saint Anthony.

"We'll get your pills," she says, "then go to a hotel for the night."

She leads me by the hand through Costco and stands me in front of the pharmacist, who hands me a vial of help. Then we drive. I stare ahead, holding my pillow and pills, grateful someone else is in charge of me. We check into a Marriott Courtyard. Jane pulls back the bed covers and tucks me in. We watch HGTV for six hours straight, eat takeout, and don't talk about my business or husband. She holds me with her presence and returns me home a little stronger, a little less desperate, two pills making their way into my bloodstream, chemical sustenance for what's ahead.

Still on my calendar is the twice-yearly meeting with the Target book buyer to show her new ideas for fall. Do I keep the meeting? We're out of business. But a part of me also knows if they like something, we'll find a way to get it done. Three manuscripts sit on the floor next to my desk with rough cover ideas. *Beautiful Blue Eyes* inspired by Cole and Julia, *The Night Night Book*, a rhyming bedtime story, and *If I Could Keep You Little*, a book I wrote after school clothes shopping with Will.

A few months earlier, we were at the mall, him trying on pants. "Stop growing," I told him, playfully pressing my hand on his head. "I just want to keep you little." As soon as the words were out my mouth, I recognized a sentiment—and book title—every mother, parent, and caregiver would understand, the bittersweetness of time passing. The message flowed easily: "If I could keep you little, I'd keep you close to me. But then I'd miss you growing into who you're meant to be!"

A few weeks later, Jim and I sit on a couch in the Target lobby. Across from us is a man waiting for his appointment too.

"Hi, there." He leans forward to introduce himself. We shake hands. His name is familiar.

Jim excuses himself to go to the restroom.

"I got your email," he continues, his voice lowering. My email. Yes, the one I sent to book publishers worldwide.

"How are you?" he asks.

"Not great," I reply.

"Your note traveled through our office," he continues, "And our CEO is interested in acquiring your company. She acts fast when she wants something."

"Fast would be good," I respond. And then it's my turn with the buyer.

"We definitely want this," she says, reading through my stapled-together text for *If I Could Keep You Little*. "For Fall reset."

In August.

Today is April.

"That's amazing!" I say while my brain wonders how.

When I return to my office, an email from the CEO is waiting in my inbox. The next day, she and I talk for an hour.

"And so, I'm at the end," I summarize.

"Actually, Marianne, you're just at the beginning," she counters.

My eyes, tears welling, connect with my desk calendar. It is April 1, Mom's birthday and April Fool's Day. I hope this isn't a joke.

Jim and Sally send reams of paperwork to the publisher. Due diligence, they call it. I am flown to Chicago, where everyone is lovely and enthusiastic. I hear myself saying things in a voice that sounds like mine, but my body feels detached. George and Linda's house is ten minutes from the publisher, so I stay there for a night, the distance from home a needed respite. That morning, George had pasted a Post-it Note on my purse. *M, show them your "you-ness," and you'll be fine. Show them the talent that sustained your company for sixteen years. Love, G.*

After the meeting, I don't want to go back to my life. Curling into a ball on the downstairs guest bed, I rest my body on soft black and white checkered flannel, a warm hug for my psyche. On the bedroom wall is a framed picture of a large paper turkey, a Thanksgiving Day craft project from years ago. I get up to read the personalized feathers and see Mom and Dad's handwriting among them. There was a time when they ate Thanksgiving dinner with George and Linda. Now they sit in their apartment, unaware what day it is. Dad's feather is jam-packed, a mini novel in cursive, giving thanks for his parents who sacrificed to no end, his wife and kids, hearing aid, TV, car, and his Catholic faith, which promises *we'll always be together in heaven*. Mom's feather is far less verbose, instead a list of four gratitudes: her immigrant parents; her kids, *whom I love dearly*; her husband, *whose care has been tremendous*; and her daughter-in-law, *whom I love dearly*.

I could use a mom right now, one to hear every ugly truth, rub my back, and tell me everything will be okay. When my brain considers all of it, I can't put the words into the atmosphere. It is too suffocating. In the morning, Linda makes me a fried egg sandwich and takes me to Massage Envy, where she has a coupon. I want to move in and be their kid. But my problems are Jim's and mine to solve.

Twenty-six days later, we sign the paperwork formalizing the publisher's acquisition of every book I've written.

"Just your assets, not your liabilities," they confirm.

Sideways Rain

OUR LIABILITIES ARE LARGE.

We decide to sell our house.

The Realtor pounds the sign near our big tree out front.

"Why are we moving?" the kids ask, confused.

"Mom and Dad's business is winding down, and we need to pay some bills," I say, trying to sound like it's no big deal to sell the home we bought when they were little, personalizing every square inch. The one with a front-yard swing set and homemade wiffle ball field. And the one with the peaceful deck where I read by candlelight, listen to the splashing fish, and greet Harry the Heron every morning. One afternoon, my neighbor friend Brad knocks at my front door. We've lived next to Brad and Shelly for nine years. Our kids are friends too.

"Can I pay your mortgage for you?" he asks, his eyes red with emotion. "You know, just 'til you work things out."

"You don't have to do that, Brad," I say, my eyes watering in reply.

What I do accept is using their quiet house—ours in growing disarray—to illustrate my three newest books the publisher acquired in the sale. They are fast-tracking *If I Could Keep You Little* to make the Target deadline, and I have one month to finish sixteen art pieces. It's a welcome distraction and hopeful reassurance that what I valued most about our business—my ability to touch others through my writing—is continuing amid the concluding.

Slowly we disassemble our life. Jim and I coexist. Some days, I pack boxes at home. Other days I descend into the ten-thousand-square-foot basement of our building to bundle shelf after shelf of greeting cards into boxes for donation. Every inch of space needs to be emptied, and the enormity of the task paralyzes me. June is sunny, sunny, sunny until I have a garage sale. Then it rains sideways like the sky is crying for me, saying, "Forget this, Marianne. Take everything to Goodwill and be done." But no, I dutifully sit in my driveway holding an umbrella for the two hundred dollars I'll make, manning my tables filled with the miscellaneous stuff we accumulated over a decade. I don't know where we're going, so I'm committed to streamlining. The basketball hoop, wet suits, and patio set sell right away; the six-foot plastic Santa we strap to our roof every Christmas stays until the end, water dripping from his fake beard, his painted eyes staring down anyone who peruses.

"Where are we going to live?" the kids ask.

"Working on that right now!" I say, light and breezy, while fear and *hell if I know* keep me up at night.

Jim isn't worried. "We'll be fine." He continues his optimism, yet I don't see him doing enough to solve our problems. And certainly not at the pace my anxiety needs him to. We will be fine because I am the one scrolling Craigslist daily to find a rental to make sure we have somewhere to go.

"We need to be out of our house in exactly seventeen days," I tell Jen, a potential landlord, during a quick tour of her four-bedroom place in the same school district. She and her partner are moving to Florida to rescue dogs, she tells me, before opening the door to a messy laundry room, where five cages are stacked up to my left, a tiny barking chihuahua in each. "So that's why we're offering a short-term lease." Jen continues talking to my blank expression. "If we get down there and it sucks, we want the option of coming back."

I nod. "Makes sense," I say even though nothing makes sense. "A short-term thing sounds good to us too. We're winding down a business and need a place to regroup," I tell her. I've started using the phrase *winding down* thinking it sounds more casual and voluntary than, "Our business ended on a Tuesday when Walmart returned two hundred and fifty thousand dollars worth of books and the bank slashed our credit line, and we're in debt up to our eyeballs. Oh, and I'm depressed and feeling suicidal, and I hate my husband right now."

Jen doesn't pry. "Yeah, so after six months," she continues, "we can check in with each other and see where we're at, and if we want to extend the lease or not."

I can do six months, I think. I did nine months of pregnancy four times. Six months is a blip.

Jen head motions toward the front door. "There's a lockbox next to the water faucet so when you decide to leave, you can just put the keys in there and call us and let us know you're gone."

It has been years since we rented a home, and I don't remember it as loosey-goosey and covert as this. But loosey-goosey is what we need. No yearlong commitment. No probing or background checks or credit report screenings. Almost a quiet understanding we are both dealing with crap much bigger than this transaction and "let's just make it easy on both of us."

She leads us up two steps to our left and into the kitchen, a dark room given its lower-level location. Jen proudly points out its features with a sweep of her hand. "We redid this room a couple years ago," she says, "with a new fridge, granite countertops, and a copper ceiling."

I take in the orangish brick wall to my left, the dark-brown cabinets, white scuffed linoleum floor, and faux-copper ceiling tiles. I hate everything about it. The windows at ground level peek out above the concrete patio, giving the room an underground cell sensibility.

"The TV's coming with us." Jen gestures to a wall-mounted unit. I size up the dining area and figure our kitchen table might fit. Up two more stairs and we are standing in a smallish family room with vaulted ceilings and two tall arched windows. Light streams in to offer encouragement. "We fit so many people in this room!" Jen chuckles at some memory.

"This all sounds great," I force out, "but remember we need to be out of our house in seventeen days." I figure most people try to secure their renters a month or so in advance.

"Perfect," says Jen. "Because we and the dogs are moving in fifteen, so the house'll be empty for you."

Maybe God is real.

⤚⤙

The night before our closing, the six of us sit on a back step facing the lake. It is mid-July, the humid dusk alive with the smells and sounds of summer: grilled burgers, boat motors, laughing kids. All evidence of our family's life here is packed up or sold, countless memories stored inside each of us. Jim and Cole are quiet. Julia and Will make small talk. Adam cries, his head on my shoulder, his body shaking with sorrow.

I sit in stunned silence.

⤚⤙

Two weeks after moving, I drive to Wisconsin to meet up with George and Linda to move Mom and Dad from Maple Meadows into Franklin Terrace, a memory care center. Mom's decline is worsening, and Dad needs more help now too.

Except they don't know we're coming.

"What brings you all here?" Dad asks us gleefully, sliding open his back patio door. He wears his usual summer outfit—a baggy white sleeveless undershirt with dark Wrangler jeans cinched with a brown leather belt—and smells like Old Spice. My stomach sinks seeing Dad's joy. He has no idea a U-Haul is parked around the corner awaiting their belongings.

"It's moving day!" George says, feigning excitement.

We follow Dad inside as he sits on his love seat. A month earlier, George wrote Dad a letter preparing him for today, but we knew he'd forget. Sure enough, he looks at us, head tilted, forehead wrinkling in question. George hands Dad a copy of the first letter. When he looks up after reading it, George hands him a second one telling him today is the day.

Three quiet seconds pass; then Dad gets up and walks over to Mom in her recliner.

"Mary," he says with a gentle shake of her shoulder, "Mary, we're moving today." Just like that, he accepts what we tell him. What else did he have planned for his Saturday if not to move into memory care?

"Hey, Mom," I say, helping her upright as she steadies herself on her walker.

"Mary, Mary, Mary, why must you get so old." Her automatic refrain.

Days earlier, I arranged for Mom and Dad to spend moving day at their new place. I load and buckle them into my van for the drive, Dad in front, Mom in back. Their rosaries hang around their necks like name tags for a field trip.

"Bye, Maple Meadows," I say, waving. Mom and Dad wave too.

I glance sideways to check for tears. None. They stare ahead, departing in the clothes they put on earlier today, no thought about toiletries, pajamas, or furniture. Twelve minutes later, I pull into the circular drive of Franklin Terrace, where an aide greets us and escorts them in for "a delicious lunch and activities." Like dropping my children at day care.

George, Linda, and I tackle separate rooms, the spaces tinged with melancholy.

"Look familiar?" George laughs, donning Dad's favorite flannel plaid cap and gold winter coat. He holds to his chest a doll-sized wool sweater-vest Dad shrunk in the wash.

"Look out," I say, circling the tiny family room using Mom's walking sticks.

We pitch expired yogurt and discover a robust inventory of apple juice, Depends, and Hydrox cookies stuffed in closets. Linda scrapes *Proud to Be a Veteran* stickers off the windows and doors with a razor blade, erasing Mom's legacy.

In one afternoon, we whittle down their belongings into three piles: 1) move to Franklin Terrace, 2) Goodwill, and 3) junk. And by day's end, Mom is napping in her motorized chair and Dad in his love seat in their new home, a one-bedroom suite in Spring House, the cheery name for the not-so-cheery memory care floor. The scene is quiet and antiseptic, wheelchairs filled with slumped and sleeping figures. Others wander aimlessly, further down the road of dementia. It is the last stop on Mom and Dad's life road, the alarmed door a one-way ticket to eternity.

I sleep to escape reality and every morning relish the split second before remembering what is true: We owe a lot of money. We live in a borrowed home with, we soon discovered, leaky windows and carpenter ants feasting on the rotting deck. The carpeting that was supposed to be cleaned for us wasn't. "I think they're on the run," said the Chem-Dry man about Jen when I called.

I still want to disappear, but four kids need me. Being the mom is hardest. Pretending I am okay when I'm drowning in depression but don't want to pull them into the abyss with me. Pretending for them to save myself. Someone sends me a direct message on Facebook from a made-up username—URThieves, he or she accuses me of "knowing all along" the financial truth of our business. Of "screwing" our employees. URThieves doesn't believe I didn't know. I couldn't believe I didn't know. Which of our ex-employees would hide behind anonymity to do this? The intentional meanness nauseates me.

Jim gets a job that sends him overseas in three-week chunks to oversee product production. Across the ocean is best, my mind still believing our mess is mostly his fault. Weeks earlier, I made an appointment for the two of us with a marriage counselor. "Jim did not intentionally create your situation," he said. "And he's sorry." A therapist who talked for my husband. We didn't go a second time.

Nights when I can't fall asleep, instead of sniffing lavender oil or drinking warm milk, I get up and scroll the internet, reading random articles and blogs. "How to Climb out of Debt." "The 'Are you Depressed?' Quiz." At 3:00 a.m. one morning, I click my way onto the website of Sue from Colorado, a "career intuitive" who promises to see the "destiny work" I've already signed up for based on my birth date and time. At two hundred and fifty dollars an hour, this isn't what I should be spending money on. But I make an appointment and charge it to my one Visa not connected to the company. Because equal opportunity to anyone who knows my future.

"You're a master soul meant to be a powerful speaker, teacher, and leader," Sue says, "here to use your energy, intuition, and writing to enlighten the world to live and heal in a new way."

"How am I going to do that, Sue?" I ask skeptically.

"The conventional life doesn't get you where you want to be," she says. "It's more spiritual, more using and embracing your intuition than you have in the past."

Sue asks me why I think we're all here on earth.

"Great question," I say. "I think about this all the time."

"Are we really energy beings?" she continues. "Are we here to make Jesus happy?"

I don't have answers.

"Your mom is still holding you back from a larger worldview."

What does Sue know about my mom?

"We didn't exactly see eye to eye," I say.

"Let me tell you that story in a different way," Sue replies. "This lifetime is about how your differences are your gifts. You are the enlightened one. You are the one with the higher frequency, the higher consciousness. Your mom was hired by a soulmate agreement with you that she was going to push the 'you're not worth it' message at every possible moment to help you finally see the insanity of carrying that negative belief around and break through it to find your own power."

I laugh out loud, thinking about hiring my mom.

But as bizarre as it sounds, I can't deny Mom's beliefs and opinions made me question everything about myself—and yes, especially my worth.

"You are in a place where you can step out and do the work your mom never would have embraced," says Sue. "By doing that, you end the karmic chain."

Fascinated, I glance at my watch. Our hour is nearly up, and Sue's increasing speed of talking tells me I'm not getting a minute more.

"Your spiritual journey is not one path. Expand your idea of spirituality and see where it takes you," she says, giving me homework. "Visit a Buddhist ashram. Chant with the monks. Visit a Unity church. Study quantum physics. Hinduism. Get out of your small box."

"Do we stay in Minnesota?" I ask.

She sighs, exasperated at me missing her point.

"When you change your thinking, your geography falls away."

I didn't know what to expect when I made the appointment, but it certainly wasn't this. More "I see you at a pottery wheel. Be a graphic designer. Take a calligraphy class." And yet, maybe Sue is on to something. That my uncertainty and skepticism about one path to God is an opportunity to explore and claim what feels truest to me.

The following Sunday morning while Jim and the kids eat pancakes, I go alone to a Unity church across town. The sanctuary is large and bright, curved pews descending toward an altar below. I slip into a back row and look around. Arm in arm, same-sex couples mingle with singles young and old and traditional mom-dad-kids families. Hugs, warmth, and laughter abound.

"God is love," the female reverend says, "available to everyone." And we are love too, because we are an expression of God. There is no mention of me being a faulty transgressor in need of a savior. As for Jesus, according to Unity, he wasn't the actual son of God but a wayshower who expressed his divine potential and invited others to do the same.

"Like we can do today," says the reverend.

My curiosity ignites, quickly snuffed by guilt. "Upon this rock, I will build my church." I hear Mom's voice, her disapproval running in my veins whether I want it there or not. She doesn't even need to talk anymore; I can self-sabotage on her behalf. Maybe Sue is right about Mom pushing me toward a larger spiritual view. Getting my entire family on board feels like too big a detour and effort right now. A tentative explorer myself, I'm not certain how to explain with conviction a new way of believing after a decade of Sunday school and Wednesday night Bible club.

"How was it?" the kids ask when I get home.

"Different in a good way," I say.

Months pass. Winter becomes spring. My days are a mix of kids, work, and debt settlement over the phone. Week after week, I barter dollars with uncaring creditors who assure me we'll never recover.

Exhausted by the relentless dance, I ask Mr. Nelson from a big scary bank, "Can I call you by your first name?"

The question prompts a pause.

"Because I'm an adult, and you're an adult."

"Fine," he agrees.

Soon we are two people—Bill and Marianne—talking about life and its challenges, and he accepts a much-reduced settlement with my promise to send him one of my books for his children.

One afternoon, I go out to check the mail and find a note stuck to our front door. *Foreclosure* says the small type. Turns out Jen hadn't paid the mortgage since we moved in, our monthly rent apparently subsidizing their dog rescue efforts in Florida.

Loss abounds. Everything that brought structure and consistency to me—our house, marriage, business, savings account—is precarious or gone.

"As long as you're together, you'll get through," people say.

The problem is getting through. And I'm not sure about together.

I am here.

But barely.

I need help.

My lifetime of self-sufficiency is no match for anxiety and depression.

Life Bus

I SIT ON A BEIGE COUCH, my hands folded in my lap. A miniature fountain bubbles on a nearby table, a bowl of smooth rocks offering etched solace: *trust, faith, love*. Life goals, perhaps. Laura, the therapist, sits in a straight-backed chair across from me. A robust woman with ruddy cheeks and an easy laugh, she holds a clipboard, poised for intake. Her website invited me *to my truest self*, and I'm hoping it's someone besides the angry, resentful, fearful person I currently inhabit. After Jim's and my single meeting with the marriage counselor, I decided I need to help me before helping us. My laptop is next to me, ready to capture Laura's wisdom.

"What brings you here?" she asks.

What doesn't?

I unload everything: my seizures, my brain tumor, Mom, our disconnection, her Alzheimer's, Jim, our business, my anger, shame, blame, fear...and my confusion about who the hell I am in all of it.

Laura listens quietly, an encouraging nod here and there. She jots a few notes. Then rests her pen before speaking.

"You have a lot of lack in your history," she says gently. "Emotional and nurturing gaps in ways that mattered to your heart."

My shoulders drop, resonance buzzing through me, my watering eyes concurring. No one has ever captured my experience quite this succinctly.

Laura nudges the tissue box closer to me.

"You learned pretty early on that life was up to you," she continues, "and unfortunately, you didn't have the best inner resources to navigate it."

Tears obscure my vision now, her validation a balm to my deepest self. Life has felt up to me for as long as I can remember. Hiding in bathrooms. Fleeing St. Al's and Eau Claire when the shame was too great. Choosing medication against Mom's wishes. The wrong faith too. Moving alone to Connecticut, brain surgery, my endless productivity and procreation. My drive to prove my worth and right to exist. Physically and mentally running for decades, fueled by fear, humiliation, and self-doubt.

"Our goal is to reintegrate all parts of you—mind, body, and soul," Laura says. "To rediscover your original design."

I don't know my favorite food or color let alone the intricacies of my being, though I'm fairly certain I wasn't delivered onto the planet a ball of anxiety and hopelessness. I learned early on my body wasn't a safe place to be, Mom not a safe person for my heart, and now, is Jim untrustworthy too?

"When you can't trust yourself, everyone else must be right," Laura offers, "and when they're not, huge betrayal, huge resentment."

Yes, and *yes*.

There were times I trusted myself. When I first sat in front of doctors and knew my seizures weren't my doing. When I watched Ray Clark and knew I had epilepsy too. And, of course, choosing Dr. Spencer as the one to open my brain. When I finally felt "fixed" after surgery, my first creations came from that elusive authentic place, words and art flowing through me, for me. Heart to hands to paper. But the hurt of feeling unseen and unsupported through my epilepsy and beyond created a deep well of self-doubt that no amount of productivity or procreation could fill. And as our family and business grew—and the weight of responsibilities quadrupled—I lost myself in the needs and opinions of others, trying to find worthiness in busyness and achievement. I answered one need and three others popped up.

"You realize this is your stuff," Laura breaks it to me.

I nod.

What is up to me, she kindly notes, is my life, my happiness, and my response when things go awry. To live congruently with what I know, tentative as it is.

"Is there hope for me?" I ask.

"We need more sessions for that," Laura says, laughing.

I would have moved into Laura's office if I could have, sleeping under her desk, making lunch in her hot pot, and crawling to the Comfort Couch for my weekly appointments. Being in her presence is the most understood I've felt in my entire life. Every Monday at 10:00 a.m., I learn a new way of being based on the truth of my worth versus what I pieced together from the worst of what happened to me. And learn to see where I need to accept responsibility. My part. In our business, I gladly let Jim handle what I didn't want to. It was fine until it wasn't.

"You get tripped up when you're confused or feeling pressure," Laura says. "Then you give away your power to someone else to decide, making it about them and getting pissed off in the victim role."

Well, there was that.

"No matter your circumstances, you're addicted to the longing for things to be different," Laura says, "but it's the very thing keeping you from the present. You're missing your life."

I didn't want to get to eighty and realize I missed my life bus.

"The more you relax into the unique expression of God in you, the more you'll challenge the belief you're defective," Laura says. "When your soul feels heard, you can move forward."

God in me versus out there. Here it is again.

"How does a soul talk?" I ask.

"Through your three centers of knowing: head, heart, and gut. Check in with each and see what answer comes."

Maybe other people already live this way, but her counsel feels revelatory.

"The whole work of therapy, Marianne, is growing the pause," Laura summarizes. "The space between stimulus and response is where your freedom lies. Connect to your ability to choose."

Free was not a word I'd ever used to describe me, and I imagined it in my body: A shoulders-down weightlessness. Heart-opening expansiveness. Possibility. Strength and surrender all at once.

⁓

Weeks later, our family sits in metal folding chairs in the back of a high school cafeteria. A pastor we knew and liked had started his own church, and we go to check it out. It is an uncomfortably small crowd, maybe forty people. "Welcome!" says a smiling lady holding bulletins, delighted with our half dozen new faces. I don't want to be noticed. Black drapes define the gathering space, a coffee and donut table along a back wall.

The room darkens, and a scene from Terrence Malick's movie *The Tree of Life* fills a large screen, a beautifully crafted visual montage of creation. Simple text appears, ancient words spoken by God.

Where were you when I laid the foundations of the earth? ...
When the morning stars sang together, and all the sons of God
shouted for joy? Job 38:4, 7.

The on-screen O'Brien family—Brad Pitt the dad—plays in the backyard of a 1960s neighborhood as Mrs. O'Brien's whispery voice reverberates around the room in an opening monologue introducing two ways through life—the way of nature and the way of grace. And how we must choose which one to follow. The voice describes the way of nature as being about pleasing ourselves at any cost, whereas the way of grace is more about being selfless in our pursuits and accepting being slighted, forgotten, and disliked.

The clip ends, lights come up, and Pastor Kevin appears on a small makeshift stage. "I have watched people die," he says. "Some people die like caged animals. They are so wounded. So angry. So disappointed life didn't give them what they wanted, they lash out at anyone who will give them comfort. But I've been in the presence of people who have died in the way of grace. They welcome you into all the experiences of their life. The good, the bad, the difficult. They accept everything they have faced, and they are full of dignity, respect, and hope. They offer what they can. And sometimes that's just praying or saying a kind word. You are changed by their presence. It's my goal that every one of us here can choose the way of grace. Because the alternative is dangerous and ugly and so eternally damning that it's not worth going down that path."

My mind leaves the high school cafeteria. If I die tomorrow and need an autopsy, the pathologist won't find grace inside me but rather disappointment and bitterness for the lack.

"When something happens that truly hurts, and we feel betrayed," Pastor Kevin says, reading my mind, "the ability to look human failure in the face and to forgive is the greatest power on Planet Earth."

Recognition zings through my body. I strain my eyeballs sideways at Jim, the other bookend to our four kids in between. This is my life, my family, the most solid, enduring thing I have. I don't want to die a caged animal, forever snarling about how Mom, Jim, God, and life have let me down. Life lets everyone down. It's what we do in its wake that defines us.

Head bent, I will the tears to stay inside my eyes, the battle visible on my reddening face. Adam looks up at me, his little hand moving to my knee. He is a feeler too, and my distress triggers his empathy no matter whether he understands its origin.

The musicians regather at the front of the cafeteria; soft piano music imbues with poignancy Kevin's final plea.

"What are you holding on to?" he asks. "We can all be open to God doing something new with what is broken, turning the mess into something magnificent."

Everyone stands, and I stay sitting.

Magnificence from the mess.

Provision in pain.

Beauty from broken. Not the God Cave or Vending Machine God, but an indwelling presence and power working through humans to inspire love of self and others.

This I can rally for.

If I am a divine expression, everyone else is too. No two camps of saved and unsaved.

So often I had begged God to take away my seizures and change my circumstances. To give me a different mom. To heal me as the angel promised nine-year-old me on my bedroom floor.

I am my own healing, though my river of self-compassion is dry. Rarely am I kind to myself, feeling other and less-than for a lifetime. And yet I know blessing and protection and provision.

I know God.

Through the skilled hands of Dr. Spencer. Through Jim and my family's love. Through the practical care and gentle wisdom of friends. Through our foreclosed rental house, which offered a timely and affordable option when we needed it most. Through the acquisition of our company, which allows me to keep writing and creating. Through

Laura, my therapist. And yes, through Mom, whose own story keeps me searching for the truth of mine. I keep looking into my valley of loss, instead of at my mountain of blessing. My heap of grace.

A week earlier, Laura asked me, "How do you become willing to see the fallibility of others and learn to accept it?" The answer, elusive then, is clearer now:

By believing I, too, am a chosen channel with life lessons to grow my soul, only then will I love myself enough to fully love others. It sounds easy and foreign and impossible all at once.

I need to forgive to move forward. To trade anger and resentment for the reclamation of myself. "When you belong to yourself, your belonging with others matters more," Laura said.

"Amazing Grace" fills the cafeteria. Of course. Thematically perfect and Mom's favorite song, and no doubt my official invitation.

"I did the best I could with what I had...under the circumstances." Mom's life refrain that, to me, annoyingly absolved her of the aftermath of her efforts. I could say the same. I did the best I could with what I had...under the circumstances. Can I do better by forgiving both of us?

"To offer forgiveness is instant," says Pastor Kevin. "To feel forgiveness takes time."

Back home, Jim and I fold laundry side by side.

"I took you down from the cross today too," I say.

"I'm glad about that," he says simply.

We don't talk about whether he thinks he needs forgiveness or what's changed inside me. My words simply hang between us.

I am tired. Weary of round and round conversations, me needing his apology and actions to look a certain way that involves him sobbing on bended knee, promising me a trouble-free future, an impossible commitment for anyone. And it isn't lost on me that Mom spent decades forgoing her present in search of accountability for her past. Missing her life bus, perhaps.

⟋ᴼ

One Saturday morning on my way to watch kids' soccer, I drive by an *Open House* sign on the lawn of a small yellow ranch house with white shutters. House shopping is not on my to-do list today, yet I turn around to park and go inside. The earthy smell of linseed oil greets me in the tiny foyer. To the right is a small galley kitchen behind swinging wooden saloon doors. Avocado-green appliances contrast the gold linoleum floor. The house is clean and well-kept—and another huge project. I turn to leave when my eyes connect with the large south-facing picture window in the straight-ahead living room. Sunlight pools on the gleaming wooden peg flooring. Something in my gut feels good and long-ago familiar. The view isn't a lake but rather a roomy backyard where four kids can jump on a trampoline and play tag. My knowing knows we are supposed to be here, with one problem—our credit is wrecked.

From my car, I call Steve, our Realtor. "Ask the sellers if they'll consider contract for deed." It's a long shot. In the throes of our debt settling, I had researched how one buys a house with a bleak FICO score. Contract for deed lets a seller be the bank and offer financing to the buyer. Most sellers, however, want their cash ASAP. Steve calls me back. Lo and behold, it turns out the homeowner, an elderly woman, has died, leaving her single, well-off son to handle the sale. Sure, he'll take a small down payment and be our bank. Fresh out of rehab, he is eager to be done with house-selling duties.

Magnificence in the mess. Provision in pain. Beauty from broken.

A few months later, I email our landlord. *The key is in the lockbox*, I say. It is the happiest sentence I've typed in a while.

One Little Cookie

MY TOES ARE FROZEN. I warm myself in front of a fireplace at Red Lodge resort in Montana after a day of January skiing in negative-ten-degree temps, thirty degrees colder than fun. It is the kids' winter break, and we are traveling with friends. Three years have passed since the beginning of the end of our business, my nervous system grateful. Jim's changed jobs, and I'm writing and illustrating from my downstairs furnace-room-turned-office. My books are thriving, and *If I Could Keep You Little* is a bestseller at Target—a validating phoenix rising. Turns out customers around the globe do want Marianne Richmond.

I download my email on my phone. A message from George appears. *Subject: Mom and Dad.* I click warily and read.

This past weekend I enrolled Mom and Dad in hospice, he says, *to give them an extra level of nursing care and attention beyond what Franklin Terrace can provide.* Mom is eating less, sleeping more, and can't stand without help. *Dad is the bigger surprise,* George continues, telling his caregivers to *leave him the hell alone and let him rest in peace.* Apparently, Dad tried to hit one of the nurses, he says. *Doctor thinks they have less than six months to live,* George concludes before signing off, *Happy Freakin' New Year!*

What the hell? I type back. Two months earlier, I visited Mom and

Dad before Thanksgiving. Zipping down the hallway with his walker, Dad was his usual alert self. He and I colored together in the dining room, an outlined turkey our project. My heart sank watching his shaky hands grip his brown crayon, unable to stay within the confines of the feathers.

But when Dad and I "talked" in his room using his dry-erase whiteboard, his tone was dejected. He and I had developed a strategy for conversing. I wrote on the board where he could read my question and audibly answer. "This is no way to live," he said, his eighty-nine-year-old head motioning toward his doorway and the disheartening scene beyond it.

By Christmas, things had deteriorated. I found Mom and Dad sitting in the quiet dining hall well after lunchtime—a sparsely decorated tree in the corner—both slouched in wheelchairs, staring at the table.

"Dad?" I said tentatively. Who was this man who looked like Santa Claus, his clean-shaven face replaced with a full gray and scraggly beard?

"Jean, Jean," he mumbled, calling me his sister's name.

I asked a nearby aide what happened.

"He's giving up," she replied. Dad yelped in pain when they tried to dress or shave him, and he didn't want to get out of bed anymore, often sleeping until noon.

Two days after George's email, my phone rings on our drive back to Minneapolis. "You need to get here," George says. "Dad doesn't have much time."

Things are speeding up faster than I am ready.

"I'm scared," I say as George and I pull into Franklin Terrace. Tony has arrived too. A white-haired hospice nurse is camped in their small living space, Dad's love seat command central. A portable table holds her paperwork and laptop, a stethoscope encircling her neck.

"How is he?" I ask.

"Resting comfortably," she says, handing me a *What to Expect When Someone Is Dying* brochure. *As death approaches, skin color is likely to change from the normal pinkish tone to a duller, darker, grayish hue. The fingernail beds may also become bluish rather than the normal pink...*

I toss the pamphlet on the counter and walk cautiously into his bedroom. The shades are drawn, a single lamp casting a gentle glow. Dad is lying on his back in his twin-sized bed on black-and-white-flowered sheets, eyes closed, mouth open, a washcloth on his head. His beard is gone, his mustache still bushy. His white Hanes T-shirt hangs loosely on his frail body, thin arms crossed on his stomach. Dark bruises cover his wrists. I inspect his fingernails. Are they pink or bluish? Dad looks older without his glasses, his forehead mottled with liver spots. A little black prayer book, rosary, and air freshener sit on his nearby bedside table.

I lower into a folding chair next to his head, watching his chest rise and fall with raspy breaths. How many more will there be?

"Dad," I whisper, "it's Marianne-o." No reaction. I sit and stare at him for fifteen minutes, taking in this man whose life was one long worry. And now it was almost over. Lifting the flowered sheets, I peek at the rest of him, his legs skinny sticks, a loose cloth for modesty. He looks like Jesus on the cross, maybe one hundred pounds.

"You can let go now, Dad," I say, resting my forehead on his bony shoulder. "No more hearing aids in heaven. No more worries, no more struggles. All peace. Thanks for everything, Dad. The cribbage games, the camping trips, the being proud of me. You tried really, really hard, and I love you." My tears drip onto his shirt, and his eyes flutter.

It's his "You're welcome," I know.

Tony and George take turns with Dad, and I wander down the quiet hallway in search of Mom, finding her in one of the common rooms.

She is sleeping in her wheelchair, her gray hair clean and brushed. The elderly group around her is playing hangman. A leader awaits guesses, her large paper pad propped on an easel, a partial stick man depicted.

"A!" a woman shouts.

"We already have an A," says the leader.

"A!" a second voice pipes in.

"Has your mom seen Jerry?" a nurse asks me.

"Not since I've been here," I say.

"You should bring her to him," she encourages me. "He's probably waiting."

Of course. Her husband. It didn't dawn on me, the fifty-two years between them. I pluck Mom from the semicircle and wheel her into Dad's bedroom, parking her in the narrow space between his head and the wall. She wakens from the movement.

"Do you know who this is, Mom?" I ask.

She shakes her head, lips pressed together.

"It's Jerry, your husband."

"Oh?" she murmurs, tipping her head on the *oh*.

"He's dying, Mom," I say. "Going to heaven to meet Jesus."

Another murmur.

"Let's pray."

Mom nods.

"Our Father, who art in heaven..." I start, and she joins in, Alzheimer's be damned. We move to a couple Hail Marys and a Glory Be, her tracking word for word. I snap a photo of them with my phone, the dying husband with his beloved wife, gazing down from her wheelchair, imagining their deep spiritual connection in this moment, when Mom pipes up.

"I want a cookie, one little cookie, that's all I'm asking for, and no one will give it to me."

It is a fitting farewell.

Ten hours later, at 8:00 a.m. on a January Monday, Dad dies. I am already back home when George calls me with the news. I wasn't sure what to do about leaving, but Tony and George encouraged me to keep my flight.

"Do you feel complete with your goodbye?" asked the nurse.

I scanned my insides, head to toe. My centers of knowing agreed, yes.

"Then go back to your family," she said.

We hang up, and I curl up on the living room couch, my sobs piercing the quiet. Was Dad scared when he breathed for the last time? Did he feel loved when he let go? I ask God to make his transition easy and give him new ears. After school, Julia and I sit on her bed. "He was ready, Mom," she says matter-of-factly, then jumps up and grabs her giant pink blow-up cell phone propped in a corner, a prize from the Minnesota State Fair. Punching the enormous numbers, she waits for an answer. "Oh, hey God, it's Julia," she says. "Is Papa Jerry there?" She nods, feigning receipt of an answer. "He's in heaven, Mom," she confirms, hanging up her phone face down on the bed.

Tony and George elect me to give the eulogy. I'll look through his memoirs for material, I figure. Years earlier, he mailed me a copy that I put somewhere. But now, multiple moves later, I can't remember where.

Do either of you have Dad's book? I email my brothers.

What book? they reply.

Shit. I am the keeper of his life story, and I've misplaced it.

⌣∘

The six of us pull into the St. Charles parking lot two hours before the service. It is a gray, wet, and chilly morning, most of the world at work and school. Inside the quiet narthex, I spy Dad's casket across the room—it's open—a wall of gorgeous stained-glass windows behind him. Roses and tulips with fancy bows and messages adorn the casket's bottom half: *Beloved Dad. Loving Husband. Proud Grandpa.* I can't imagine who sent them, Dad's social circle nonexistent. Slowly I walk over, afraid of what I'll see. I've been to a random wake or two but never for someone I can stare at as long as I want. And, certainly, never my parent. Mom and Dad prepaid their funerals and picked out their caskets years before—his light blue, hers gray. They visited their crypt too, typically after lunch at Taco Bell and before grocery shopping.

"Doesn't it creep you out," I asked Mom, "to look at your name on a drawer in a wall and know you're going to be in there?" It did not, she assured me.

Dad wears a gray suit, white dress shirt, and maroon tie, a perfect outfit for a lifetime government employee. Plastic-rimmed glasses rest over his closed eyes, crossed hands on his middle. I expect him to pop up.

"Just kidding, Marianne-o!" he'd say with a smile.

But he doesn't. Dad is really dead, his cheeks smooth, his lips the pale pink of unflavored Chapstick. I haven't seen Dad's upper lip in years. He looks too still and perfect, not the baggy undershirt guy who padded around his apartment in corduroy slippers.

"He looks weird," Adam says, wandering over, and I agree. Death is new for all of us. Cole and Adam are pallbearers, adorned in their school-concert button-down shirts and ties.

The priest emerges from the sanctuary, his hand outstretched to shake mine.

"I'm Father Jerry," he says, except it comes out "Jeh-wee," two obvious hearing aids explaining his modified speech. How perfect that hearing-challenged Father Jerry is officiating the funeral for hearing-challenged father Jerry.

"Keep your eulogy to five minutes," he says.

"Sure, Father," I say, knowing I won't. My five pages of recollections need more time. Plus I've tucked the giant pink God Phone behind the podium as well for an reenactment of Julia's call to heaven.

Familiar faces trickle in. High school friends. Dan, the Laura Lane neighbor who talked lawn care with Dad and whose wife had the home birth when Mom was in her "desert." And Dad's Sheboygan nieces and nephews—our first cousins. Tony, George, and I finally got to know them at a family reunion a few years earlier.

"Do you remember visiting us when you were three or four?" my cousin Sue asked me. "Your mom did yoga poses for everyone. Brought her own healthy food too and had you kids eat in the car, instead of enjoying the meat, potatoes, and marshmallow salad inside with everyone else." Decades later, my face flushed, feeling both embarrassed and impressed by Mom's fortitude.

"They didn't like me." Her words rang in my head.

They didn't understand you, I quietly countered.

I take a last peek at Dad.

"Watch over me, okay?" I say, touching the polyester sleeve covering his stiff forearm before turning from his face a final time. Halfway through mass, I walk to the pulpit to share my memories of Dad's quirks and qualities, personalizing his ninety years. Jelly donut over glazed. Malt-o-Meal over Cream of Wheat. His beloved garden, the Packers, and *Reader's Digest*. And his lifelong worries and faith, an incongruous duo.

After mass, our cars follow the hearse to the cemetery for a brief service in the mausoleum, a high-ceilinged room filled with gold muted light, the white marble walls dissected with grid lines; behind every square is an urn or body. Dad will be in the very top row—a mini forklift is needed to access it, the funeral director tells us.

The higher the location, the cheaper it is.

Peony Pink

SEVEN MONTHS LATER, DEEANN FROM Franklin Terrace texts me. I am standing outside Will's fourth-grade classroom door waiting for his end-of-day bell to ring.

"Your mom is asking when she's going to see Tony, George, and Marianne," she says. Deeann is now baking and bringing in cookies herself. Mom isn't on a restricted diet, Deeann says, and if Mom wants a cookie at ninety years old, she should "damn well" have one.

Mom hasn't put our three names in one sentence in eight years; she is telling me she is going to die too. I wondered how long she'd hang around after Dad's passing. Though oblivious to her surroundings, I think she knows he is gone. That the guy on the couch is missing.

"I'll come next weekend," I reply.

On a steamy August Saturday, I pull into Franklin Terrace just after lunchtime. This drive is second nature now, an audiobook my usual company. Wheelchairs flank the front door, frail bodies soaking up the warmth and light.

"This feels good, doesn't it?" says a woman to her elderly companion.

I sprinkle my hellos over the small crowd and receive their smiles. Inside the double doors, I nod at the receptionist and walk my usual route past the mailbox to the elevator. *Bingo! Dance Party! Ice cream social!* shout the posters taped to the walls.

I played bingo once with Mom in their dining room. "All Card" was the goal but no one understood because they have dementia. Every thirty seconds, one resident gleefully announced, "Bingo!" only to be told, "No Florence, you need to fill your whole card." Two seconds later, confused Florence called bingo again.

Just give her the damn prize, I thought. Winners chose from a wicker basket a travel-size shampoo, toothpaste, or mini tissue pack likely donated from people's travel extras.

The elevator door opens. Unused treadmills on the left. Beauty parlor and blood pressure check to the right. I walk straight to the locked and secured door and punch in *321*. The usual smells prick my nose—urine and cleaning solution. Glancing right and left down the quiet hallway, I read the name plaques of the residents, mostly women. *Lorraine. Mary. Fran. Mary*. Lots of Marys. Each unit displays photos in a glass case outside the door, highlighting memories of a younger, active life. A dashing husband in military uniform. A young beauty with a 1950s coif and ruby lips. On one door is a big colorful poster, *Welcome to the neighborhood, Jean!* Code for *Someone died, and a room became available*.

Unit 131. I gently push open Mom's door, noticing her name sign has been changed to reflect her single status. Peeking around the corner, I expect to find her in her chair, but the room is empty. Dad's absence is palpable. He was always my first sight, his reading spot in direct view from the door. Now his gold love seat sits unused. No newspapers scattered about. No rosary or water glass on the side table. No more dry-erase board awaiting my scribbled questions.

I locate Mom in the dining room. Well after lunchtime, she is alone and asleep in her wheelchair, head slumped on her chest. She is missing eleven teeth now, all pulled because of decay and infection. Purple bruises mottle her face. George asked for an explanation.

"A fall in her room?" the aides surmised, clearly guessing.

My chest aches at the scene.

"We like to get her out," says a nearby worker. "You know, for a change of scenery."

I nod. "I'll take her back," I reply, grabbing the handles and turning her wheelchair around.

Mom stirs, her head lifting at the movement.

"Hi, Mom," I say, curving my head to put my face in front of hers.

"It's Mar-i-anne," I enunciate. "Your daughter."

"Oh!" she says, cheerful but without recognition.

I push her slowly back down the hall. Two women gossip on the couch, gray heads bobbing, hands aflutter. I'm tempted to sit between them and delight in their stories. A gentleman powers by in his wheelchair, carrying a wad of toilet paper.

Inside Mom's room, I gingerly slide her into her recliner.

"Can I have a cookie?" she says promptly, straightening her posture as if to convince me she'll be awake for bit. According to the nurses, Mom is pulling the emergency cord at all hours to ask for cookies.

"I bet you had a cookie after lunch," I say.

"Mary, Mary, Mary, why must we get so old?" she asks instead.

A valid question. I plop down in Dad's spot on the love seat, wondering what to do the next couple of hours. Mom is nodding off already. I flip television channels. Read my book for five minutes. An elderly neighbor pops in thinking it's her room. This is likely the last time I'll see Mom alive. How do I spend such a day?

I stare at her for a while, taking in her form, her large bosom resting on her lap. She is wearing a light-blue shirt today with sparkly gems around the neckline. It looks newish, and I wonder where it came from. Her pants, khaki colored and shapeless, appear easy to pull on and off. My eyes zero in on her swollen bare feet, the skin taut and shiny. I walk over and crouch down next to her. Picking up her right foot, I hold it in my hand, feeling its warm weight. Her bunions bulge. I inspect her toenails, cracked and yellowed. Her pinky nail is tiny for such a robust woman.

I study her without her knowing, my face inches from her papery cheek. Her bruises tell me she is close to done with this life. I cannot recall ever being this physically close to Mom, so unlike my daughter and me, Julia noticing my errant nose hair while side by side watching movies in my bed. Mom's forehead is smooth for nine decades of living, her cheeks still plump, her hair more brown than gray. Moles dot her complexion.

"Why don't you get rid of those?" I asked her as a kid, analyzing the bumpy blights on an otherwise smooth landscape.

"They don't bother *me*," she'd reply.

I run my index finger across her cheek, the skin thin and dry. My mother. My *mother*. The person I have longed for a lifetime to evoke feelings of warmth and closeness. Instead, it is like sitting with an aunt or neighbor, a woman familiar but not intimate.

Do I love her?

I'm saddened by my asking. I feel compassion, yes, but love? Mom told me she loved me through the years. Signed her cards with the words, and I believe she meant it, though her unavailability and judgments felt mismatched to my needs. I rarely felt supported or affirmed. Perhaps our definitions of love simply differed.

"Thanks, Mom," I say to her sleeping eyes.

I exist because of her. I have my beloved family because she gave me life. She modeled generosity and tenacity...and her version of religion and faith. God lives in her too.

I lift her right hand, the skin translucent and crisscrossed with knotty blue veins. Her fingers are slim and pretty with long nail plates.

These hands worked hard through the years—typing school papers, laundry, ironing Dad's shirts, counting beads on her rosary.

I stand up and head back to the dining room.

"Do you have stuff to paint fingernails?" I ask an aide mopping the floor.

"In that cabinet," she points across the room.

Behind white laminate doors, I fish through saltine crackers and hot chocolate packs to find a ziplock bag full of polish, cotton balls, and emery boards.

Back in Mom's room, I sit on the arm of her recliner and move her right hand to my left thigh. I clip, file, and smooth...and accidentally pinch her skin.

"Ow!" she yelps, suddenly awake.

"Oh, sorry, Mom! Just trying to clip your nails."

"You're a tough cookie," she murmurs.

Our history floods my conscience.

"You have no idea," I say to the quiet room.

Choosing Peony Pink from several corals and reds, I paint two coats of polish plus one top coat and arrange her hands on her lap to dry. Still restless, I wander into the small walk-in closet, Dad's side now empty. We divvied up his few belongings after his funeral, the aides donating his clothes to the other residents. I kept his gold Timex watch, military dog tags, and the green photo album, of course. George took his journals and Green Bay Packers sweatshirt. I can't remember if Tony took anything.

Mom's few shirts and one dress hang tidily, a black and white floral I hadn't seen before. The fake birchwood dresser—the same one I stood at before my first big seizure—occupies a corner, housing her underwear and pajamas. I open the top drawer. Inside is a small jewelry box holding necklaces, rosaries, St. Christopher medals, and cheap beads.

This tangled mess of mementos reflect her priorities: Catholic, devout, simple, nonmaterialistic. I go into her bedroom. Her twin bed looks lonely in the room without Dad's nearby.

The sun is starting its descent. Mom will eat dinner soon at her usual table. I can't think of anything else I want or need to do. Gathering my purse and book from the love seat, I stop at the side of her recliner and ponder her for the last time. Leaning down to kiss her temple, I pause to imprint this moment in my memory.

"Bye, Mom," I say. "I love you."

I want these words to be the last I say to her, even if I'm not sure they fit.

Nine days later, Mom dies. I find out by email.

It is Labor Day afternoon, and I am walking my dog with a friend.

"Talk to you soon!" I say, parting ways in front of her house and my car. I slide into the front seat and grab my cell phone from the glove box. No texts, but eight missed calls from George. Not a good sign. I dial and get his voice mail. Redial twice. Panicky, I check my email instead and watch a couple messages download. And that's when I see it. Subject line: *Mary Helf*. Sent by Tony ten minutes ago at 3:08 p.m. to our seventeen cousins and me.

I stare at the words. The passing of our mom. Before I went for a walk, she was alive. While I was walking, she died. Was it so urgent for Tony to tell our distant cousins before he knew I knew? Apparently, her funeral is Friday, and my name is included in the email signature.

I reach George on my drive home. He is already on his way to Franklin Terrace.

"She died in her chair this afternoon," he says. "The nurse went to check on her after lunch. Said she hadn't been feeling well."

"The nurse just found her there?" I squeak through tears.

"Yeah, said she looked like she was sleeping. Tried to wake her up and when she couldn't..." He trails off.

"Should I be coming too?" What is normal for a daughter to do when her mom dies?

"I don't think you need to," George says. "I'll call you when I get there."

When I hang up, I am in front of my house. Jim appears in my window, and I roll it down.

"My mom died." I say. Emerging from my car, I rest in his hug. My street is quiet while my insides reel, the finality of her death working its way through me.

Two hours later, George calls me back.

"I'm in the apartment now," he says. "With Mom."

I gasp. "She's still in her chair?"

"Where's she going to go?" he says sarcastically. "I'm waiting for the funeral home guys." Right.

"What does she look like?" I ask.

"Like her. Peaceful." He texts me a photo while we talk. She looks like she did a week ago, napping while I sat on the love seat. But knowing she is dead in the photo changes peaceful to vacant.

"What does she feel like?" I ask. "I mean, is her body still warm?"

"Really, Marianne?" George says but obliges me.

"Kinda coolish," he reports.

A knock on the door interrupts our conversation. "Funeral home guys are here," George says, and we hang up. They put Mom in a purple velvet body bag to wheel her out of Franklin Terrace, he tells me later. "She looked regal."

That night in bed, I ponder Mom's earthly journey. All the emotional miles we'd traveled together have finally reached a destination. I ached for how beat-up she was in the end. But I'd be damned if God didn't take her exactly as she'd requested many times.

"I just want to go in my sleep."

It was the least he could do for someone named Mary Magdalene.

⌒

Mom gets to her funeral before us; the hearse is parked out front, her casket already open on the far side of the church lobby. I feel like I was just here, which I was, seven months ago. Same church, same priest, same funeral director.

Our family chatter interrupts the quiet narthex; the midmorning September sun flooding the space with a golden glow. I stop at a small wooden table where Mom's framed obituary and prayer cards sit and empty the large yellow envelope I carried from Minnesota. Loose photographs slide out, and I arrange them in order: Mom's ninety years in five snapshots.

Steadying myself, I walk over to her casket, the echoey click of my black high heels on tile punctuating the stillness. I look better for this funeral, my haircut cuter, my dress more flattering. It's not about me, but it is. When parents die, the kids are front and center as greeters, memory sharers, and explainers.

Besides an apology from the CIA, Mom finally got what she wanted most—to meet Jesus. Eight years past schedule though. "Not to be morbid, but I'll be ready to go by eighty-two," she repeatedly announced at a family supper when we were kids, preplanning her usefulness on the same timeline as her mother's. "I'll have done everything I needed to do."

What if I still need you? I wondered.

She looks like a version of herself, someone related maybe, but not the woman I saw two weeks ago. The funeral home erased her bruises with makeup, but she never wore foundation, so she looks thick and tan like a pancake. Her lips are lined and colored mauve, her hair trimmed, brushed, and sprayed. So put together—and so not her. She should be wearing loose cotton pants and her *Proud to Be a Veteran* sweatshirt instead of a dress and big round, plastic-rimmed glasses. To see what exactly? I know they try to make people look like they did in real life, but this being all dressed up strikes me as silly. Why not pajamas and slippers for the hereafter?

A small white pillow cradles her head. A silver crucifix hangs inside the casket lid and an American flag, folded into a tight triangle, is propped next to her, part of the military funeral package she preordered. A fake crystal rosary wraps around her left hand, her manicured fingernails still Peony Pink.

Glancing over my shoulder to make sure no one is watching, I poke the back of her hand several times with my right index finger. It is cold and wooden, with little give. She is gone, her soul in the Great Beyond. I imagine her sitting front row at Jesus's feet, singing hymns and hanging out with her family and grade school buddies. Possibly with George Graham, too, her first crush, whose going to war ended things. Her people, finally reunited. Would she look for Dad or use heaven as a divine do-over?

My eyes scan the lobby. A small crowd is gathering. Mom couldn't care less if anyone came; she didn't go to funerals herself.

"I prefer to remember them living," she said whenever someone died.

"It's actually not about you, Mom," I'd tell her. "You go for the people left behind."

Today that is us—her three kids and six grandkids, a beautiful legacy, but her interests were elsewhere. I reach into my purse for my cell phone and snap a few pictures of her in her coffin, knowing someday I'll be glad I did.

Jim's arm comes around my shoulder, and I look up. The funeral home guys hover respectfully, waiting to close the casket and wheel it into church for mass. Jim steers me toward the back of the sanctuary where my four kids wait. Halfway there, I about-face, striding back to where the two men are closing the lid over Mom's face.

"Wait!" I urge. They look up, eyes wide, a "what the heck" between them.

"I want to see the other half," I said. "Her legs. I want to see if she has shoes on."

They hesitate, but I don't budge. The older guy moves first. He fiddles with the lock and raises the lid to show me Mom's whole body. No shoes. Just nylons. And a tag with her body's ID wrapped around her big toe, pushed taut against the beige pantyhose.

We lock eyes. No one says anything.

They didn't want me to see it. I'm kinda sorry I did.

We are all passing through, and when we die, our body is numbered and tagged so it doesn't get mixed up with somebody else. I hear Mom's voice in my mind. "In heaven, I'll have a new body without bunions."

I had rehearsed this day countless times, pretending she was dead, then asking myself, *Am I sad? Relieved?* I couldn't know until I knew. Both. The answer is both. Sad for what I didn't get and relieved because I can quit expecting.

"Thanks," I say to the funeral guys, "I'm good."

Mom and Dad are together with the Lord, Father Jerry assures us during mass. The sound of taps filters in from outside. Tony gives the eulogy this time, speaking of Mom's selflessness, sense of humor, and love of sports, recounting the time he watched a middle-school basketball free-throw contest she and I had entered. I missed my ten attempts while Mom sunk every single basket. "She strutted off the court proud as could be," Tony tells the small crowd. A defining moment for her, and I have no recollection.

We pick and choose what to hold on to.

Back at the mausoleum, I walk to the marble wall where Dad lies four stories up. Their square is open, waiting for Mom, the door slab resting on the ground nearby. I feel badly leaving them both in the wall forever; at least they have each other. For all their differences, Mom and Dad's birth and death years are the same: 1923–2013.

As we ready to leave, my cousin Linda signals my attention.

"I was helping your aunt Jean clean out her filing cabinets the other day," she says excitedly. "And we found a copy of a book your dad wrote."

What? I throw my arms around her. Dad to my rescue. He had worked too long and too hard on this book only for me to lose it.

After lunch with the cousins on the outdoor patio of a Milwaukee restaurant, we head back to Franklin Terrace to divvy up Mom's belongings. The kids run on the hallway treadmills and motor themselves up and down in Mom's recliner. Mom and Dad's furniture is pushed to one side of the room for a Goodwill pickup. I sift through a laundry basket full of stuff: Dime store jewelry. Jesus statues. The cookie jar with the dancing pig. A dozen toilet paper rolls and bottles of hand soap. I grab some hangers; we never have enough at home.

Then I choose two more things: The first a large blue-painted rock with the word *smile* on top that I made for Mom when I was in third grade, perhaps an effort to make up for the "I hate housework" drawing I made that same year. My rock adorned various places in our Laura Lane house—Mom's dresser, a paperweight on the counter, a door-stop. When they moved to Maple Meadows and Franklin Terrace, and Mom gave away eighty percent of their stuff, including Dad's antique Christmas ornaments, she took my rock with her. If only shepherding one another was as easy as toting a blue rock from place to place.

I take her holy water bottle from the basket too, a small square plastic container with a black top, the *L* and *Y* on its side worn away from years of holding and blessing.

"Here," George says, reaching into his pocket and pulling out Mom's gold JCPenney wedding band. "The funeral director gave this to me if you want it."

I turn the thin metal circle in my fingers and slip it on my right hand for safekeeping on our drive back to Minnesota. It isn't the solitary diamond Dad put on her finger fifty-two years earlier, but it is certainly a more honest memento of Mom's journey.

Back home, I feel surprisingly empty and untethered, Mom and Dad's care and demise my emotional side job for years.

"Do you feel like an orphan?" friends ask.

No. Orphan is not a new feeling with their death.

"More like the top rungs on my life ladder have disappeared," I reply.

When they were alive, I belonged to someone further up. Now Tony, George, and I are the top rungs. I wonder where Mom and Dad are, if they know they are dead, and if they are watching over me with newly acquired supernatural abilities, assisting God and the angels to divinely orchestrate my life.

A few weeks after the funeral, Dad's typewritten book comes in the mail from Cousin Linda. One morning, the kids at school and the house quiet, I sit on the living room couch to read it start to finish. Flipping to its end to check page count, I notice this version is a few pages longer than I recall mine being.

The extra pages are Dad asking Mom to marry him.

It was April 1957, he writes, and he's visiting Wright-Patterson Air Force Base in Ohio for Mom's birthday. *Walking back to Mary's quarters, we stopped under a tree, and I presented her with a small cube-shaped gift. Of course, she knew what it was before she took off the wrappings. She slowly took it out of the box, started to slip it on her finger as I said those words:*

"Will you marry me, Mary?" She began to weep. We kissed. Mary's tears were tears of indecision. "I really don't know what to do, Jerry," she said. "I'll take the ring for now, I'll wear it, but I'm not sure. I may have to give it back sometime in the future. Please give me time to decide. I'll let you know." That's the way we left it—up in the air.

Up in the air.

It is the first time I hear the story from Dad's side, his big brave moment met with Mom's tears and indecision. From the get-go, Dad was sure. Mom said she wasn't sure, but it seems she was too.

"I never wanted to be married, but your dad's sisters talked me into it."

Reading Dad's words make me newly sad for him, his earnest devotion unrequited. But it stirs in me new understanding for Mom too. Her centers of knowing seemingly had a consensus, and she ignored them to please someone else—said yes to avoid hurting Dad at the expense of hurting herself and, years later, her daughter, listening with a sinking stomach to her frequent verbal regrets. And yet, they lasted fifty-two years together.

I grab my laptop. *Dottie Chialastri in Philadelphia*, I type into my browser. Dottie was Mom's oldest childhood friend from North Street, both from immigrant families, and the one person with whom Mom still traded letters until her Alzheimer's set in. George wrote Dottie to tell her mom died, and she typed back a note of sympathy. Mom was the fun-loving one, she wrote, the one who arranged blind dates for anyone needing a partner for a dance and who had introduced Dottie to her husband, Russ. *I'll miss hearing from her,* she signed off.

A few clicks land me on an address and phone number. There is but one Russ Chialastri in Philly. I dial. Three rings.

"Hello?" answers a sweet elderly voice.

"Dottie, this is Marianne, Mary Sokas Helf's daughter."

"Oh, hellloooo," she enthuses, meeting my random call with lovely expectancy.

"Do you have a little time to tell me about my mom?" I ask.

Dottie chuckles, delighted to access her remembrance. "Your mom could never sit still. She was always doing."

Me too, I think.

"She worked three little jobs at once, just to keep busy."

Me too.

"Your mom kept in touch with everyone…including kids she went to grade school with!"

Me too.

"Your mom loved to walk and exercise."

Me too.

I listen and ask, learning more about a younger woman always up for adventure, looking out for her friends, and making something out of nothing. For all my perceived differences, a lot like me.

Hanging up with Dottie, I wish I would have known more of that free-spirited mom in my life versus the one lost in her own pain and regret. Staring out the window, phone still in hand, my insides stir with empathy for her struggles and sadness for the missed opportunity to know the best version of her.

Soul Door

THICK SNOWFLAKES FALL ON MY windshield. It is a Sunday night in early March—nearly midnight—and I am driving to the twenty-four-hour Walgreens to get a prescription for Julia's bladder infection after she crawled into my bed crying that it hurts to pee.

Sitting at a red light, I watch in my rearview mirror as a black pickup truck gets closer and closer until *BAM*, he slides into my back end.

"Shit." I jolt forward against my seat belt.

"This has never happened to me before," a round-faced teenager in a backward baseball hat appears in my driver's-side window to hand me his information on a crumpled-up napkin.

"Really?" I reply. "Because this is my thing."

It's my second car accident in two weeks, the first with Will on our way to Cole's basketball game when my U-turn at a yellow stoplight coincided with a truck's decision—the driver an off-duty police officer—to bolt from behind a snowbank to beat the light and send my front-end car parts onto the road. The officer showed me his badge and offered we both go on our way. His truck was fine; my car, Dad's Corolla, not worth much. "I'm glad our dad has a good job," Will said, and I didn't explore his logic.

Jim's good job is two thousand miles away in California. Two months after Mom's funeral, his employer had a layoff. "Workforce reduction," they explained. When an opportunity came up in San Jose, we agreed Jim would move in January and fly home every three weeks. The kids and I would follow after the school year. The big reasons keeping us in Minnesota—our business, Jim's job, proximity to my parents—had fallen away, and the kids were open to change.

"I'm game," I said too, but second-guessed the decision a zillion times, and after the fifty-third night of negative temps, relentless blizzards, a broken snowblower, and single parenting, I started resenting Jim living solo in sunny California.

"Remember, you chose this together," Laura reminds me. She and I still meet twice a month because I am a work in progress. "This isn't easy for Jim either."

"And what if I hate it there?" California's *different*, friends warn.

"And what if you don't?" Laura counters. "People's comments pull you off track. You're so quick to give your power away. You get to decide how you want to be."

Here it is again. Growing the pause. Choosing my response. She reminds me of our solid reasons for moving. We reaffirm them with my centers of knowing. I pray fewer begging prayers and more affirming God's presence and provision through people and circumstances. More recognizing I am loved and guided versus hanging on a cliff, begging God to notice if he isn't too busy with his billions of other humans. We are still at Kevin's church but barely. His sermons had moved more into evangelistic territory, and my insides rebelled.

"Part of your heart still isn't healed," Laura says. "Choosing faith in uncertainty is a scary thing for you."

Between appointments is my practice time, Laura's reminders my daily mantras for finding inner congruence. Becoming an integrated, self-responsible human is a ton of work. When I feel resentment bubbling up, I consider what boundary I'm crossing. When my stomach churns, I ask what's not in alignment. I keep opening my soul door to God, but a bigger version of God, one without so many rules about access. My head, heart, and gut agree on resisting the belief that only certain people in certain churches have access to a boundless God.

"Do your goodbye well," Laura offers during our final session. I had booked two full hours to revisit all I had learned since I first sat on her Comfort Couch, dazed and empty. It felt important to mark my growth. "Be intentional. Take photos. Spend time with who you are and what you want. Leave feeling complete in the experience." Complete versus cut and run. "Gratitude opens you, so you have capacity to transition and receive what's waiting in California."

Standing in Laura's doorway, I wrap my arms around her middle. "Thank you for every minute," I say, my eyes tearing. "You helped me find me." Releasing my grip, Laura and I stand face-to-face, inches apart. Closing her eyes, she wishes for my safety and well-being, then gives my hands a final squeeze. Back in the waiting room, I look at the chair I've sat in so many times, my mind filled with three hours of issues for our one-hour appointments. The decent magazine selection. The Keurig, tea bags, and dish of stale candy. I stuff a soft peppermint circle in my jeans pocket and ascend the stairway two steps at a time. Walking into the sunlit parking lot in the quiet early afternoon, I hope I've absorbed enough truth to carry me through whatever is coming.

To pass time and counter my winter isolation, I join a small artists' group, six of us seeking a kindred community in our work-from-home lives.

"I wonder if my mom and dad know I'm moving," I say over coffee and a bran muffin at a local café.

"Ask Liv," jokes one of the five women.

Liv (pronounced *Leev*), recently came out to us as a lifelong intuitive. Ever since she was a little girl, she confided, she's seen and talked to angels. Liv knows things about people before they happen. Gets signs and messages from the other side through her spirit guides. Sitting there, I recall my own angel vision at nine years old, the ethereal larger-than-life being assuring me I'd be healed.

We lean in to hear more. With her Norwegian blond bob and practical wardrobe, Liv is the furthest thing from who I'd imagine someone with mediumship abilities to be. More purple robes, long painted fingernails, and crystal balls, less Minnesotan suburban. She is officially launching a new business and offering one-on-one calls to channel divine guidance.

"I'm in," I say without hesitation.

⌒

A couple weeks later, on a Friday morning, I nervously sit on my bed, cell phone in hand, door closed. The kids are at school. Jim is home from California for the weekend, busy changing light bulbs and pounding in new baseboard trim to ready our house for sale. Do I light a candle or burn incense? Put on airy music?

At eleven o'clock sharp, my phone rings, and my stomach flutters.

"You ready?" Liv asks after a few minutes of conversation.

"I am," I say.

"Take a few deep breaths while I go into a short meditation," she instructs.

The line goes quiet while I inhale and exhale, holding my air extra long to make sure I'm as open a channel as possible.

"You there?" Liv comes back on the line.

"Yes," I say, "and *very* relaxed." Closing my eyes, I press my phone to my ear to shut out Jim's pounding and to ensure I hear every word.

"So. What's really funny is as soon as you started talking, your mom pulled out these rosary beads," Liv says. "She turned to your dad and said, 'Should we tell her?' and your dad's sort of noncommittal, like, 'Whatever.'"

My heart quickens. The rosary? Mom's defining accessory.

"Yes," I say. "Catholic was the only way. We argued about it."

"Your mom's nervously stepping forward with her rosary beads and trying to find the right words for how she wants to put this for you," Liv continues. "What I've heard her say multiple times is, 'I still believe what I believe.'" Liv's voice jumps to a higher pitch as she channels Mom's words.

"Oh, my goodness," I respond. "You sound just like her. Is she in heaven? Is she with Jesus?"

"Yes. She is saying, 'However, I have met people here who did not believe the same things as me, and they're here.' Your mom feels like she is raising the white flag, and she can't believe she's surrendering. Like it hurts."

"Does she love me?" I ask.

"She said, 'Don't be silly.' She's with lots of old friends from Philadelphia and church. It's been fun to reunite, but she's also gotten to know this one lady and become great friends. Your mom just whispered, 'She's Jewish.'"

I glance at my clock next to my bed, wanting the ticking minutes to slow down.

"'It doesn't change anything for me,' your mom is saying, 'but I suppose it means you can believe what you believe...that there is a higher power but maybe not so many rules.'"

Exactly what my gut has been telling me for years.

Mom keeps talking through Liv.

"'I'd really still like for you to go to church. There is a God, you know that, right? I've only been here a short time, but what I've learned is that people come to God in so many ways.'"

"She's saying that this has been a shocker for her," Liv says. "She got what she wanted. She's showing me a giant image of Christ. She says she had a vision of what heaven would be like. That she'd meet Jesus. And she's saying she got it, and it's all she needs."

"It sounds like everything she wanted and lived for," I reply.

"Yes, and then some," Liv says. "Because what she didn't count on was that she could have that and there would be other people finding their own heaven. 'So,' your mom just said, 'before you move on, I don't want you feeling guilty even though I made you spend your whole life feeling that way. I admit it. I get it. I wasn't the easiest person to live with. Your father keeps telling me that.'"

I shift on my bed and look out the window at the spring sky. Is Mom up there, out there, one with all?

"Spirit wants you to know," Liv says, "you don't have to go where you do not feel called. Allow for a transition in your faith that is not a closing off but an opening up. Move outside your comfort zone and find where you feel your fit.'"

Divine permission granted.

"Ask her if her fingernails are still painted?" I interject.

"She's putting out her hands," Liv says, "and saying, 'You're changing the subject on me.'"

"Do my parents know I'm moving to California?" I ask.

"Your mom just said it doesn't matter where you live; she can follow you. She keeps making sure you're not forgetting things. Do you have her china? She's watching over this to make sure it gets on the truck because she wants the dishes to go with you."

This is crazy.

I have Mom's china in boxes in the garage. Besides the few things I took after the funeral, it is the largest keepsake I have. There is *no way* Liv can know this without hearing it from Mom. I lean my head back against my pillow. The conversation feels like a heavenly olive branch, the beginnings of reconciliation between us. An hour zooms by. Before we hang up, Liv promises a recording of the call.

"Oh, and be on the lookout for red cardinals," she adds. "That's a sign from your mom that she's hanging around."

Later, Jim and I take our dog for a walk around Central Park. I tell him about my call with Liv and her messages from Mom. I tentatively use my new vocabulary—*angels, divine guidance, spirt, the Other Side.* And as if on cue, a red cardinal lands on a tree branch in my right periphery. I stop midstep, goose bumps dotting my arms.

"Oh, hi, Mom," I say, Jim giving me a sideways look.

She is certainly freer to travel now.

Finding the Bright

Y'ALL WILL HATE THE SUMMERS here," says the Budget rental car lady upon our arrival into Nashville's airport, sliding paperwork over the counter. Why do people feel a need to point out what sucks about a place? Dolly Parton's recorded voice welcomes us to Music City through overhead speakers while my eyes scan the crowd. So. Many. Beards. Sure enough, outside the thick August air envelopes us, my eyeglasses fogging.

After three years in northern California, our family moved to Tennessee when a good job appeared for Jim. As much as we loved the West Coast sunshine and low humidity, we welcomed the return to four seasons and a lower cost of living. California enlarged me, painfully at times. Creating a new life wasn't easy, but I found aliveness in the redwoods and ocean. I made friends. I accepted opportunities to share my books at schools and moms' groups. And I wrote new stories.

It's okay to be afraid, I typed one afternoon. Then what? *Courage,* my brain answered. But what *is* courage exactly? A muscle or superpower? An intention? Tossing my laptop aside, I headed upstairs and found Will in his room folding laundry. "Hey," I said, "What do you think it means to be brave?" Will was familiar with my pop-up inquisitions. "Because you moved across the country and started a new school."

He stood in thought, a blue sock in hand. "I guess," he said, "but I didn't have a choice about that. I think brave is when you choose to do the thing you want to do, no matter what anyone else says."

I stared at him in wonderment, this little boy soul who knew already at age eleven how to listen to himself. "A *choice*," I repeated. "You're exactly right." Hugging his narrow shoulders, I thanked him for articulating in one brilliant reply what I wanted to convey—and crystallizing for me how I, too, have been brave. Am brave. Deciding in partnership with my inner voice is courage. I returned downstairs and typed in a flurry the beginning of what would become my next book, *Be Brave Little One*.

> *Be brave to begin*
> *to listen inside*
> *to the voice of your heart,*
> *so truthful and wise.*
> *How far can I go?*
> *What things can I be?*
> *When I get to choose*
> *what brave is to me?*

We drive twenty-five miles south to a rental property, the landscape turning rural as the miles pass. Three of our four kids are with us, Cole staying in California for college. Trees and rock walls line the highways, green and lush. When we find our house—a three-bedroom with a landscaped yard and small carport—the sun is setting. A wide front porch holds a weathered bench and wooden swing. Jim runs out for beer. Later, I sit outside with a Bud Light and watch the lightning bugs blink in the steamy blackness, the buzz of cicadas a jarring soundtrack. Thunder rolls in the distance, and I smell skunk. This move feels different, because I feel different, a deeper internal certainty where anxiety and confusion had long lived. A growing confidence between my now and not yet, and an emboldened belief that my mom, dad, angels, and spiritual team are along for the adventure.

And I have one in mind.

Months later, our train pulls into the Philadelphia Amtrak station. It is late afternoon in mid-October, fall break from school for Julia and Will. After two days exploring New York City, we arrive to my real reason for this trip. I dial an Uber, and ten minutes later, we are on our way to an Airbnb in Old City, close to Philly's historic district.

Our first morning in Philadelphia, we walk the few blocks to Elfreth's Alley, the oldest continuously inhabited residential street in America and a National Historic Landmark. A picture of the alley hung crooked in our Laura Lane living room my entire childhood.

"My house was three blocks from Elfreth's Alley, where Betsy Ross made the first American flag," Mom explained, overtly proud of her Betsy connection. *Who'd name their son Elfreth?* my kid brain wondered, but the large welcome sign at its entrance tells me the street is named after Jeremiah Elfreth, an eighteenth-century blacksmith and property owner. And sure enough, Betsy, Benjamin Franklin, and William Penn were frequent passersby.

Along this street William Penn's message of tolerance was widely adopted as shopkeepers of different nationalities, races, and genders worked side by side, something that was almost unheard of in the eighteenth century.

We stroll down the narrow cobblestone lane, taking in the renovated colonial-era row houses with bright-red doors and shutters, bloom-filled window boxes, and quaint courtyards.

"I'd hate to have all these people walking past my house all the time," Julia pipes up, eager to move on.

Next, we walk to 5 Cherry Street, Mom's first address, a quick stroll from the famous alley. In her folders of paperwork, I found a list of her childhood addresses, which first sparked the idea for my Mom Tour.

The one-way blacktop road is quiet. Redbrick brownstones line one side, parked cars the other. I stand on the sidewalk directly across from her once-upon-a-time front door, an arched window above like it's wearing a cute hat. Three steps connect the sidewalk to the entrance, a single metal railing between her home and the neighbors'.

I imagine Mom's life here in the late 1920s—no indoor plumbing, shared outhouses in the backyards. It's hard to fathom that life with toddlers, bringing them out back to use the bathroom in the middle of winter. I imagine, too, the comfort of a community of similar circumstances.

"We'd sit outside on our steps in the summer humidity, drinking lemonade and playing jacks," Mom said. A young girl and her people. Solidarity. Community. Belonging. Like the Air Force, perhaps. And what she never felt or found in Greendale, her marriage, or motherhood.

After lunch at a bustling hamburger place, we drive to North Street, to Mom's house after Cherry, and where she lived from age three on. It looks much the same as Cherry Street, well kept red brownstones with front doors more spaced apart, but the same slice of sidewalk out front where my grandfather died of a heart attack after shoveling snow. Mom was twenty-three by then, a college graduate out in the working world. Six years later, she'd join the military, and five after that, she had her electroshock therapy. I have been on a journey to comprehend her for as long as I could remember, starting with sneaking into her bedroom as a kid to examine her bras.

Holy Cross Cemetery is my final stop.

My cell phone alarm rings.

Our last morning in Philly. I've envisioned today for decades. The kids sleep in while Jim makes coffee, grabs our duffel bag, and we head to the elevator. Inside our bag is a metal detector we bought online, small enough to fit in our luggage, but capable enough for our basic metal-detecting needs. Just in case, I tossed in two tablespoons from the kitchen drawers to use as shovels. Then we call an Uber to the airport to rent a car.

"I buried it at my mother's grave site." Mom's words about her wedding ring revisit my brain as Jim navigates us over well-worn streets to Yeadon, an adjacent borough, and through the pillared entrance of Holy Cross, a huge Catholic cemetery on more than 225 acres. I've been holding the mystery of her ring for decades. Winding through hundreds of gravestones, we find the small office where Lois, the friendly office manager—a woman I've talked to numerous times over the phone—instructs us on my grandma's whereabouts: plot HCJ45.

"Joe'll take you to the grave site, Marianne," she offers.

A man has slipped in while we talk. He wears a suit and gold badge that communicates his role: *Family Services Director*. I don't want company, but Joe insists, and we follow his car to one of the most conspicuous headstones in the entire place. Grandma rests in the center of a busy roundabout while clumps of cars drive by, and crowds gather to begin burials around us. The drone of bugles mixes with the deep intonations of ministers offering solace.

"Youse guys have two plots still availerbul," Joe says in his Philly accent, his right hand resting atop the marble cross, the other in his pants pocket. I'll let the family know, I promise him before we part ways.

Jim turns on the detector.

Beeeep, a high-pitched signal pierces the air.

"Turn that thing down!" I insist, curving my body over the machine to dull the noise while glancing at the nearby mourners thankfully engaged in their praying.

"I lost my ring last time I was here," I'll say if anyone asks. It feels morally acceptable.

Jim begins circling the wand around the grave. We look and scrape and search and dig. Nothing. We go wider, imagining Grandma six feet below. Still nothing.

Nearly an hour later, I sit back on my heels, slow acceptance settling in while Jim gives a final effort. Maybe it's not even here. Maybe the rain washed the ring away. Maybe the landscapers mowed it up, or Mom disposed of it elsewhere. And maybe she wanted her ma to have it, and what am I doing here thinking I have the right to retrieve it?

BEEP. BEEP. BEEP.

The detector is squealing. Jim and I meet surprised eyes. Springing into action, I dig up the grass with bare fingers and pile it to the side.

The beep dissipates.

Jim moves the wand over to my grassy pile.

BEEEEEP.

Sifting through my grass clump, I feel metal.

But it isn't round, dainty metal with a diamond stone; rather it's a three-inch piece of thick wire—dark, bent, and rusted to rigidity.

"Here's my ring," I say with a wry smile.

It's a fitting metaphor for Mom's and my relationship, me digging for one thing and getting another. I have preimagined my unlikely, dramatic, and remarkable ending (I find the diamond ring! It's in perfect condition! Mystery solved!) like I prescripted so many of Mom's and my interactions according to my ideal desires, longings, and expectations. My invitation, the same as it has been all along, is accepting what is and choosing the meaning and momentum I give it. For years, I adopted and internalized a faulty takeaway in response to Mom's doings: *I am unworthy of love.* Every interaction I viewed through this distorted lens, my psyche's calling card. Finding and wearing Mom's ring wouldn't change the truth of her experience or mine—or suddenly solidify what's been valid all along: I'm good as is. Always was. All my outward searching was never going to uncover what could only be found within.

I am because Mom was, both of us continuums of a story started long before us and full of the mystery, drama, conflict, and suspense of a compelling tale. It's up to me—though so difficult at times—to choose and change my trajectory based on the characters, trauma, and plotline I inherit through ancestry. Rescript my part to tell a new narrative about and for myself. For my children. And for others too. From my first book, I offered words of love and belonging. Initially aspirational and now—more often than before—embodied. From writing *for* my healing to writing *from* my healing, an ongoing and layered process.

Jim and I tidy the grave site, patting the uprooted grass into place like two golfers repairing divots. I repack the detector in its bag and toss in the tablespoons. "Bye, Grandma," I say. If I've somehow missed the ring, I feel good about leaving it, as well as Mom's discontent when she buried it with her own ma. It was never mine to own.

Back in our car, I examine the rusted wire in my palm. Though unexpected, it's a spot-on souvenir of my search—my search to know and be known by Mom, but moreover, a lifetime quest to know my own value. Once upon a time, Mom, like this little wire, was a brighter version of herself. Happily unscathed. Same as me. But life's elements had tarnished our spark. The opportunity is to reclaim instead our divine brightness, less a destination and more an inner pathway beset with choosing. Choosing to believe we're on purpose. Choosing to trust our soul voice as guidance. Choosing to love and be loved as is. And choosing to forgive who and what impedes our way. It's a big ask.

The unearthing of this wire mirrors my own excavation from the mistruths long burying me in self-critique and second-guessing. Whole and free doesn't mean untouched. What traits we embody in the aftermath—hardened and inflexible, or strong, resilient, and open-hearted, depend on our faith, perspective, and willingness to trust the rust—to believe our exposure can transform us into something new—less perfect and more patinaed with a purposeful backstory of becoming.

Jim starts the car and begins winding us back out of the cemetery. I didn't find the ring, but I found clarity, resolution, and peace—treasure of a deeper kind.

Reading Group Guide

1. "The stories we're born into shape the ones we tell about ourselves" is a major premise of the book. In what ways does this resonate for you in relation to your own life and upbringing?

2. Mary is convinced she is a victim of mind control experiments by the CIA, a narrative that dominates her life and limits her emotional availability to her daughter. Similarly, Marianne carries the belief of unlovability. What beliefs might be holding you back from a truer version of your story?

3. Marianne feels she and her dad are most alike and yet her father is uninvolved in her life and health journey. What do you make of his role in the family?

4. What emotions do the main characters in this book evoke for you?

5. *If You Were My Daughter* explores the impact of the author's emotional trauma, the result of terrifying seizures without the accompanying psychological support. Do you believe our society recognizes the impact of emotional trauma as readily as it does physical abuse?

6. Self-trust is a theme of this book. Marianne struggles with knowing how to trust herself after being dismissed by doctors and her mother. What's your relationship with self-trust? Do you find yourself a confident navigator of your life?

7. The title of the book—*If You Were My Daughter*—came from a doctor saying these words to Marianne which made her feel, at long last, seen and understood. In what ways can we offer one another the gift of validation?

8. There are times we may never receive an apology for the ways we have been hurt. Can you relate to this in your own life? How have you chosen to move forward?

9. Multiple children can have vastly different experiences of their parents and upbringing—and each is telling the truth. The author described her upbringing as five individuals fending for themselves versus a family experience. What does the word "family" evoke for you?

10. "*If You Were My Daughter* explores the covenant of motherhood" (from a review by Jeannette Walls, *New York Times* bestselling author of *The Glass Castle*). How do you interpret the agreement of motherhood? Do mothers sign up for certain responsibilities by taking on the role?

Acknowledgments

A heartfelt thanks to my Sourcebooks team for your longstanding partnership; to Dominique for continuous new beginnings, deep belief, relentless enthusiasm and diligent IPad notetaking; and to my editor Shana for being my caring, trustworthy and pragmatic (thank goodness) constant. Thanks, too, for receiving this memoir exactly as you did because you knew how much it would matter. A huge thank you to Brittany for your expert artistic nudging toward the perfect cover and for being consistently in sync with my brain. And to Heather and Kay—I'm the luckiest to have your support.

To the booksellers, retailers and gift shops who support my work, my sincere thank you.

Biggest gratitude to my advanced readers and reviewers Dr. Gillian O'Shea Brown, Ami McConnell, Kelly McDaniel, Vicki Kopplin, and Jeannette Walls. Your yeses meant more than you know. To Jenni and Stacy for your early reading and encouragement that kept me moving forward. And to Diane for your tenacious library research that unearthed *the* elusive newspaper article featuring the interview with my mom.

Thank you to my Nashville writers group, Elly, Betsy, Courtney, Victorea, Adam, and Paul, who listened to many chapters with helpful feedback. A special thanks to Paul, for saying, "*That's* your title," when I read the words, "If you were my daughter." You were right.

To my dear and beautiful friends whom have held my story with care and compassion, I appreciate you endlessly. And to my childhood pals for giving me true belonging and countless laughs through the secret hard.

Thank you, Jane, for holding my hand in Costco and my heart through every day of our friendship. JAMA club forever. To Sue for planting seeds of a bigger faith and narrative. And to Liv, my trustworthy angel conduit and soul guide. Thank you, Laura, for helping piece me back together.

To Dr. Richard Mattson, Dr. Dennis Spencer, and the Yale Comprehensive Epilepsy Center, thank you for dividing my life into the best before and after. To the one in twenty-six people living with epilepsy, the fourth most common neurological disorder, you have my deepest admiration, empathy and support. I hope my story helps shed insight into the mental, emotional and physical toll that epilepsy takes on individuals and families as well as the need for continued research and answers.

To my mom for modeling tenacity and my dad tenderness. Without you, there'd be no me to continue our story. Thanks for keeping heavenly tabs on me. And to Tony and George, I'm grateful we've rediscovered one another.

Most of all, thank you Jim for being my biggest supporter since the day we met. Your willingness to listen, love, learn and grow together is such a gift. Thanks, too, for the thousands of listening hours you've given this project. I can *finally* say there's a book with a title.

Lastly, to my beloved four: Cole James, Adam Jon, Julia Rose, and Will David, a.k.a. CAJW. Thank you for teaching me more than you know. Being your mom is my greatest joy.

About the Author

© Shoott Photography

Beloved author and artist Marianne Richmond has touched the lives of millions for nearly three decades through her bestselling children's books that help people share their heart and connect with those they love. Inspired by her childhood journey with epilepsy, Marianne is passionate about the power of storytelling and creative self-expression to learn, heal, and grow. She recently completed her master's degree in clinical mental health counseling. Marianne, a mom to four young-adult children, lives near Nashville, Tennessee, with her husband, Jim, and senior dog named Otis Adventure who isn't very adventurous. To learn more, visit mariannerichmond.com.